YOUR CHILD'S *BEST* TEACHER

A FATHER'S PERSPECTIVE ON HOME EDUCATION

CRAIG HARRISON

SILVERSMITH
PRESS

Published by Silversmith Press—Houston, Texas
www.silversmithpress.com

Copyright © 2023 Craig Harrison

All rights reserved.

ISBN 978-1-961093-03-4 (Softcover Book)
ISBN 978-1-961093-04-1 (eBook)

In loving memory of my parents,
Ben and Lyn.
My mother, who was the teacher.
My father, who set the example.

ACKNOWLEDGEMENTS

This book has been a lifetime in the making, and I am grateful to those who have helped me and contributed to my journey and experiences.

First on my list of people to thank is my wife, Edelweiss. She is a Proverbs 31 woman and has kept faith in me through life's peaks and valleys. She has provided constant support and encouragement during the writing process, proof-read the manuscript countless times and challenged me to express my thoughts more clearly. Her input has improved this book tremendously, and I have appreciated her advice even when I haven't agreed with it. "Her children rise up and call her blessed; her husband also, and he praises her" (Proverbs 31:28). As I was finalizing this manuscript, I read Proverbs 4 and thought it encapsulated what I wanted to say to my sons, Ethan and Jesse: "Get wisdom; get insight; do not forget, and do not turn away from the words of my mouth. Do not forsake her [wisdom], and she will keep you; love her, and she will guard you" (Proverbs 4:5-6). Thank you for helping me become a better person, and for allowing me to test my ideas about learning on you. You have both worked hard and accomplished a great deal, and I am so grateful that God placed you in our family.

During these last few years, we have been sensing the importance of our family team and our gratitude for our wider family has grown. I am grateful for the life-long friendship of Shane, Chérie and Darren, and appreciate my most excellent in-laws and out-laws on both sides of the family.

My childhood friends, Simon Kay and Waitārehu Hoyle, encouraged me during the writing process and gave invaluable feedback on the first draft. I'm delighted to join them and Stacy Gregg in the Ngāruawāhia Writers Guild. My appreciation also goes to Charlotte Silva, Lee Nelson, Anne Marie Ezzo, JD Linder, Todd Anderson and David Sluka who reviewed sections of the manuscript and helped whip it into shape.

During this project, I have received advice, assistance and input from many people. Some of this help was practical, some clarified my thoughts, some enhanced my writing and research, and some provided material that I needed to develop my thinking. Thank you to

ACKNOWLEDGEMENTS

Joanna Hunt at Silversmith Press, Darren Jones at HSLDA, Brian Ray at NHERI, Chris Boyer, Steve Turley, Israel Wayne, George Wieland, Malcolm Elliott-Hogg, Andy McGuire, Rory Groves, Hans Hettinga and Maximilian Cunnings.

Our lives are touched by people in ways big and small. On occasions, seemingly insignificant events can make an enormous impact. David Lamason, I'm grateful for your email. If I had read it at the time, I may not have written this book. Michelle Harrison, thank you for the *Oxford English Dictionary* which I refer to frequently here in the land of no "u." Anna Harrison, you demonstrated the character of a great teacher which I wish to emulate.

Finally, I acknowledge tyrants around the world who are shaking us out of comfortable complacency and forcing us to think about self-determination and values in a way that hasn't happened for a century, leading to the rise of great faith, family, and freedom-loving enterprises such as Silversmith Press and Turley Talks as well as the explosive growth of home education. My prayer is that as parents become more deliberate in teaching the values of faith, liberty and life to their children, this next generation will reclaim the freedoms we have lost.

CONTENTS

Part 1: About Home Education

The journey I took to become my children's teacher, an overview of education, and a defense for home education.

Part 2: About Fathers

Exploring the challenges of transitioning from a career to a calling as the full-time educator of one's children.

CONTENTS

Part 3: About Foundations

*As we begin on more practical matters related to home education,
I discuss some fundamental issues such as purpose, priorities, program,
and assessment.*

Part 4: About Teaching

*Lessons that I learned about teaching boys, about training children,
and about managing time effectively.*

Part 5: About Subjects

*Tips and tricks, lessons learned, and advice for the various subjects
we have studied over the years.*

CONTENTS

Part 6: About Perspective
*My wife and children provide their perspective, and I finish up
with encouragement and key thoughts to take away.*

Appendices

LIST OF FIGURES

INTRODUCTION

Home Education

For the last century, it has been standard practice to outsource education. While parents are accountable for the welfare of their children and are considered negligent if they fail to provide adequate schooling, few have questioned whether sending them to school is the best way to educate them.

In the case of missionaries, schooling may be the deciding factor for where in the world they go and when they return home. Those working in remote locations often face a choice between sending their children away to boarding school, teaching them at home, or returning to their own country to ensure they receive a quality education.

However, home education has surged in popularity during the last few decades. The modern homeschooling movement gained force in the USA during the 1980s as pioneering families fought legal battles to regain the freedom to fulfill their responsibility of providing education to their children as they thought best. Over the ensuing years, comprehensive home education materials have been developed, while advances in technology enabled a proliferation of video and online resources.

A significant juncture was reached in early 2020 when schools throughout the USA, and in many other nations, closed their doors and sent all students home. As instruction was attempted online, many parents were confronted with their responsibility to educate their own children. Parents learned that they needed to take an active role in the process. Sitting in front of a Zoom call was often not enough for effective learning. While some motivated children thrived in this environment, many needed extra assistance. And as always, it was the disadvantaged families who suffered the most, being the least able to provide additional support or resources.[1]

Parents also learned with shock what the public-school system was actually teaching,[2] leading to tension with school authorities. Rutherford County Schools in Tennessee asked parents to sign a document stating they would not listen during their children's online lessons.[3] As parents objected to curricula choices at public-school board meetings, the National School Boards Association compared them to domestic terrorists and requested assistance from federal law enforcement agencies.[4]

During this time of reckoning, many parents discovered they were capable of taking on the task of education. Some found that their children learned better in a home environment than at school. And when schools reopened, with a concerning number of students six months to a year behind in their education, many did not return.[5] The percentage of households in the United States choosing to educate their children at home increased from 4 to 11 percent.[6]

My Context

Our family's decision to educate our children at home was made in 2015. The initial choice was not a long-term commitment. We were not evangelical about the movement. It was simply an approach that made sense at the time, and one which we were happy to revisit each year. But we are still at it. Now, looking back, we are grateful we decided to homeschool.

In this book, I am sharing with you the lessons I learned over eight years of teaching my two boys. Boys are different than girls. That's just reality. And fathers are different than mothers. That's a reality too. So sharing my experiences as a father educating his boys will be interesting to other fathers, but I hope it will also be informative and provide a useful perspective for mothers. I focus on boys because that's what I have, but I'm sure most insights will be relevant to girls as well.

More significant in my view is that I am an engineer. Engineers have a particular way of thinking about the world. I believe that more than teaching boys, more than being a father, what I can contribute the most is sharing what I have learned about home education from an engineer's perspective.

But going back to fathers. Studies have shown that at least 90 percent of homeschooled children are taught by their mothers.[8] In many cases, it is simply assumed that mom is the teacher. The support group at my church is called "Homeschool Mamas," and I receive many Mother's Day notes from homeschool organizations. In reviewing literature, podcasts, and conferences, I have found only a passing reference to fathers who are the full-time teacher. There is plenty of discussion about how dad can help mom out by teaching mathematics and doing science experiments or by being the "school principal," but almost no mention of dads who have taken on the role of primary teacher.

It's not that I think Homeschool Papas are being unfairly ignored. The reality is that most teachers are women. And we men don't need a support group, do we? I mean, how many times have you heard a man ask for directions? But with homeschool households in the USA numbering over 3 million and growing, there is an increasing number of dads taking primary responsibility for teaching their children. Maybe there is a need for more recognition and support.

About this Book

But that is not what this book is primarily about. It's not about championing the cause of Homeschool Papas. It's not saying we should be given greater recognition. I do have a lot of important things to say to fathers who, like me, are teaching their children. But my message is to fill a gap, not to complain about being overlooked.

And this book is not about telling you how you should go about teaching your children. Although engineers are always happy to tell others how to do their job, I've tried hard to avoid this! You are responsible for your own children.

What **is** this book about, then? It's about the way I look at education as an engineer and a father. It's about what I have learned on the journey so far. Because I am not the typical homeschool teacher, I have brought my unique point of view to the role. I trust you will find this perspective interesting; that it will stir your imagination and make you think and perhaps even have you disagreeing with me at times. If you disagree, it means you are thinking, and have a different opinion which you will attempt to justify. That's great! I want you to reflect on what you're doing and what you believe and how you can better educate your children.

But mostly, I want to encourage you on your journey, whether you are homeschooling or just thinking about it or even if you conclude that it's not for you. It is not my place to decide what's best for your children. That's your task. No one has the opportunity to love and nurture and train them the way you can. I trust this book will help you as you seek what's best for your children.

A View from the Shoulders

As a good scientist, I believe that any worthwhile publication should clearly outline what will be covered along with constraining aspects that may have influenced or affected the work. Let me therefore explain the scope and limitations of this book.

Scope

The scope of this book is what I have personally learned about educating two boys. There are things which I have tried that worked. There are things which I have tried that didn't work. There are things I wish I would have tried, which in hindsight may have been beneficial. I have learned a lot about myself. I have learned a little about how students learn. I am happy to share my experiences in the hope that you will gain insight and perhaps a new perspective on educating your children.

In addition, I present a defense of home education, and there is a section on the impact on dad when he is the principal homeschool teacher. When I began writing, these were expected to be minor chapters. They have grown in both importance and magnitude during the development of this book, for similar reasons.

In Part 1: About Home Education, I narrate the story of how I stumbled into homeschooling. While writing, I realized how important it is to know and be able to articulate why I am doing it. That led me to think deeply about the purpose of education, and the more I researched and reflected, the more there was to say. From being something I kind of thought I knew, the writing process has allowed me to express clearly my "why" for home education.

In Part 2: About Fathers, I confront the questions that have plagued me for years about being a stay-at-home dad. Once the dam burst, the suppressed emotions flowed out in a torrent. I am grateful for the opportunity to come to terms with being a father educating his children and believe there is plenty here that will be helpful to you. Moms, you will find much in this section that will be of interest, particularly if you have sacrificed a career to be home with your kids.

And at the suggestion of my oldest son, my wife and children have contributed a chapter to offer their perspective. Let's see whether or not they agree with me!

Limitations

A limitation of this book is that it is anecdotal rather than academically rigorous. In other words, it is based on my experience rather than objective research. I did undertake research for Parts 1 and 2 as I thought I needed to understand these topics better before presenting my views. However, the remainder of the book consists almost entirely of sharing what I've learned. I know studies have been done, such as in the different ways boys and girls learn and at what age various subjects should be introduced. I have come across some interesting and relevant information, but it would take much dedicated investigation to present a rigorous and comprehensive position on the various aspects of teaching I am going to cover. I won't attempt to do so and don't claim this book to be anything other than my experience.

The sample size is also a limiting factor. My entire teaching experience comprises the eight years I have spent educating my two boys, along with three missionary children a day a week for three months, and a two-week mathematics intensive with my nieces. I have worked with youth groups at church, taught mission courses, and coached junior football. But my direct experience of children's education is limited.

I am writing from the perspective of a father and an engineer. I don't know what percentage of homeschool families have the dad as the primary teacher. I have heard that a number of us are around but have never met or talked with any. We are either rare, or shy, or both. In a straw poll of a few local groups, it seems that maybe 25-50 percent of homeschool moms have a background in STEM (science, technology, engineering, or mathematics). That is more than I expected, but very few are engineers. Again, I have never met or talked with an engineer who is the primary homeschool teacher.

I did not grow up in the United States of America but have lived here for the last decade. While I guard against being US-centric, my teaching experience is here and most of the research I have seen is related to the USA. Although many of the sources I cite are specific to the USA, my experiences should be applicable anywhere. Parents are still parents, and children are still children in other countries as well. And if my publisher allows (Publisher's note: Nope!), my spelling will be the Queen's English. "Honour" is spelled with a "u," "tomato" does not rhyme with "potato" and I don't include the Oxford comma. But I do have an *Oxford English Dictionary* within reach.

INTRODUCTION

This book is written for both parents. Fathers, I hope you will learn to value and leverage your unique skills and mindset to better educate your children. Mothers, I hope you will find many ideas in this book that will provoke your thinking and provide greater insight into home education. I'm not advocating that anyone should try to emulate my teaching style. You are not me, and your children are not mine. But by looking through a different lens, you will see an additional view of your objective and understand your world more clearly.

Worldview

The lens through which I view the world is that of a Bible-believing Christian. This is fundamental to who I am and to the educational program I teach. I do not consider this a limitation. Everyone has a worldview; every teacher has a paradigm. It is a fallacy to believe that any instruction is unbiased and value-free. I can no more detach my writing from my faith than separate it from being a father and an engineer. My identity, all of who I am, is inevitably expressed in my writing. But in the same way that I hope mothers can learn from the perspective of a father and artists can learn from the perspective of a scientist, so I hope both Christians and non-Christians will benefit from this book. The Bible speaks to human nature, and you are certainly human.

If you are not a Christian, then I'm delighted you're reading this book and hope that when I discuss a Biblical perspective and quote Bible verses, you will think about how that aligns with your beliefs and worldview. We both want the best education for our children.

A great quote, attributed to C.S. Lewis, Albert Einstein, and others, says, "*What you see depends on where you stand.*" I see home education differently than you. My goal is that through this book, you will benefit from how I see the world. You don't need to become an engineer or a physicist. I studied calculus and quantum mechanics and theology to save you that effort! Isaac Newton (quoting a well-known adage)

> *Psychology and theology are not opposed to each other, any more than science and faith are opposed to each other. One deals with things from earth's perspective, while the other . . . presents heaven's perspective.*
>
> —Dan Delzell, *The Christian Post*[9]

said, *"If I have seen farther than others, it is because I have stood on the shoulders of giants."* You will see your task more clearly and overcome the challenges you face more easily if you listen to the experiences of others.

The Engineer Mindset

The Scientific Method

Even though I worked as an engineer, I trained as a scientist. Operational science is experimental; it's about trying to figure out the correct explanation for why something happens the way it does.

The scientific method is grounded in the ideas of repeatability, falsifiability, and testability. Here's how it works. First, you suggest an idea that can be disproved, which is called a falsifiable hypothesis. Next, you conduct an experiment that others can repeat in order to test your work. This experiment is designed to either fail or succeed. Failure means you have proven that your idea, your hypothesis, is false, in which case you throw out the idea and come up with a different one. The second possibility is success, which means your result supports your hypothesis. But here's the important point. If the experiment is a success, you haven't proven the idea to be true. You've merely shown that it has not yet been proven false. Science cannot **prove** anything to be true, and anyone who claims otherwise is not speaking as a scientist. Science can only suggest, by repeated experimentation, that something is increasingly unlikely to be false.

> *Scientific knowledge is a body of statements of varying degrees of certainty—some most unsure, some nearly sure, none absolutely certain.*
>
> —Nobel Prize-Winning Physicist Richard Feynman[10]

> *The demand for scientific objectivity makes it inevitable that every scientific statement must remain tentative for ever. It may indeed be corroborated, but every corroboration is relative to other statements which, again, are tentative.*
>
> —Sir Karl Popper[11]

Engineers

Engineers are a little different. They use the tools of science and mathematics and logic to build stuff. They view the world as a series of problems to be solved or processes to be improved. They learn by trial and error, with failure simply eliminating a poor design and increasing the chance of success next time round. Their basic process is to think, research, test (that is, try things out), evaluate, change, and try again.

Engineering applies scientific knowledge to the real world.

Engineers have a particular way of thinking. They don't do anything randomly. Everything is thought through, because there's a bad way to do something and a good way; a less efficient and a more efficient; and even effective solutions can be made better.

My brother-in-law illustrates this mindset. He is an engineer at an aerospace company. While staying with him once, I noticed he had a specific way of putting dirty dishes into the dishwasher. He used a deliberate dishwasher-stacking technique—he had thought about how the water cleans the dishes and had developed a particular method of stacking dirty plates and utensils to maximize the cleaning potential of the dishwasher. He had weighed up the efficiency of cleaning against the ease of emptying and putting dishes away. I noticed this because I had done exactly the same—I had thought through the problem and arrived at what I thought was the best solution. But what I find most interesting is that we loaded the dishwasher differently because we had reached different conclusions. And in some respects, that makes a better point than if we had both done it the same way. The point is not that there is only one correct answer but that we had both thought through the problem. To engineers, stacking the dishwasher is not a random activity.

Scientists look for a single answer, the eternal search for the grand unifying theory that explains the workings of nature. But for an engineer, there may be multiple correct approaches. There could be constraints on cost, size, and available materials. The design may optimize for efficiency, simplicity, or aesthetic beauty. Different engineers might come up with different solutions that balance competing requirements and limitations. That is why bridges do not all look the same. You can be confident, however, that whether driving over a suspension or a cantilever or an arch bridge, the engineer designed it to carry the load of the traffic. The various designs may look different and be suitable for different applications, but they still work.

And the same is true for educating children. I approach this as an engineer, not a scientist. I would never claim there is one right way to do it, and that I have found the best solution. But I have thought through the process using the tools at my disposal and experimented to find the best way to go about it.

Yes, I did experiment with my children. I approached teaching with the mindset of an engineer and made deliberate choices early on that have had long-term impacts. Some may not have been the best solution, and I was limited by only having two test subjects, but overall I am confident my experimentation has been more beneficial than detrimental. Both of my boys have scored in the top 5 percent, and frequently in the top 1 percent, in nationally normed tests every year, despite testing a couple of grades above their age. And at eleven and thirteen years old, they are working steadily through a high school curriculum and are well on their way to producing university-level assignments. More importantly, they are growing into delightful young men with whom my wife and I, as well as others they encounter, enjoy spending time. What we're doing is working.

Every parent experiments to some extent, even non-engineers. You will try different ways of incentivizing or disciplining your children. And you know what works for one child does not necessarily work for another. So it's a natural process, though perhaps I have done it more deliberately than most. I hope that by sharing what I tried, and more importantly, explaining the thought process behind my experiments, you will learn some new ideas and gain the confidence to deliberately attempt things outside the box. Your children are different to mine, but I hope you will learn to think like an engineer and find solutions that work well in your situation as you educate them.

Oh, and engineers believe they are experts in everything, not merely their own field of expertise. Here's a secret: they don't know it all. And I don't know everything about educating children. But I hope you will benefit from this insight into my way of thinking and my approach to home education.

NOTES

1. Katherine Lewis, "What the Covid-19 Pandemic Revealed about Remote School," *Smithsonian Magazine* (14 July 2023), https://www.smithsonianmag.com/innovation/what-the-covid-19-pandemic-revealed-about-remote-school-180982530.

2. Debbie Veney, *Never Going Back: An Analysis of Parent Sentiment in Education*, National Alliance for Public Charter Schools (August 2022), https://www.public charters.org.

3. Johnathan Jones, "School District Under Fire for Asking Parents to Vow Not to Sit In on Children's Online Learning," *The Western Journal* (22 August 2020), https://www.westernjournal.com/school-district-fire-asking-parents-vow-not-sit-childrens-online-learning.

4. Viola Garcia and Chip Slaven, "Letter to Federal Government," (National School Boards Association, 29 September 2021). https://www.mdjonline.com/nsba-letter-to-federal-govt/pdf_4b147a5a-26b2-11ec-8e78-8b9b2977ef49.html.

5. Lawrence Wilson, "The Great Dropout: Why 1.4 Million Children Left Public Schools in 2020 and Where They Went," *The Epoch Times* (18 January 2023), https://www.theepochtimes.com/the-great-dropout-why-1-4-million-children-left-public-schools-in-2020-and-where-they-went_4991654.html.

6. According to the US Census Bureau, national homeschooling rates had remained steady since 2012 at around 3.3%, before interest exploded from 2020. The October 2021 Household Pulse Survey reported that 11.1% of households with school-age children were homeschooling: Casey Eggleston and Jason Fields, "Census Bureau's Household Pulse Survey Shows Significant Increase in Homeschooling Rates in Fall 2020," *United States Census Bureau* (22 March 2021), https://www.census.gov/library/stories/2021/03/homeschooling-on-the-rise-during-covid-19-pandemic.html.

7. Homeschooling rates appear to be significantly lower in other countries. The Home School Legal Defence Association website provides information internationally at https://hslda.org/legal/international, as does the International Center for Home Education Research: http://www.icher.org

8. Patricia Lines, "Home Instruction: The Size and Growth of the Movement," in *Home Schooling : Political, Historical, and Pedagogical Perspectives*, ed. Jane Van Galen and Mary Anne Pitman, Contemporary Studies in Social and Policy Issues in Education: The David C. Anch Series (Norwood, NJ: Ablex Publishing, 1991).

9. Dan Delzell, "Comparing Psychology to Theology," *The Christian Post* (11 July 2018), https://www.christianpost.com/voices/comparing-psychology-to-theology.html.

10. Richard Feynman, *The Pleasure of Finding Things Out: The Best Short Works of Richard P. Feynman*, ed. Jeffrey Robbins (Cambridge, MA: Perseus Books, 1999), p. 146.

11. Karl Popper, *The Logic of Scientific Discovery*, English ed. (New York: Basic Books, 1959), p. 280.

HIGHLIGHTS

Part 1: About Home Education

We all acknowledge the value of education, but parents seldom consider how their children may best be educated. In the first part of this book, I describe the journey that led to me teaching my children and discuss education in general while taking a close look at public schooling. My conclusion is that children will flourish best when they are educated within the family.

- Home education is the best choice for your children, because it nurtures them within the structure of the family which is the ideal place for them to grow, learn, and flourish.
- Homeschools are the lighthouses of the New Dark Age.
- Modern society has more knowledge but less wisdom.
- Ideas have consequences.
- Parents should be responsible for their children's education.

Part 2: About Fathers

In the second part of this book, I grapple with the challenges I needed to overcome in order to embrace the calling of being the full-time educator of my children. I speak specifically to fathers; however, women who have sacrificed their careers in order to raise their children will also identify with many of these struggles and will find value in the solutions offered.

- There is a fundamental difference between being involved and taking full responsibility.
  - Spiritual Solution 1: Affirm your God-given calling.
  - Spiritual Solution 2: Answer the question.
  - Social Solution 1: Recognize that your identity is not your job.
  - Social Solution 2: Talk to your family.
  - Social Solution 3: Model hard work to your children.

- Homeschool dads forgo their own ambitions for the sake of their children.

  - Psychological Solution 1: Recognize that your dragon is sacrifice.
  - Psychological Solution 2: Talk with your wife.

- Between stimulus and response, there is a space. In that space lies our power to choose our response. In that choice lies our growth and freedom.

  - Emotional Solution 1: Embrace the space between stimulus and response.
  - Emotional Solution 2: Find companions on the journey.
  - Emotional Solution 3: Don't reject the support that is offered.
  - Emotional Solution 4: Keep your focus outward.
  - Emotional Solution 5: Be grateful.
  - Emotional Solution 6: Keep a journal.

Part 3: About Foundations

Part Three marks a transition to more practical matters related to home education. I discuss my thoughts regarding some fundamental issues such as purpose, priorities, program, and assessment. I have taught my children that the goal of education is to prepare them to succeed in life, but that it is more important they know they are part of a family that loves them. Of greatest importance, however, is that they follow Jesus closely.

- Decide to homeschool because you're FOR something, not because you're AGAINST something.
- Our purpose for educating our children at home was to allow the flexibility to travel.
- Teach your children HOW to think, not WHAT to think.
- Choose a curriculum that you are excited to teach.
- The objective is to learn, not to get a satisfactory grade.

Part 4: About Teaching

I offer some ideas about teaching boys and training children, and highlight what I consider to be the most important lesson of all. I also talk about time management. Homelife is inevitably busy. Time is always in short supply and it needs to be managed effectively. I share that curriculum creep is the enemy, structure is your friend, and there is a hidden danger to organization.

- A child will remember how you make them feel much longer than they will remember what you taught them.

Part 5: About Subjects

Part Five covers tips and tricks and friendly advice and lessons learned regarding the various subjects we included in our curriculum over the years.

- Develop a love for great writing by reading great writing.
- Focus on quality of penmanship at a young age.
- Include plenty of hands-on science while children are young.
- In our school, we teach logic.

Part 6: About Perspective

The final part of this book provides an opportunity for my wife and children to offer their perspective on home education. I finish up with encouragement for your journey and reiterate the key thoughts for you to take away.

- You are your child's best teacher.

> **A child will remember how you make them feel much longer than they will remember what you taught them.**

PART 1

ABOUT HOME EDUCATION

The journey I took to become my children's teacher,

an overview of education,

and a defense for home education.

CHAPTER ONE

THE RELUCTANT JOURNEY

Teaching Genes

I was not meant to be a teacher. My personality was just not cut out for it, and I had no desire to become one.

My mother was the teacher. She was wonderful at it, and taught at a public school for a couple of years either side of marrying my dad. Kind, sincere, and patient, she loved children. She was a natural, and even though the arrival of my older brother ended her formal career, she continued to make use of these skills, teaching Bible-in-school classes for the rest of her life and frequently serving as a chaplain at children's camps. She would have been a great source of advice and encouragement, if only she were still alive when I began educating my boys. Teaching was her thing, not mine!

My older brother inherited Mum's teaching genes and would have made a great teacher if he had chosen that career. He is encouraging, sympathetic, and understanding. But not me. I mean, I can be all those things. I think. But he is easy-going, patient, and tolerant, while I am the world traveler and the daredevil. I climb tall trees and kayak over waterfalls. Teaching was simply not something I ever wanted to do. Maybe you can relate?

And I am the academic. Learning comes easily to me. I grasp concepts and assimilate them quickly. It leaves me confused if people don't "get it" when "it" seems so plain and obvious, and when I've explained it so precisely. I am not patient. I am not empathetic. If someone doesn't understand my explanation, I repeat the exact same thing, but louder and with a slight edge in my voice. Strangely, it doesn't seem to help.

I have always been keenly aware of my lack of teaching skills, which is why I knew I would never, ever be a teacher. I was destined to be an

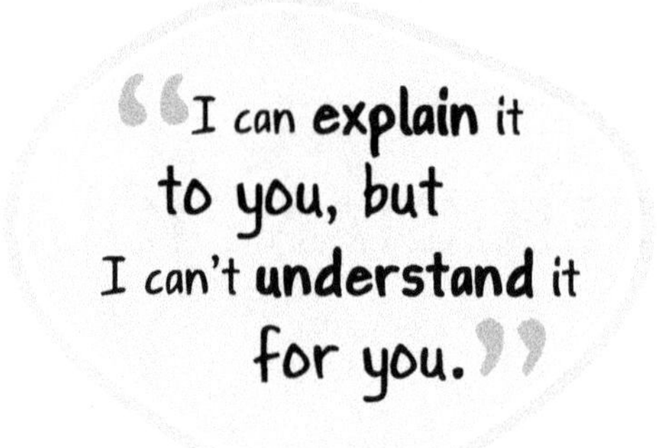

"I can explain it to you, but I can't understand it for you."

Figure 1. I Can Explain It[1]

engineer. Growing up, my mother was also keenly aware of this and was amused by the irony when, on a mission trip to North Africa, I wound up substitute-teaching three missionary kids on Fridays to give their mother a break. But when you're on a short-term mission, you serve in any way you can. So I did my best, and maybe I didn't do such a bad job. It was a valuable experience in any case, and I made it through, comforted by the fact that it was only one day a week for three months. It wasn't something I would do long-term.

Then I found myself married with two boys. . .

As our eldest neared school age, we began investigating local options. At that point, my wife and I had never thought about educating our children ourselves. But I started to hear murmurings from my wife's family, and homeschooling began to be mentioned. It soon became clear I was going to become a teacher. Like a square peg in a round hole, like a fish out of water, like Arnold Schwarzenegger in *Kindergarten Cop*, I was going to become a teacher.

My mother knew God has a sense of humor.

My reluctant journey into homeschooling had begun.

Career, Interrupted

Going to university was a foregone conclusion, although I was torn between studying languages and science. I had split my time in high school by taking English, French, and German as well as physics, biology, chemistry, and calculus. I toyed with the idea of pursuing languages at university, but physics and mathematics captured my imagination.

I progressed through a bachelor's degree with a physics major, a Master of Science and Technology, and a PhD for which I developed a mathematical model of high-energy pulse transformers. My doctoral supervisor was brilliant in his field, but a terrible lecturer. Being an awful teacher clearly did not disqualify someone from a career as an academic. In the USA, an academic career is almost assumed after completing a PhD, but that was not the expectation in my home country of New Zealand. Becoming a professor was never in the forecast.

I studied because I was curious about the world, and there was a problem I wanted to solve. I always said the only reason to study physics was because you loved it, since it didn't offer many career options. I did love physics and pursued it for the sheer pleasure of discovery, but I guess I still hoped it would be useful in some way during my career.

For sure, teaching was the furthest thing from my mind.

During my time in North Africa, when I wasn't helping to homeschool missionary kids, I coached football with various groups of disadvantaged children. I guess coaching is a kind of teaching, and I've done a bit of that over the

> *The popular image of the lone PhD in a lab coat, seeking discovery of the unknown, is quite attractive—almost romantic.*
>
> —Akio Morita, founder and former CEO of Sony

years which has required me to grow in patient endurance. However, helping young people improve their football skills is still very different from being a teacher.

I worked as an engineer for twelve years in the Research and Development Department of a large manufacturer. I was young and single, and learned much about life and human nature. I went skiing and white-water kayaking and played football. I taught a Bible class and ran a youth program. I traveled around the world and went on mission trips to Fiji, Cambodia, and North Africa. But learning was my passion, and a year before marrying, I resigned from my job to attend Bible College. Two years later, I had completed a Bachelor of Applied Theology.

My wife worked as a business consultant, and God gave us a vision for using our training and skills to assist mission organizations. The first few steps toward that goal went to plan. We returned to school, where

I completed an MBA and my wife gained a Master of International Business. During this time, in addition to junior football coaching, I picked up some freelance consulting contracts which provided me with useful experience. I gained computer and technology skills managing IT for several small businesses.

The final step was for me to spend a few years working at a large company to gain further professional and corporate experience. We moved from New Zealand to the USA in pursuit of this dream, with our son less than a year old and a second soon to be on his way.

Career, Ended

And then, it all seemed to fall apart. I spent five years job-hunting, and was utterly unsuccessful. My $600 interview suit has never been worn. We were reaching the end of our savings, and of the favor of relatives with whom we lived.

The defining moment for me occurred at 3:15 p.m. on 1 January 2013, when my life abruptly ended. One of our boys had a very public meltdown in Taco Bell, and I knew immediately that I needed to focus on our children. My attention had been consumed by the job search, and my wife had been working part-time in consulting to keep us afloat. In that split-second, I knew one of us had to take primary responsibility for our children, and it needed to be me. And I knew my career was over. No one wanted to employ me as a forty-year-old. By the time our children were independent, certainly no one would hire me as a fifty-five-year-old.

My wife accepted a full-time position.

Educating our children at home had not even crossed our minds. My wife and I both attended public schools and were generally of the opinion that the quality of a child's education had more to do with how hard he applied himself than with how expert the schooling was.

I grew up in a small township twenty minutes from a larger city. Our town was big enough for a secondary school, but affluent families sent their children to the city schools that had better facilities, sports teams, teachers, and support. I later learned that my primary school principal had met with my parents to urge them to send me to the city. But they resolutely (and cost-consciously) resisted. My mother once asked me whether I thought that was the wrong decision. I responded that while I would definitely have done better during high school, it would have made no difference once I reached university. Perhaps my first-year grades may have been a little better, but I wouldn't have earned any more degrees.

And so, the default thinking for my wife and I was that our children would attend a local school. The elementary school nearby was well-regarded and within walking distance. And there was a private school at a nearby church.

It was quite a paradigm shift to consider home education. My heart sank when the in-laws began talking about it, because I knew it would tie me down for the next decade and more. At least if our children attended public school, I would have the chance to do other things during the day. But not if I were their teacher.

It was the final nail in the coffin for my career.

But let's finish this chapter on a positive note. Educating our children at home is the best decision we could have made. It wasn't a particularly thoughtful choice at the time—in some ways, it was just easier to take care of their education ourselves rather than deal with navigating an unfamiliar school system in a foreign country. Yet there have been no regrets.

NOTES

1. This slogan is a variation of a quote attributed to former New York City Mayor Edward Koch, who is said to have told a reporter, "*I can explain it to you, but I can't comprehend it for you.*"

THE NEW MONASTERIES

The Responsibility of Parents

Raising a child is a wonderful and difficult assignment. While parents are usually tasked with this job, there have been times in history when they have enlisted the help of professionals or when experts have taken over entirely.

In Genesis, we read that the Egyptian princess who adopted Moses as her own child hired a nursemaid for him. During the Greek golden age, Plato recommended that children be raised by the state. Nannies responsible for childcare became prominent in Victorian England. Jean Jacques Rousseau (1712–1778), whose philosophy of education influenced the founders of modern schooling, gave up all five of his children. The Nazi Lebensborn Project, which sought to breed a master race of Aryans to secure Hitler's vision of a thousand-year Reich, kidnapped children from throughout German-occupied Europe and gave them to Nazi families to raise.

> Of course, there are no perfect homes or perfect mothers. But neither are there perfect schools or perfect teachers. And there are clear indications that a concerned, loving mother who is willing to learn can usually do more for her child than can any stranger, regardless of training and ability.
>
> —Raymond Moore[1]

These are not examples I believe we should emulate. I think that it is the responsibility of parents to raise their own children, whether or not they are professionals or experienced at it. God has given you children and entrusted you with them, not because you are an expert but because your children need nurture and love, and you are the best person to meet their needs in a holistic way.

Some work is best outsourced to specialists. You would likely take your car to an auto-mechanic for an engine rebuild. But while raising a child is an important undertaking, that doesn't mean we should outsource it to a specialist. I don't believe children are like cars. God trusts us with our children; He will help us with the task. And while there are always exceptional situations, exceptions are, by definition, not the norm.

In this book, I challenge you to view education in the same way, to understand it as part of raising a child rather than as being a job for the professionals. It is a responsibility given to parents, not because they are experts but because they are parents.

The Best Choice

Jordan Peterson proposes a vision for the future that includes a family policy which encourages long-term, child-centered marriages.[2] Being a clinical psychologist, he is no starry-eyed idealist but explains his position in this way:

> *I do think we have to have an ideal at the center of every concept. But the ideal can't be too rigid, you know, because people, people aren't perfect. . . . Nobody attains the ideal, the ideal has to be surrounded by a fringe of tolerance, but that doesn't mean you sacrifice the ideal.*[3]

Knowing that reality requires us to consider, tolerate, and accept less than ideal situations doesn't mean we should discard our notion of the perfect solution. As Peterson says, we can both laud an ideal while also accepting that, at times, some compromise is necessary.

What is the ultimate model for education? The following chapters make the case that this ideal is centered on parents taking personal responsibility for their children's academic learning. I accept home education is not always possible in every family situation. Nevertheless, I will not shy away from the position that it should be the first choice as it provides the greatest benefits to children, families, and society.

My primary argument is that children learn best within the family structure. They are holistic human beings, and their education should not attempt to separate knowledge from faith and virtue. Proverbs 4 encourages us to acquire wisdom above all else. Wisdom is not simply

> *Who and what comes first—parents' liberty or their children's welfare? True freedom implies responsibility to protect another person's liberties. If the young child develops best at home, then it is the greater loss for him, and ultimately society, if he is sent elsewhere.*
>
> —Raymond Moore[4]

knowledge; it is knowledge within the context of a moral framework. In other words, children will not develop wisdom by academic learning alone. It is the task of parents to discipline and train their children, to pass on their principles and beliefs and moral standards. Homeschooling allows parents to impart their values through consistent mentoring and discipleship, enabling their children to not only grow in knowledge but also in wisdom. It allows children to spend their critical formative years with their parents, creating a strong generational bond benefitting society. I believe this is the model endorsed in the Bible. And with advances in technology and the explosive growth of homeschool resources, no parent need feel inadequate for the task of teaching their children.

I do think there are significant concerns about the modern school system which should trouble every parent, and I will be discussing these particularly in Chapter Five. However, the position I take is that a decision to homeschool should be made because of the benefits it brings to your children, not because of the dangers school poses to them. My most important message in Part 1 is this:

Home education is the best choice for your children, because it nurtures them within the structure of the family which is the ideal place for them to grow, learn, and flourish.

Problems at School

Parents know the importance of education for their children. "Education" and "school" are often thought of as synonyms, and for generations, the prevailing mindset has been that education means attending school. We have assumed public schools do a reasonable job; although if we can afford it, we might send our children to a private school for which we would have higher expectations.

Today, however, evidence is mounting that the education system is failing our children. Ron Paul, never an advocate of big government, notes that *"The state's schools are visibly failing. . . . 'The more we pay, the worse it gets.' This is a basic rule of thumb and can generally be applied to everything run by the state."*[5] Test scores have been declining in recent years, a trend accelerated by school closures in 2020–2021. The US National Assessment of Educational Progress, known as the nation's report card, recently published results from 2022 and recorded a significant drop in reading ability and the largest decline in mathematics since assessments began in 1990.[6] Emily Oster of Brown University, who studied the effects of remote learning on student achievement, said, *"The general patterns are that the losses are big, they're much bigger in math than in reading, and they're much bigger in more vulnerable kids."*[7] In my home state of Minnesota, reading proficiency at grade level decreased from 60 percent in 2019 to 51 percent in 2022, and math proficiency from 54 percent to 44 percent.[8]

> *Every generation imagines itself to be more intelligent than the one that went before it, and wiser than the one that comes after it.*
>
> —George Orwell

Should parents be concerned that half of all public-school students do not meet the expected academic standard for their grade? What does the general public think about the state of education?

A September 2022 Gallup poll reported that only 42 percent of US adults are satisfied with the quality of education students receive. Among more conservative Republican voters, trust in the education system has plummeted in the last two years, with satisfaction dropping to only 30 percent.[9] And concerns are not limited to conservatives. In a monologue lambasting the intelligence of Americans, liberal talk-show host Bill Maher said, *"This country simply has no education standards anymore. They will let you out of a public high school and give you a diploma and you don't have to actually know anything."*[10]

Not only are academic outcomes on the decline, but public education also seems to be increasingly antagonistic toward traditional values. Parents are taking notice, as are some politicians. In the state of Virginia in September 2021, candidate for Governor Glenn Youngkin made school choice a platform of his campaign.[11] The incumbent miscalculated the strength of the parent vote by stating that *"I don't think parents should be telling schools what they should teach."*[12] Youngkin surprised many, but probably not parents, when he won the Governor's race.

More Engaged than Ever

An August 2022 report[13] by the National Alliance for Public Charter Schools found that for 83 percent of parents, education has become a more important political issue to them than it was in the past, while 82 percent said they would be willing to vote outside of their preferred political party if they agreed with the candidate's education platform.

Parents are a powerful voting bloc in our country; and those currently serving or seeking political office would do well to listen to them.

—Nina Rees, President and CEO of the National Alliance for Public Charter Schools[14]

School Options

Most educators would agree that intentionality in parenting is highly predictive of academic success, regardless of the school choice. Students will do better if their parents are involved. How involved should parents become in their children's education? And if they have concerns about public schools, how should they respond?

I see four options.

Option 1: Hope for the Best

The easiest option, the path of least resistance, is to "soldier on manfully," to ignore the problems and persevere with public education while trying to counteract any unwelcome influences by providing an edifying out-of-school environment: home-life, church, youth group etc.

But parents' tolerance is being stretched to the limit. I believe we have reached the point where it is no longer an option to ignore the problems and hope schools will improve.

Option 2: Private or Charter School

In response to these concerns, more parents than ever are choosing to send their children to a private or charter school.[15] This does not require greater involvement by parents but may address many misgivings and provide an easy alternative to public education for those who can afford the tuition and have a suitable establishment nearby.

Option 3: Engage with Public Education

For most of us, then, two options remain: engage or withdraw. And this is the fundamental choice we face as Christians. Do we engage with the world, or withdraw from it? Are we to be the "salt of the earth" and the "light of the world" (Matthew 5:13-14)? Or are we to "go not in the way of evil men. Avoid it, pass not by it, turn from it" (Proverbs 4:14-15 KJV), for "what partnership has righteousness with lawlessness? Or what fellowship has light with darkness?" (2 Corinthians 6:14).

I respect those who feel their calling is to become involved in their children's school, to stand for the Parent-Teacher Association or School Board and seek positive change that not only benefits their own children but also many others in their community. That requires effort and commitment. It is a noble cause, and such parents are desperately needed.

Option 4: Withdraw from Public Education

But when times are dark, withdrawing from the system is also a valid approach, one which should not be dismissed without careful consideration.

Proverbs 27:12 says, "The prudent see danger and take refuge, but the simple keep going and pay the penalty." History shows us that withdrawal can not only be prudent, but may also ultimately benefit society. During the so-called "Dark Ages," monasteries preserved classical knowledge, cultivated the arts, developed agriculture, and fostered literacy.[16] Ben Shapiro argues that *The age of scientific progress didn't begin with the Enlightenment. It began in the monasteries of Europe.*[17]

More recently, faith and culture survived fifty years of communist rule in Eastern Europe through withdrawal from the system. Czech activist Václav Benda wrote:

> *Totalitarian power has extended the sphere of politics to include every-thing, even the faith, the thinking and the conscience of the individual. . . . The first responsibility of a Christian and a human being is therefore to oppose such an inappropriate demand of the political sphere, ergo to resist totalitarian power.*[18]

He recognized that totalitarianism mandated *"the abandonment of reason and learning* [and] *the loss of traditions and memory."*[19] His solution was the *parallel polis*—an alternative set of social structures within which social and intellectual life could be lived outside of official approval.

Monastery or Lighthouse?

Homeschools have been described as the monasteries of the New Dark Age.[20] But aren't Christians supposed to influence society rather than withdraw from it? The idea of a monastery will cause many to envisage disengaging from the world and establishing a fortress to keep evil out. It may create the impression of retreat, of withdrawal, of survival. That understanding of the role of monasteries is deeply flawed—they were much more active and influential in the society of the Middle Ages than most people realize and often functioned as the hub of community life.

Perhaps it is a false dichotomy to think we need to either be in the world to influence society (like salt) or else build a fortress to protect ourselves from the world (like a monastery). Maybe both can be achieved simultaneously. If it's true that homeschools are the monasteries of the New Dark Age, it is also true that homeschooled children are often highly engaged in the wider culture. It's a myth that they are socially isolated. In reality, homeschoolers are usually more socially connected than their public-school counterparts, who are cloistered in a classroom five days a week amongst a small group of their peers. Monasteries are an appropriate analogy because they were places of nurture and centers of learning. But the term itself may summon the wrong image to our minds.

A better metaphor may be a lighthouse. Jesus compared the influence we should have in society to a light set in a prominent place (Matthew 5:14-16). We are to shine brightly to illuminate a dark world. But when culture opposes our message, we need a strong tower that will withstand this opposition so we can continue to shine.

A lighthouse is built as a fortress against the elements, not so that its light will be hidden but so that it will remain standing during the fiercest storm and still shine brightly in order to save the lives of sailors. I suggest that homeschools are the lighthouses of the New Dark Age. We need to build a strong fortress to protect our children against a culture that is trying to destroy their faith, so that they remain firm in their convictions and able to shine their light brightly to those around them.

Homeschools are the lighthouses of the New Dark Age.

The Battle Is Real

Let me again make it clear that my primary reason for advocating home education is the conviction that it is a better way to teach children: that family is the foundation of civil society, that children belong in the home, and that you as a parent have the responsibility to educate them. It is more a case of being convinced of the benefits of homeschooling rather than reacting to the failings of the school system. Even if public education were without fault, I would still argue in favor of home education. More on this later.

But am I also suggesting public education is beyond redemption and it's time to retreat to our cloisters? Yes. In a way, I am. Understand that even if you feel education needs to be reformed, you are not the one being sent to the front lines. You are sending your children. They are the ones who must face the onslaught each day, and they are the ones who are falling in battle. Our responsibility as parents is first and foremost to our children. Even if you feel your calling is to redeem public education, you surely wouldn't sacrifice your children for the sake of your mission.

This battle is real, and it is measurable. A 2014 study conducted by the National Home Education Research Institute found that home-schooled students are twice as likely to retain their Christian faith into adulthood compared to public, private and even Christian school pupils.[21] Of course there are quality schools and wonderful people who maintain their principles and thrive in a hostile environment

despite the challenges they face. But we must avoid forming our conclusions by comparing the best of public school with the worst of home
education. Something is wrong, and as parents we need to be honest
about how education is affecting our kids. Certainly your child is not a
mere statistic, but there are plenty of statistics to indicate the influence
that public education including university is having on the values and
worldview of young people.[22] Professor Robert George, director of the
James Madison Program in American Ideals and Institutions at Princeton
University, commented:

> *It used to be that liberal professors in higher education licked their
> chops at the prospect of challenging the conventional and conservative
> views of their incoming students. Today, it's the opposite. Conservative
> professors like me lick my chops at the opportunity to challenge incoming
> students who have already been indoctrinated by the "woke" Leftist edu-
> cational system. Especially in the past decade, the kids show up already
> indoctrinated.*[23]

The 10,000-Hour Rule

If we withdraw our children from public school because of the influence it may have on them, where do we draw the line? Does the
same argument apply to sports teams and drama groups? Should
we pull our children out of all organizations that don't proclaim
wholesome values? What about other children they interact with at
the library or the playground? Or even church—not all the kids there
are perfect angels.

It is easy to explain why school choice is different from everything
else. Simply do the math. If a child spends 5 hours a day inside
a classroom, 5 days a week, for 36 weeks a year, this amounts
to 900 hours.[24] In 12 years from first to twelfth grade, that is
10,800 hours.[25] Including kindergarten and non-classroom activities,
Pete Hegseth suggests the total time at school might be more like
16,000 hours.[26]

In his 2008 book *Outliers*, Malcolm Gladwell introduced the concept
of the "10,000-Hour Rule." He suggested you will become an expert
in any field of endeavor if you dedicate 10,000 hours to it.[27]

Yes, if there are negative influences in a sports team or youth group,
then I think any responsible parent would consider whether their

child should be in that environment. But the issue is the amount of time devoted to school, and that's what makes the question of school choice so different from other activities. Your child won't be nearly as impacted by the values of the drama teacher after 3 hours a week, 20 weeks a year for 3 years in the theatre club (180 hours total) as by 10,800 hours in class.

Ron Paul recognizes this principle when he writes the following:

All sides in this conflict understand that the future will belong to those teachers who are most influential in shaping children's thinking. . . . Tax-funded educators reinforce the belief in students that they are under the life-time authority of the state, and that they should not seriously question that authority. . . . In effect, they want the state to replace the parents in shaping children's lives.

This is why there is a growing battle between parents and the state with respect to education. This is why the revolution of liberty I propose must start with the educating of children. The educational system is at the center of the struggle for the commitment of its graduates."[28]

Why Have Schools?

Although home education may sound counter-cultural, it is helpful to ask the basic question, *"Why do we have schools, anyway?"* Public schools are not sacred. There is no "Thou shalt establish a school" in the Bible.

They may have begun as a noble idea, with the intention of ensuring no one missed out on an education. In times past, the poor could not afford to educate their children and free public schooling was a virtuous and charitable enterprise. It was notably supported by the church and became a fundamental component of the missionary endeavor.[29]

Changes in family dynamics have also come into play. Over the last century, public schooling has become increasingly necessary as families have disintegrated and mothers have moved into the workforce. Today, even in two-parent families, almost half of all mothers work to sustain the expectations of a consumer lifestyle. The industrial revolution moved the father out of the home. The consumer lifestyle has moved the mother out of the home. Public schooling has become both education and baby-sitting.

Work Arrangements in Two-Parent Households
percentage of couples

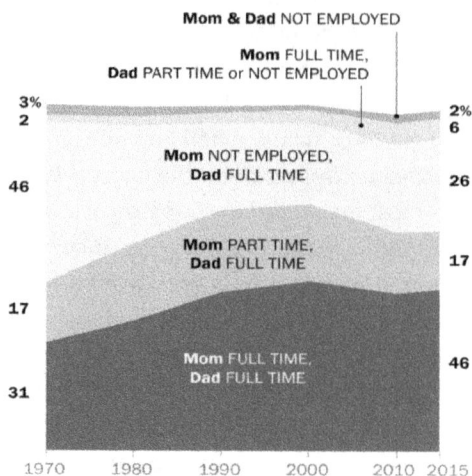

Figure 2. Family Work Arrangements. Pew Research Center (2015)[30]

Has this been a deliberate strategy? Is there some secret agenda, some vast conspiracy to separate parents and children in order to indoctrinate the young? I believe so. The founding figures of modern education were open about their goal of replacing the traditional Christian worldview with a progressive ideology by means of public schooling. And the immense social changes evident in the last few years would not have been possible without removing children from their families for most of the week. I will return to this question in Chapter Five and cite evidence in support of the view that public education has been an intentional strategy to influence the worldview of children.

But first, let me emphasize this point again: schools are not sacred. They may have fulfilled an important role in the past when access to education was limited. They may have been necessary when specialized teaching was required due to an exponential growth in the body of knowledge following the scientific revolution. They may have provided an essential service when materials and resources for learning were not widely available or were prohibitively expensive.

But that is not the case today, and I now question the need for schools. To explain, we must first understand the purpose of education.

The Household and the War for the Cosmos:
Recovering a Christian Vision for the Family

—C.R. Wiley[31]

Before the industrial revolution, when economic work was performed within the household, both men and women spent most of their time in the home and its outbuildings. Fathers were able to be far more involved in childrearing than today. And mothers were able to be involved in economically productive work without putting the kids in day care. . . .

The change started with the industrial revolution, which took work out of the home. The household was no longer the center of economic activity. Fathers had no choice but to follow their work out of the household and into factories and offices. As a result, they were simply not present at home enough to continue the same level of involvement in teaching and disciplining their children.

As for women, when household industries were transferred to the new factories, mothers at home were reduced from producers to consumers. Eventually not only economic production but also a host of social functions were moved out of the home—education was removed to schools; care of the sick and elderly was transferred to institutions; grandparents and singles moved out into separate homes and apartments; recreation become something you buy at the movie theater or engage in alone on your private electronics. Even family devotions were given up and parents came to rely on churches and youth groups. What remained in the home was little more than housework and early childcare.

No wonder feminists sensed that many of the rewarding and interesting activities of life had been transferred to the public realm! . . .

But feminism has not provided a solution. Just the opposite: it has urged women to strip the home still further by working outside and putting the kids in hired day care. . . .

Today the true revolutionaries are . . . families who are intentionally working to restore at least some of the traditional functions of the household. Most obvious are homeschooling families who are bringing education back into the home.

NOTES

1. Raymond S. Moore, Dorothy N. Moore, and Dennis R. Moore, *Better Late than Early: A New Approach to Your Child's Education* (Reader's Digest Press, 1975), p. 43.
2. Tamás Orbán, "Jordan Peterson and the Program for an Alternative Future," *The European Conservative* (8 February 2023), https://europeanconservative.com/articles/commentary/jordan-peterson-and-the-program-for-an-alternative-future. Peterson's initiative was announced on the Joe Rogan Experience podcast on 28 Jan 2023: https://www.jrepodcast.com/episode/joe-rogan-experience-1933-jordan-peterson.
3. Jordan Peterson, "An Invitation to the Future," (YouTube, 2 February 2023). https://youtu.be/L_cjujecPsE.
4. Moore, Moore, and Moore, *Better Late than Early*, p. 5.
5. Ron Paul, *The School Revolution: A New Answer for Our Broken Education System* (New York: Grand Central Publishing, 2013), p. 8. Used with permission.
6. "Reading and Mathematics Scores Decline During COVID-19 Pandemic," *The Nation's Report Card*, https://www.nationsreportcard.gov/highlights/ltt/2022.
7. Kevin Mahnken, "Nation's Report Card Shows Largest Drops Ever Recorded in 4th and 8th Grade Math," *The 74* (24 October 2022), https://www.the74million.org/article/nations-report-card-shows-largest-drops-ever-recorded-in-4th-and-8th-grade-math.
8. Republican Party Senate District 50, 22 September 2022.
9. Lydia Saad, "Americans' Satisfaction with K-12 Education on Low Side," *Gallup* (1 September 2022), https://news.gallup.com/poll/399731/americans-satisfaction-education-low-side.aspx.
10. Bill Maher, "New Rule: The United States of Dumb-merica," (YouTube, 3 June 2022). https://youtu.be/6dMOfwUP0F0.
11. Trey Gowdy commented on Fox News that education played a significant role in Republicans winning the Governor, Lieutenant-Governor and State Attorney General offices as the candidates campaigned on giving parents more control of their children's education: Trey Gowdy, "Trey Gowdy Goes 1-on-1 with Winsome Sears on Education," (YouTube, 4 September 2022). https://youtu.be/HvrVLIbqxUA.
12. Paul E. Peterson, David M. Houston, and Martin R. West, "Parental Anxieties over Student Learning Dissipate as Schools Relax Anti-Covid Measures: But Parent Reports Indicate Some Shift Away from District Schools to Private, Charter, and Home-schooling Alternatives," *Education Next* 23, no. 1 (2023), https://www.educationnext.org/parental-anxieties-over-student-learning-dissipate-as-schools-relax-anti-covid-measures-2022-education-next-survey-public-opinion.
13. Veney, *Never Going Back*.
14. National Alliance for Public Charter Schools, "New Report Shows Parents More Engaged than Ever in Education, and "Never Going Back."" Press release, 24 August 2022, https://www.publiccharters.org/latest-news/2022/08/24/new-report-shows-parents-more-engaged-ever-education-and-never-going-back.
15. Wilson, "The Great Dropout."
16. Ben Shapiro, *The Right Side of History: How Reason and Moral Purpose Made the West Great* (New York: Broadside Books, 2019), pp. 63-65.
17. Shapiro, *The Right Side of History*, p. 70.

18. Václav Benda, *The Long Night of the Watchman: Essays by Václav Benda, 1977-1989*, trans. Barbara Day, ed. F. Flagg Taylor (South Bend, IN: St. Augustine's Press, 2018), p. 218.

19. Benda, *Watchman*, p. 218.

20. Rory Groves, "Building Monasteries in the New Dark Ages," (28 August 2021). Audio Recording. https://gatherandgrow.us/product/building-monasteries-in-the-new-dark-ages, quoting Fr. Joseph Fessio on the Hugh Hewitt Program, 5 January 2006.

21. Brian Ray, *Gen2 Survey: A Spiritual and Educational Survey on Christian Millennials*, National Home Education Research Institute (Generations with Vision, January 2015).

22. As an example, 70-88% of evangelical teens will leave the faith within two years of graduating high school: Thomas C. Pinckney, *We Are Losing Our Children: Remarks to the Southern Baptist Convention Executive Committee*, Southern Baptist Convention (Nashville, TN, 18 September 2001), https://dev.schoolandstate.org/Knowledge/Faith/Pinckney-WeAreLosingOurChildren.htm.; Jon Walker, "Family Life Council Says It's Time to Bring Family Back to Life," *Baptist Press* (12 June 2002), https://www.baptistpress.com/resource-library/news/family-life-council-says-its-time-to-bring-family-back-to-life.
A Barna Group survey found that 83% of those surveyed started doubting the Bible in middle school and high school: Ken Ham, Britt Beemer, and Todd Hillard, *Already Gone: Why Your Kids Will Quit Church and What You Can Do to Stop It* (Green Forest, AR: Master Books, 2009), p. 32.

23. Pete Hegseth and David Goodwin, *Battle for the American Mind: Uprooting a Century of Miseducation* (New York: Broadside Books, 2022), p. 9.

24. According to the National Center for Education Statistics, most states require between 900 and 1,000 hours of instructional time per year: "State Education Practices," *National Center for Education Statistics*, https://nces.ed.gov/programs/statereform/tab1_1-2020.asp, accessed 4 January 2023.

25. Israel Wayne, *Education: Does God Have an Opinion? A Biblical Apologetic for Christian Education & Homeschooling* (Green Forest, AR: Master Books, 2017), p. 19.

26. Hegseth and Goodwin, *Battle for the American Mind*, p. 9.

27. Malcolm Gladwell, *Outliers: The Story of Success* (New York: Little, Brown and Company, 2008), p. 40.

28. Paul, *The School Revolution*, p. 15. Used with permission.

29. D. James Kennedy and Jerry Newcombe, *What if Jesus Had Never Been Born? The Positive Impact of Christianity in History*, revised ed. (Nashville, TN: Nelson Books, 2001), pp. 41-43.

30. The data until 2010 describes the employment status of married couples with at least one child younger than eighteen in the household. Both married and cohabiting couples are included since 2010. "In Nearly Half of Two-Parent Households, Both Mom and Dad Work Full-Time," *Pew Research Center* (2 November 2015), https://www.pewresearch.org/social-trends/2015/11/04/raising-kids-and-running-a-household-how-working-parents-share-the-load/st_2015-11-04_working-parents-01, accessed 9 December 2022.

31. Chris R. Wiley, *The Household and the War for the Cosmos: Recovering a Christian Vision for the Family* (Moscow, ID: Canon Press, 2019), pp. x-xii. Used with permission.

CHAPTER THREE

THE PURPOSE OF EDUCATION

Education Defined

For a few years, I was an Uber driver during my spare time. I listened in on the conversations of passengers and was shocked at the way many people "communicate" these days. We're accustomed to impressive-sounding but essentially meaningless rhetoric from politicians. What I came to realize is that this is also the style of communication amongst many in the general population (essentially meaningless, I mean; not impressive). During numerous rides, most of the conversation consisted of swearing and nebulous language with a healthy helping of catachresis. The listeners seemed to understand, and maybe their level of perception was sufficient for them to infer meaning through emotion and non-verbal cues, but I doubt it. I bet that most of the time, the listener heard whatever they wanted to hear and simply created their own meaning from the words spoken. Here's an example:

> "Hey, I saw Joe the other day. You wouldn't believe what that #$%@ is doing now! He's doing, you know, like he's really gone and done it."
> "I knew it!"
> "Yeah, it's like, what was he thinking?"
> "Wouldn't put it past him. He always was a #$%^."

Catachresis:	an incorrect use of words; the misuse or strained use of words, as in a mixed metaphor
Equivocation:	shifting from one meaning of a word to another within a single argument
Etymology:	the derivation of a word; the study of historical linguistic change
Nebulous:	hazy, vague, indistinct, or confused
Rhetoric:	the art of making persuasive speeches; oratory

What Is Education?

Before we can even talk about teaching our children, we need to know what it is we are trying to do. But don't we all know what education is? Isn't it obvious? I'm not sure it is, and wonder if it's one of those concepts we all think we know but have never stopped to articulate. Defining what we mean by education might seem trivial. It's not. In an era in which the logical fallacy of equivocation has been elevated to an art form, what Martyn Iles calls *"the paganization of words,"*[1] I want you to know clearly what I mean when using this term.

And it's quite interesting when you look at the etymology to see how the meaning has changed over the years. We have two dictionaries in our home learning center: Noah Webster's original *American Dictionary of the English Language* as published in 1828, and the *Oxford Dictionary of English, Third Edition* published in 2010. This is a perfect example of why we have both.

First, education is not synonymous with schooling.

"School" is derived from the Greek *skholē*, meaning "spare time, leisure, rest, ease; idleness; that in which leisure is employed; learned discussion" while "education" means "to bring up (children), to train" and comes from the Latin verb *educare*, "to bring out, to lead forth."[2]

In the Greco-Roman world, learning was a leisure activity available to those privileged few who did not need to survive through manual toil. It is only in relatively recent times that schooling has been available to the general population. However, the sense of the word "school" to mean a building rather than a leisure activity or learned discussion has been common in English since the late sixteenth century, which is clear by the comparable definitions in both the Webster's and Oxford dictionaries.

In contrast, the definition of "education" retained its original Latin meaning of raising a child until after the 1828 Webster's dictionary was published. But by 2010, the connotation had changed to that of gaining knowledge and receiving instruction. While the Oxford definition of "educate" does include moral and social instruction, the emphasis is clearly on academic knowledge gained at school. Webster's definition leads with "bringing up a child" and includes the radical statements that educating children is the duty of parents and that religious instruction is more important than academic.

Noah Webster 1828

school *n.* [L. *schola*; Gr. σχολη leisure, vacation from business . . . in Sax. *sceol* is a crowd, a multitude, a school [shoal,] as of fishes, and a school for instruction. . . . This word seems originally to have denoted leisure, freedom from business, a time given to sports, games or exercises, and afterwards time given to literary studies. The sense of a crowd, collection or shoal, seems to be derivative.]

1. A place or house in which persons are instructed in arts, science, languages or any species of learning; or the pupils assembled for instruction . . .

2. The instruction or exercises of a collection of pupils or students, or the collective body of pupils while engaged in their studies . . .

educate *v.t.* [L. *Educo, educare* . . . to lead . . .]
To bring up, as a child; to instruct; to inform and enlighten the understanding; to instill into the mind principles of arts, science, morals, religion and behavior. To educate children well is one of the most important duties of parents and guardians.

education *n.* [L. *educatio.*] The bringing up, as of a child; instruction; formation of manners. Education comprehends all that series of instruction and discipline which is intended to enlighten the understanding, correct the temper, and form the manners and habits of youth, and fit them for usefulness in their future stations. To give children a good *education* in manners, arts and science, is important; to give them a religious *education* is indispensable; and an immense responsibility rests on parents and guardians who neglect these duties.

Oxford Dictionary of English, Third Edition **2010**
school *noun*
1 an institution for educating children . . .
2 any institution at which instruction is given in a particular discipline . . .
3 a group of people, particularly writers, artists, or philosophers, sharing similar ideas or methods . . .

—ORIGEN Old English *scōl, scolu*, via Latin from Greek *skholē* 'leisure, philosophy, lecture place', reinforced in Middle English by Old French *escole*.

educate *verb*
give intellectual, moral, and social instruction to (someone), typically at a school or university . . . • provide or pay for instruction for (one's child), especially at a school . . . • give (someone) training in or information on a particular subject

—ORIGIN late Middle English: from Latin *educat-* 'led out', from the verb *educare*, related to *educere* 'lead out'

education *noun*
1 the process of receiving or giving systematic instruction, especially at a school or university . . . • the theory and practice of teaching . . . • a body of knowledge acquired while being educated . . .
2 **(an education)** an enlightening experience . . .

—ORIGIN mid 16th cent.: from Latin *educatio(n-)*, from the verb *educare*

Defining Terms

This book defines school as "a place for instructing groups of students," while education is "the raising and instructing of a child." School is specifically an institution for teaching knowledge, while education refers to all aspects of raising a child including intellectual, moral, and social instruction. Clearly, as parents, our aim is to educate our children, not merely school them.

Working Definitions

School: a place for instructing groups of students in academic subjects

Education: the raising of a child and instruction in religious, moral, social, and intellectual matters

The term homeschooling is widely understood to mean "educating a child at home." When we think about how meaning has changed in the last two hundred years, we must guard against simply transferring school into the home. We don't want to merely copy the classroom while moving its location. We really ought to be **educating** our children and reclaiming Noah Webster's definition of bringing a child up in the knowledge of the LORD.

Education is the lighting of a fire—not the filling of a bucket.

—William Butler Yeats

The mind is not a vessel that needs filling, but wood that needs igniting.

—Plutarch

To educate a man in mind and not in morals is to educate a menace to society.

—Theodore Roosevelt

The function of education is to teach one to think intensively and to think critically. Intelligence plus character—that is the goal of true education.

—Martin Luther King, Jnr.

"My son, if you accept my words and store up my commands within you, turning your ear to wisdom and applying your heart to understanding . . . then you will understand the fear of the LORD and find the knowledge of God. For the LORD gives wisdom; from his mouth come knowledge and understanding" (Proverbs 2:1-2, 5-6 NIV).

Education is not a subject and does not deal in subjects. It is instead a transfer of a way of life.

—G.K. Chesterton

Schools have not necessarily much to do with education. . . . They are mainly institutions of control, where basic habits must be inculcated in the young. Education is quite different and has little place in school.

—Winston Churchill

The end . . . of learning is to repair the ruin of our first parents by regaining to know God aright and out of that knowledge to love Him, to imitate Him, to be like Him.

—John Milton[3]

Because the word "school" refers to the building rather than the education and is more closely linked to instruction in knowledge than raising a child, I prefer the term "home education" to "homeschooling." An early goal for this book was to avoid using "homeschool" altogether, but that proved impractical and confusing. However, please know my emphasis is on education rather than schooling.

The purpose of a child's education then is to prepare him or her for adulthood—to provide the training required to become a responsible and productive member of society, grounded in a Biblical worldview and instructed in the knowledge and skills necessary to make a successful contribution in life.

Three Models of Education

In the next two chapters, I look more closely into home and public education. When examining the details though, it's sometimes hard to grasp the big picture. I will be referring to three models of education, and the following basic overview of these models will be helpful.

Hebraic Model
Key distinctive: discipleship by parents
Basis: Biblical values
Setting: home
Authority: family

Classical Education
Key distinctive: harmony between the intellectual, moral, and emotional
Basis: holistic education
Setting: academy
Authority: legal organization

Modern Education
Key distinctive: academic learning
Basis: scientific rationalism
Setting: school
Authority: state

Hebraic Model

In Hebrew culture, the education of children was the responsibility of parents and was fundamentally about increasing in the knowledge of the LORD and gaining wisdom. I hesitate to call this the Biblical model because Scripture mentions other methods of learning. However, the majority of references in the Bible suggest that the education of children was expected to be undertaken in the home through mentorship and discipleship by parents. The key distinctive is parents modeling more than teaching, setting an example more than providing information.

Classical Education

The classical model of education was normative for over two millennia, beginning with the time of Plato and flourishing under the Romans and Christendom before declining during the Age of Reason. In recent decades, there has been a resurgence in classical schools in the USA.

The goal is to bring about a harmony between the three aspects of the soul—the intellectual, moral, and emotional—which is demonstrated in an ethical life of civic virtue and results in the ideal citizen of the *polis*.[4] Wisdom and virtue form the core of Classical Education, which teaches students to love that which is true, good, and beautiful. Virtue is understood as the right ordering of our loves.[5]

Modern Education

The Enlightenment, also known as the Age of Reason, was a philosophical movement in Europe during the seventeenth and eighteenth centuries. At its core was a belief in the use and celebration of reason, the power by which humans were to understand the universe and improve their own condition.[6] Scientism, a faith that science has all the answers, provided the philosophical basis for a new model of education, which separated morality from academic instruction and redefined education as the pursuit of objective fact.

In order to better facilitate the training of children, schooling became entrusted to the state. Modern Education is closely linked with progressive ideology, which arose during the Age of Enlightenment and posits that it is possible to improve society through political action and social reform based on advancements in science, technology, economic development, and social organization.[7] The distinguishing feature of Modern Education is that it separates ethics from scientific fact, and thus leaves training in virtue and character to parents while teaching academic subjects in an organized school under the authority of the state or government.

Steve Turley notes in his book *Classical vs. Modern Education* that *"Modern education must by definition perpetuate and enculturate a dichotomy between science and religion, fact and faith, knowledge and belief."*[8]

A Note on Post-Modernism

Post-modernism is a late twentieth century movement which developed largely as a reaction to the intellectual assumptions and values of The Enlightenment, and is characterized by broad skepticism, subjectivism, or relativism; a general suspicion of reason; and an acute sensitivity to the role of ideology in asserting and maintaining political and economic power.[9]

While post-modernism is certainly impacting education today, it has not yet led to a reconstruction of the modernist structural foundation of public education.

NOTES

1. Martyn Iles, "'Babylon' - Serving God in the Fire," (YouTube, 31 August 2022). https://youtu.be/eULxjfejeMU.
2. Online Etymology Dictionary, https://www.etymonline.com.
3. John Milton, *Areopagitica; and Of Education*, series ed. Samuel H. Beer, ed. George H. Sabine, Crofts Classics, (Wheeling, IL: Harlan Davidson, 1951; repr., 1986), p. 59.
4. Stephen R. Turley, *Classical vs. Modern Education: A Vision from C.S. Lewis* (2016), p. 13.
5. C.S. Lewis, *The Abolition of Man* (New York: Macmillan, 1947), p. 10.
6. The Editors of Encyclopaedia Britannica, "The Enlightenment Key Facts," in *Encyclopaedia Britannica* (21 June 2022). https://www.britannica.com/summary/The-Enlightenment-Key-Facts.
7. "Progressivism," in *Wikipedia*. https://en.wikipedia.org/wiki/Progressivism.
8. Turley, *Classical vs. Modern Education*, p. 17.
9. Brian Duignan, "Postmodernism," in *Encyclopaedia Britannica* (23 December 2022). https://www.britannica.com/topic/postmodernism-philosophy.

CHAPTER FOUR

THE SURE FOUNDATION

Foundations

In *The Abolition of Man*, C.S. Lewis warned that the humanist world-view which removed virtue from education would inevitably lead to man being ruled by an elite class of scientific planners. We would lose our freedom and, in essence, our humanity. It doesn't matter how competent the academic instruction, or how moderate the curriculum, or how wholesome the teachers. If the foundation is humanism, then the end result will eventually and inescapably reflect the values of humanism.

For some—including C.S. Lewis, Pete Hegseth, and Steve Turley—the answer is classical schooling.

Classical Education does not seek to repair modern schooling. Instead, it returns to an approach pre-dating the Enlightenment; to an educational philosophy embracing a holistic view of learning which includes virtue, wonder, and beauty. Classical Education was founded in the Greek academy but infused with Biblical values and baptized into the Judeo-Christian ethic following the rise of the Christian church. Today, the Classical Christian Education (CCE) movement has grown in popularity enough to warrant capitalization and an acronym.

Research has shown that Classical Education produces superior outcomes compared to modern methods. According to a 2018–19 comparative study, students of classical Christian schools were better prepared for college and career, had a healthier outlook on life, and were more active in influencing society. They even indicated a greater obligation to care for the environment than public-school students![1]

Classical Education: Wonder to Worship to Wisdom[2,3,4]

The classical model of education is language-focused and educates young people at their most appropriate developmental stages. The curriculum centers on reading, writing, grammar, and math. History and science become more and more important as the child matures. A classical program follows a specific three-part pattern called the *trivium*.

1. **The Grammar Stage** (years 1–4)
   Children acquire the tools they need to learn the intricacies in the Classics later on. The rules of language, culture, math, and science are emphasized when the mind is most receptive to absorbing facts and figures. Children spend a lot of time memorizing basic facts on which they will draw in later stages.
2. **The Logic or Dialectic Stage** (years 5–8)
   Children begin to think more analytically and start to challenge facts, authority, and each other. They are given the logical tools to organize the facts and figures learned during the grammar stage and analyze them logically. Then, they begin to form arguments with these facts. Students do plenty of reading and "compare and contrast" exercises. They also talk with other classical students to solidify arguments.
3. **The Rhetoric Stage** (years 9–12)
   With a solid education in logic, students then study rhetoric, or a clear expression of grammar, logic, and self. This is where teenagers synthesize the facts they learned and analyzed in the previous two stages and discover how to apply them to their lives. Students debate and learn how to write and speak convincingly and persuasively.

Classical Education is systematic. To the classical mind, all knowledge is interrelated. Intelligent people are often thought of as those who know a lot of facts; however, Classical Education teaches children to be selective about what they learn. Not everything is equal, and truth, goodness, and beauty are valued. Other educational virtues include love, humility, courage, diligence, constancy, temperance, and perseverance. Classical Education seeks to inspire wonder and encourage curiosity. Wonder is essential in education because it leads to worship, which then leads to wisdom.

Classical vs. Modern Education: A Vision from CS Lewis

—Steve Turley[5]

*Education in the classical sense of the term was inextricably linked to
what the Greeks called* paideia. *. . . It eventually became synonymous
with the actual content of that culture, and was thus the Greek coun-
terpart to the Latin* cultura. *So,* paideia *is both the content of culture
and the educational process by which one is initiated into culture; in
short, the "cultivation of culture." . . .*
*This conception of education became very important for the emerging
Christian civilization. This is because of a key text in Ephesians 6:4,
where St. Paul exhorts fathers to raise their children in the . . . "*paideia
of the Lord." Paul brings in this paideia *idea, but this is not the* paideia
of the Greeks or the Romans; this is the paideia *of the Lord. This is a*
paideia *that is not of this world so it is bringing in a culture literally of
another world, the world of heaven itself. And so you have Christians
developing the Greco-Roman conception of* paideia *in strikingly new
and unprecedented ways.*

While I like the idea of Classical Christian Education and agree
it is an improvement over Modern Education, I hesitate because it
is grounded in the Greek worldview. My concern is that it simply
replaces one faulty foundation with another. In Plato's *Republic*, the
training of children is idealized as a way to capture their hearts and
minds for the benefit of the common good.[6] Plato wrote that children
should be taken by the state at a young age before they could be
influenced by the habits of their parents.[7] This is the very antithesis of
the Hebraic Model.[8]

In *The Right Side of History*, Ben Shapiro argues that Western civilization is a product of Jerusalem and Athens, the twin ideals of Judeo-
Christian values and Greek natural law with its foundation being the
Judeo-Christian revelation.[9] If CCE is not founded in Jerusalem but
is instead built on Greek reasoning, or even if Greek philosophy and
Biblical values are considered twin pillars of education, then in my
view the edifice will eventually crumble. The foundation needs to be
the Bible.

Hebraic vs. Greek Thought

—Craig Kirkby[10]

Western-world Christianity is unquestionably built on a Greek view of life. While we may have much to thank the Greeks for . . . the ancient Greek worldview is at fundamental odds with Hebrew thinking on many substantial lines. . . .

Many early church fathers attempted to reconcile the Gospel with their own Greek bias. . . . Augustine was an outstanding follower of Christ and his writings continue to inspire us today. However, he was a disciple of Plato before he was a follower of Christ and by his own admission, he attempted to reconcile the Gospel with his own ingrained Greek philosophy. . . .

Socrates, Plato, and Aristotle have deeply influenced our modern world; from politics, to our education systems, to business models. . . .

To be clear, there was much beauty and wisdom in ancient Greek culture, and much of that wisdom has helped shape Western culture for good. I'm certainly not decrying Greek culture as intrinsically bad or advocating for superimposing Hebraic culture on modern-day society. . . .

Hebrew values help us better contextualise and understand the ways of God as revealed through the Scriptures. In other words, our faith will be richer, deeper, and more grounded as a result. . . .

We certainly see things not as they are, but as we are. *. . .*

To again be clear, this is not to decry ancient Greek culture or bash the contribution made by Greek philosophy to our modern day. There's everything right with nouns and prose and outlines. Nothing at all wrong with ideas and logic and knowledge. Individual rights are very, very important, and without legal bodies, well run organisations, and competent directors and managers, society wouldn't work.

However, when these values essentially define our faith, our faith communities, and our leadership and ministry styles, we lose something precious and vital about who we are and what we do.

	Greek	Hebrew
Worldview	Dualistic	Holistic
Emphasis	Nouns	Verbs
Language	Prose & Outlines	Poetry & Imagery
Thinking	Abstract, Ideas & Logic	Concrete, Pictures & Stories
Success	Knowledge	Wisdom
Ethics	Individual Rights	Community Responsibilities
Community	Legal Body (Organisation)	Family
Leadership	Directors/Managers	Parenthood
Ministry	Centralised	Cooperative

Figure 3. Comparison of Hebraic and Greek Worldviews

Education in the Bible

But does God care whether we send our children to school, as long as we "train them in the fear of the LORD?" Does the Bible talk about education? Yes, it does, and I believe our children will do better if we follow its approach.

Proverbs 1:7–8 (NIV) sums up the Biblical view of education. "The fear of the LORD is the beginning of knowledge, but fools despise wisdom and instruction. Listen, my son, to your father's instruction and do not forsake your mother's teaching." This passage suggests three elements to the Biblical approach:

1. **Education is valued**. It is foolish to despise instruction.
2. **Education is founded on a knowledge of God**, who created mankind, the universe, and the laws of mathematics and logic.
3. **Education is undertaken by parents**, both the father and the mother.

Israel Wayne, author of *Education: Does God Have an Opinion*, states that the Bible only ever refers to children being taught by fathers, mothers, and grandparents. Not the government, not even the church. Just parents and grandparents.[11]

"The fear of the LORD is the beginning of knowledge, but fools despise wisdom and instruction. Listen, my son, to your father's instruction and do not forsake your mother's teaching" (Proverbs 1:7–8 NIV).

"Blessed is the man who walks not in the counsel of the wicked, nor stands in the way of sinners, nor sits in the seat of scoffers; but his delight is in the law of the LORD, and on his law he meditates day and night" (Psalm 1:1–2).

"He decreed statutes for Jacob and established the law in Israel, which he commanded our ancestors to teach their children, so the next generation would know them, even the children yet to be born, and they in turn would tell their children. Then they would put their trust in God and would not forget his deeds but would keep his commands" (Psalm 78:5–7 NIV).

"Only be careful, and watch yourselves closely so that you do not forget the things your eyes have seen or let them fade from your heart as long as you live. Teach them to your children and to their children after them" (Deuteronomy 4:9 NIV).

"These commandments that I give you today are to be on your hearts. Impress them on your children. Talk about them when you sit at home and when you walk along the road, when you lie down and when you get up. . . . Write them on the doorframes of your houses and on your gates" (Deuteronomy 6:6–7, 9 NIV).

"Teach them to your children, talking about them when you sit at home and when you walk along the road, when you lie down and when you get up" (Deuteronomy 11:19 NIV).

"Fathers, do not exasperate your children; instead, bring them up in the training and instruction of the Lord" (Ephesians 6:4 NIV).

"Don't let anyone capture you with empty philosophies and high-sounding nonsense that come from human thinking in accordance with the elementary principles of the world, rather than in accordance with Christ" (Colossians 2:8 NLT/NASB).

"For you know how, like a father with his children, we exhorted each one of you and encouraged you and charged you to walk in a manner worthy of God, who calls you into his own kingdom and glory" (1 Thessalonians 2:11-12).

The Hebraic Model of education is for parents to teach their children, and the starting point is respect for God as reflected in the very first doctrine of the Westminster Shorter Catechism, which states, "*What is the chief end of man? Man's chief end is to glorify God and to enjoy Him forever.*"[12]

As Christians, we have fallen into the trap of separating secular from sacred, of thinking that religious instruction is different to schoolwork. We have recognized the need to teach our children religion and morality while accepting that the state is best equipped to instruct them in areas of academic knowledge. But this division of responsibility is a concept foreign to the Bible, as it was to the Church Fathers. Ben Shapiro notes that "*Neither Augustine nor Aquinas would have contemplated a separation between church and state in any real sense.*"[13]

Education is Discipleship

—William Farrington, Doctor of Education dissertation[14]

The results in this study could . . . suggest the idea that education is discipleship, that education is inherently relational, and thus should be completed by the parents in a homeschooling setting where education is under parental direction.

The Hebraic Model also highlights a concern about the location of education, whether it be classical or church or government; whether it be founded on Biblical or humanist values. Where does learning physically take place? To the Greek mind, the foundation of community is the legal body or organization. The education of children is consequently the responsibility of the authorities, and learning is carried out in the academy. This contrasts sharply with the Biblical worldview in which the fundamental unit of society is the family, with education being the responsibility of parents and centered in the home.

Israel Wayne concludes, "*The fundamental problem with government schools is not ultimately what they teach; it is that they exist.*"[15] This critique of the setting for learning is applicable to all schools, whether public or private. No matter what they teach, there is a significant difference between learning from an instructor in an institution and learning from parents in the home. It is a difference between teaching and modeling, between providing information and setting an example.

As the world moved from a primarily agrarian or artisan culture to an industrial and now a technological society, it was true that the knowledge children needed to acquire to be successful in life was beyond the ability of most parents to provide. Many parents wanted their children to be given a better education than

> *The schoolmaster can at best teach morality in theory, but the mother is obliged to teach it in practice.*
> —G.K. Chesterton[16]

they had received but did not have the knowledge or resources to teach them. That is no longer the case. There is an abundance of homeschool resources which allow any parent to more than adequately educate their children, create a flexible learning program, and customize lessons to the interests and abilities of both the child and parent.

The issue we need to grapple with isn't merely whether progressive ideology has infiltrated the classroom. It isn't simply that Modern Education has separated knowledge from virtue. It's also that schooling has taken the child out of the home.

And for perhaps the first time in modern history, almost without exception, every family has the potential to return to the Hebraic Model of education. We have the resources available, and thanks to the authorities' great miscalculation in 2020 of closing schools, we now have the overwhelming incentive to do so. But it isn't only about rejecting progressive or modern or classical education. It's about embracing the importance of family as the foundational element of community and returning to the example described in the Bible of parents mentoring their children.

Objections

In 1994, I traveled around the world with an excellent friend. We drove all over the United States of America, spending countless hours together in the car. And despite the fascination of seeing a new country and the wonderful scenery all around us, the long hours on the road became tedious. So we talked. Sometimes we'd get onto a topic such as country music and discover we agreed. It was boring if we had the same opinion, and we would try to find a contentious issue since that made the conversation much more interesting. Drinking alcohol; christening babies; whether a song can be worth listening to if it has bad lyrics. We never agreed on these matters, and we never convinced the other of our point of view either, but we're still best friends. And it forced me to justify my positions—many of which I had inherited from my parents and hadn't really thought through for myself.

I'm not a big fan of people-pleasing, of being wishy-washy and indecisive, of withholding an opinion and avoiding making definitive statements in case others are offended. I'd rather hear a view I don't agree with and debate it.

This book provides me with a platform to express my opinions decisively! But I also like to be fair, and I'll be honest with you here. Writing a defense of home education was not in my original outline, but the more I read and researched, the greater this section became in size and importance. I did read a lot about the education agenda. But I admit I need to learn more about both Classical Education and the Biblical position.

The Purpose of Education

—Dr. Jason Lisle[17]

What is the purpose of education? Who is supposed to do the educating? What topics should be covered? What should be the end result of education? Do we have any moral obligations in how we educate our children or are we free to choose any method whatsoever?
These are all important questions, and people have very strong opinions on them. But the most important question has not yet been asked. Namely, what does the Bible teach regarding these issues? Let's be honest. We all have preconceptions about how the above questions should be answered. And perhaps we then look for support in the Scriptures. But such preconceptions have been formed by our experiences, our society, and even our own education. When "we have always done it that way," it is especially difficult to put our preconceptions aside and ask, "Yes, but is that way truly biblical?" However, as Christians, we must ask that question.

Biblical Alternatives

When looking at the Bible, the majority of references to education refer to mentorship and discipleship by parents in the home. This may simply reflect the agrarian culture of the time. Scripture describes other methods of learning, such as a young Samuel training under Eli (1 Samuel 3) and the school of prophets at Bethel (2 Kings 2). By the time of the New Testament, the Greek influence was evident with Paul being carefully trained in Jewish laws and customs under Gamaliel, a prominent Pharisee (Acts 5:34, 22:3).

I am not confident enough to call education by parents in the home the "Biblical Model," which is why I termed it the "Hebraic Model." While I believe there is plenty of support for it in the Bible and consider it to be consistent with Biblical teaching overall, I also accept that other views may be reached. I need to explore this question further. However, I have examined it enough to be completely convinced myself. The Bible seems to be very clear about the value of education, the responsibility of parents to provide it, and the centrality of family. The examples of Paul and the prophets do not seem applicable to children under the care of their parents.

If you reach a different conclusion to me, I'm not suggesting you are a heretic! We can still drive around America together. But please, reach your position by studying the Bible for yourself and considering what it says. Don't simply hold on to your opinion because that's what you've always thought and your pastor has never told you otherwise.

Note that there is a difference between a model and a doctrine or commandment. A model is "a standard or example for imitation or comparison."[18] In Part 2: About Fathers, I talk about a model for family roles; in Part 3: About Foundations, models for learning and assessment. In each case, these are not "the way you have to do it" but rather "a great example that will help you." Sometimes they work well, while in other situations they may not be relevant. Remember Jordan Peterson's conception of the ideal discussed in Chapter Two, that we can both endorse the perfect model while accepting compromise as sometimes necessary.

I understand the Hebraic Model to be this way, descriptive rather than prescriptive. My argument, however, is that if God did indeed create us, then He knows what works best for us. And what He describes for us in the Bible is recorded there for our benefit. Discernment is of course required; I don't wear sandals or break holes in people's roofs even though these things are described in Scripture. There is room for interpretation. However, I do take the Bible seriously and think we should carefully consider the models it provides.

Classical Considerations

As mentioned, my concern about Classical Education is that it simply replaces the foundation of modernism present in Modern Education with one based on Greek philosophy, in contrast to Biblical values. It makes me nervous to read about the twin pillars of Athens and Jerusalem.[19,20] But I do realize my understanding of Classical Education is limited.

Perhaps it is true that *"In God's providence, Christianity was born at a time when Greek and Roman thought dominated the ancient world."*[21] It is certainly true that *"Christendom, the culture of Christians after Jesus' life, death, and resurrection, was the product of Christians making sense of both Greek and Jewish heritages."*[22]

I'm open to the thought that Classical Christian Education is a huge improvement over Modern Education. I'm particularly interested in the idea of applying a classical approach to home education using a Biblical foundation, as is offered by some curriculum providers such as Compass Classroom, Classical Conversations, and Memoria Press.

However, at this point my question is the same as that of Tertullion, the church father who around 200 A.D. asked: *"What indeed has Athens to do with Jerusalem? What concord is there between the Academy and the Church?"*[23]

Objections to the Greek Model of Education

Ultimately, there are only two pedagogical models—that which was known to Abraham, Moses, and Solomon, and everything else. The former model can be described as the biblical, or Hebraic, approach to discipleship. This model sees God's Word as pre-eminently authoritative, and it recognizes and utilizes the unique and completely singular nature of the parent-child bond in the education of children from one generation to the next. "Everything else" might be described as the Greek model of education. This model comes in many shapes and sizes, and it too recognizes the strength of the parent-child bond, but it sees this bond as dangerous to the advancement of society. At the end of the day, it grants to the state a jurisdiction reserved to the family as it seeks to diminish the parents' influence on the beliefs of their own children. As an invention of man, this model is based on wrong views of the goal of education and the very nature of the child.

—Douglas Phillips.[24]

Greek society in 300 B.C. was overwhelmingly political. So was Roman society. But this was not true of the Hebrews; nor was it true of the early church. Of far greater importance were the family, the ecclesiastical hierarchy, economics, and land ownership.

—Ron Paul[25]

NOTES

1. David Goodwin, *Good Soil: A Comparative Study of ACCS Alumni Life Outcomes*, The Classical Difference (Eagle, ID, 27 January 2020), https://www.classicaldifference .com/good-soil.
2. Mark Nardone, "Classical Learning Style Yields Positive Test Results," *Delaware Today* (15 July 2014), https://delawaretoday.com/life-style/classical-learning-style -yields-positive-test-results.
3. Susan Wise Bauer and Jessie Wise, *The Well-Trained Mind: A Guide to Classical Education at Home*, 3rd ed. (New York: W.W. Norton & Company, 2009).
4. Rebecca Devitt, "8 Principles of Classical Education: A Quick Rundown," *How Do I Homeschool*, 16 August 2021, https://howdoihomeschool.com/classical-homeschooling /principles-of-classical-education.
5. Turley, *Classical vs. Modern Education*, pp. 11,12.
6. Andrew F. Wood, "Children and The Republic," *San Jose State University*, https:// www.sjsu.edu/faculty/wooda/149/summary.pdf.
7. William J. Federer, *Socialism: The Real History from Plato to the Present* (Amerisearch, 2020), p. 28.
8. Douglas W. Phillips, "What Has Athens to Do with Jerusalem?: The Deep Pagan Roots of Modern Educational Methods," in *IndoctriNation: Public Schools and the Decline of Christianity*, ed. Charles LaVerdiere (Green Forest, AR: Master Books, 2012), p. 194.
9. Shapiro, *The Right Side of History*, pp. xxiv, 20.
10. Craig Kirkby, "Hebrew Values," *A Better Future Now*, https://abetterfuturenow.com /hebrew-thinking-vs-greek-thinking. Used with permission.
11. Israel Wayne, *Is Homeschooling Just for Women?* (Christian Home Educators of California, 19 May 2022).
12. Gerald Irvin Williamson, *The Westminster Shorter Catechism for Study Classes*, 2nd ed. (Phillipsburg, NJ: P&R Publishing, 1970), p. 1.
13. Shapiro, *The Right Side of History*, p. 71.
14. William Robert Farrington, "The Lived Experience of Evangelical Christian Homeschooling Fathers in Fulfilling the Biblical Role of Disciple-Maker: A Transcendental Phenomenological Study" (Doctor of Education dissertation, Liberty University, 2020), p. 201.
15. Wayne, *Education: Does God Have an Opinion?*, p. 238.
16. The source of this quote is uncertain, but it has been attributed to G.K. Chesterton.
17. Jason Lisle, "The Purpose of Education," *Biblical Science Institute*, 18 February 2022, https://biblicalscienceinstitute.com/theology/the-purpose-of-education.
18. "Model," in *Dictionary.com*. https://www.dictionary.com.
19. Shapiro, *The Right Side of History*, pp. xxiv-xxv.
20. Benjamin Beier, "Five Defenses of Classical Education in a Time of Civil Unrest," *The Imaginative Conservative*, 23 September 2020, https://theimaginativeconservative .org/2020/09/five-defenses-classical-education-time-civil-unrest-benjamin-v-beier .html.
21. "Athens & Jerusalem," *Memoria Press*, 31 May 2018, https://www.memoriapress .com/articles/athens-jerusalem.

22. "Athens & Jerusalem".
23. Phillips, "What Has Athens to Do with Jerusalem?," p. 198.
24. Phillips, "What Has Athens to Do with Jerusalem?," p. 194.
25. Paul, *The School Revolution*, p. 179. Used with permission.

THE EDUCATION AGENDA

Now let's return to our conspiracy.

I may have given the impression that I'm critical of public education, and have perhaps even suggested there is some secret agenda hell-bent on stealing our children. But surely, it's unreasonable to take such a strong position? Aren't there wonderful schools and teachers doing a fabulous job of educating our children? Don't the benefits outweigh any concerns?

When our children reached school age, I had no qualms about public education. In fact, seven years into homeschooling when I began writing this book, I still did not have a fundamental problem with the education system. I thought of it as a personal choice for each family. But while researching the topic, my view has changed. And now, my position is that yes, there is a strong case to be made for parents taking personal responsibility for teaching their children. I agree there are some wonderful teachers and some wonderful schools. But they are operating within an educational **structure** which is at odds with both the classical and Biblical purposes of education and is deliberately seeking to establish a progressive worldview in society. The Bible envisions education as occurring within the protective framework of the family, with the law of God being central. Education classically seeks to develop virtue. In contrast, Modern Education removes the child from the home and embraces scientific rationalism, independent of objective values or traditional morality, as the only way to know the world. As such, it is at the center of the culture war between conservatives and liberals, between traditional values and progressivism.

Ron Paul explains:

> *Why is education central? It is central because each generation passes on its values, assumptions, and skills to the next generation. Parents are*

in a position to teach children about what they believe matters most in life, and what is more important than that? Because they are in authority over their children during the first two decades of their children's lives, they can transmit a system of values to them. Ultimately, education is a debate over ethics.[1]

I encourage you to refer to the cited sources if you wish to learn more about the issues I discuss in this chapter.

Heading Objections Off at the Pass

Some parents take a highly partisan position in favor of either public school or home education. And so they should—we're talking about our children, so we should have an opinion! While you may think I have swung to the extreme, please consider the explanations and evidence in this chapter with an open mind. Before outlining my position though, let me make a few comments that may address some concerns or objections.

Obviously, my views are my views, while your children are your children. Although I always attempt to defend my statements with a solid argument, I can't tell you what's best for your children in your situation. If you disagree with me, then it's great that you're engaged enough to react. I encourage you to think through your counterargument carefully and do your own research.

Understand that I am objecting to the systems and practices characteristic of modern schooling and public education. I don't have an issue with people who work within education, or parents and students who are part of the school system, unless they are in a position of authority in which case I think it's fair to hold them accountable for their actions. To put it simply, my issue is with the system, not the people.

You may find you agree with the rationale for home education, but public school is the only option in your circumstances. I encourage you to look for creative solutions. When we're convinced of the merits of a particular approach, we can often find a way to make it work. As an example which has nothing to do with school, I think owning egg-laying hens is an important step in preparing for the apocalypse, but our small suburban yard is not suitable for chickens. Instead, our solution is to keep enough fuel on hand so we can drive to a relative's farm where they do have chickens.

If owning chickens . . . sorry, if home education is simply not possible for you, knowing the information in this book will still help you be informed and make the best choice you can for your children.

A Disney Tale

And what if you think school is the better choice? Do you hold the perspective that while schools are not perfect, they're not beyond hope either? Or, that we would be better off working together to reform the school system and bring about positive change in society? Do you believe that we have an obligation to support our community as well? The following scenario may prove helpful.

For many years, conservative parents have been concerned about the ethics portrayed in Disney movies and the values promoted by the company. As far back as 1997, the Southern Baptist Convention called for a boycott of all things Disney. Their films have been normalizing same-gender couples for at least a decade, going as far as to feature an openly homosexual teen romance in the 2022 animated movie, *Strange World*. That same year, The Walt Disney Company made the news by very publicly opposing a Florida bill which limited the discussion of sexual orientation and gender identity in schools without parental consent,[2] claiming it amounted to discrimination against homosexuals.

Let's say I am convinced we should boycott Disney. I think through the reasons and articulate my best case. As a Christian, I may even find Biblical justification. I am passionate about this cause and argue that you need to join my crusade against an evil corporation that is ruining our kids; that we shouldn't give our money to a business promoting values abhorrent to our beliefs.

But you're not convinced and think a complete boycott is going too far, and we can't make much of a difference anyway. And the alternatives to Disney are no better. You prefer to avoid the questionable movies while enjoying the fun that Disney has to offer. Besides, your entire family is looking forward to a Disneyland vacation.

Or maybe you work for Disney. I think you should quit so that your efforts don't contribute to the company's success. In my view, you should offer your talents to alternatives such as Burns Family Studios and join those like Kirk Cameron and Kevin Sorbo who have left Hollywood and are creating their own conservative family films.

But you might decide to stick with your job and attempt to bring change from within. After all, Tim Allen made a positive difference by convincing Disney to acknowledge Christ in the storyline of his series, *The Santa Clauses*.[3]

Just because I might think Disney is evil doesn't mean I think **you're** evil for continuing to work for them or consume their content. I might try harder (once you're back from your trip to Disneyland) to convince you to join my boycott and would certainly warn you to be aware of subtle messaging in even the "good" movies. But despite being convinced I'm right, that doesn't mean I think you're sinning. You are simply in a different place than me; you might agree with all my arguments but simply have a different way of responding.

An Honest Assessment

So I will argue passionately in defense of home education, but if I don't convince you, be assured it's not "my way or the highway." Remember that it took me eight years of teaching my boys and a year of research and contemplation to arrive at the conclusion that home education is about more than simply personal choice. You may already agree, but if you don't and feel defensive and threatened by anything I suggest, please think through my arguments objectively before rejecting my conclusions. You're an adult and capable of thinking for yourself. And you are entitled to see things differently than me.

But don't read your own assumptions into my words or find intent that is not there. Don't interpret a statement such as "parents are the child's best teacher" to mean "if you don't homeschool, you don't want what's best for your child" or "school teachers are bad for your children." Please focus on what I actually say. I am careful with my words and try to say what I mean and provide evidence to support my assertions.

If you have children in school, or work in the education system, then this chapter will contain plenty to think about. Take your time, investigate thoroughly, and draw your own conclusions. That's what I did. But allow yourself to be guided by the thought of what's best for your children—not what is easy or convenient or possible or expected by others, but what is best for your children's education and their future.

A History of Public Education

From Greece to America via Germany

The roots of the modern education system run deep. As we have already mentioned, for fifteen hundred years after Christ, education in the West was based upon the classical understanding developed by the Greeks of the cultivation of culture—that is, *"the goal was to bring about a harmony between the three aspects of the soul—the intellectual, moral, and emotional—which was demonstrated in an ethical life of civic virtue, the ideal citizen of the* polis.*"*[4] As the church became a dominant force in society, Christian religious and moral teaching served as a unifying factor in Western civilization, and education revolved around the church. The school of theology formed the unifying discipline amongst the diverse colleges that comprised a university.

In the sixteenth century, Christianity once again impacted education as a result of the Reformation. At one time the exclusive domain of the privileged class, education came to be seen as something that should be available for everyone, because the reformers wanted the common people to read Scripture for themselves.[5] John Calvin was especially influential and believed education must have a moral source. He was emphatic that the responsibility to educate children, according to the Bible, *"rests not with the state, not with the Church, but with the parents."*[6]

When the Pilgrims and Puritans first arrived in America, they quickly mandated education so that all young people would learn the Scriptures. This early form of public schooling involved families in a community collectively hiring teachers for their children. Until the early 1800s, nearly all education in America was private, Christian, and conducted to a high standard. This impressed Alexis de Tocqueville, the French philosopher who wrote in 1831 about America's experiment in democracy. De Tocqueville observed that America's participatory system of government depended on an educated electorate.[7]

Public schooling developed in new ways under the influence of Horace Mann (1796–1859) and John Dewey (1859–1952). Their philosophy of public schooling undertaken by trained teachers laid the foundation for the modern public school system. Mann was an advocate of public education who believed that, in a democratic society, education should be free and universal, nonsectarian, democratic in method, and reliant upon well-trained professional teachers,[8] while Dewey is widely regarded as the father of progressive American education.[9]

From Whole to Part

In order to grasp the state of public education today, we must first understand a fundamental paradigm shift that has occurred in Western civilization.

As much as I admire the great mathematician and physicist Sir Isaac Newton (1642–1727), I trace many of the failings of the modern mindset to his door. Newton formulated the laws of motion and universal gravitation which established a framework that dominated scientific thought for centuries and is still deeply ingrained in our thinking, despite being superseded in the twentieth century by Albert Einstein's theory of relativity. Newton's discoveries enable a complex system to be broken down into simple constituent parts. The problem of understanding the complex system is therefore reduced to the much simpler task of understanding the individual pieces. Once we know how the parts work separately, we can reassemble them to see how the whole structure operates.

Newton's classical formulation works very well for mechanical systems such as planets and watches. But through no fault of Newton's, this mindset, this mechanistic approach of dissecting difficult problems into independent constituent parts has permeated modern thinking and is unconsciously applied where it should never be used, such as in ecology and pandemic responses, sometimes with disastrous results.

Analytical Approach:	the abstract separation of a whole entity into its constituent parts in order to study the parts and their relations
Holistic Approach:	the process of understanding the system as a whole and accepting that the whole is more than merely the sum of its parts

The following example illustrates how an analytical approach can have dire consequences.

Rabbits were brought to New Zealand in the mid-1800s for their fur and meat. Having no natural predators, they quickly proliferated to the extent that they began destroying grazing land, becoming a threat to the vital pastoral farming economy. In the 1880s, the government took action and introduced stoats to control the rabbit population. While stoats are voracious and relentless hunters who are quite happy eating rabbits, they were even happier eating the flightless birds which were a feature of New Zealand's native wildlife. These birds didn't run as fast as rabbits, and unsurprisingly, the impact on New Zealand's native bird population was devastating. By considering the rabbit problem in isolation from the larger ecosystem, the New Zealand government unleashed an ecological disaster.[10]

Education without Virtue

An analytical approach has also been used in education.

Charles Darwin's evolutionary hypothesis, published in 1859, provided humanist philosophers with their opportunity to formulate a worldview without God. (More precisely, they replaced the God of the Bible with an absolute faith in time and chance). This intellectual movement, known as the Enlightenment, sought to elevate reason and individualism and remove God from the public square and education. The Newtonian mechanistic paradigm was applied by separating academic training from the development of character and virtue, thus rejecting the classical approach that had dominated for two millennia. Dr. Ronald Nash agrees that *"Modern education in America has largely separated virtue and knowledge."*[11] As mandatory government schooling became prevalent, parents dutifully accepted that their role was to undertake a child's moral training at home while leaving academic instruction to the schoolteacher.

But children are not machines that can be taken apart and put back together. As already mentioned in Chapter Four, C.S. Lewis provided a warning. He highlighted the pitfalls that mankind would face from this analytical approach to education during a series of lectures delivered in Durham, England in 1943 and later published as *The Abolition of Man* in 1944. Lewis argues that by abandoning a holistic view of life, scientific rationalism reduces the world to mere nature so that we may control it, but *"what we call Man's power over Nature turns out to be a power exercised by some men over other men with Nature as its instrument."*[12] The result is that those with superior scientific ability inevitably take charge, perhaps initially for benevolent reasons. Nevertheless, the inevitable outcome as foreseen by Lewis is a concentration of power in a very small minority. *"Man's conquest of Nature, if the dreams of some scientific planners are realized, means the rule of a few hundreds of men over billions upon billions of men."*[13]

The End of Mankind

The argument C.S. Lewis makes in *The Abolition of Man* is summarized by Steve Turley as follows:

By sequestering the student from the objective values that formed the basis for virtue formation, modern educational practices perpetuate a mechanistic vision of the world comprised of scientifically inspired control over nature and, as a necessary consequence, humans. . . . In this modern reduction of the world as knowable only through facts, Lewis was concerned that teaching our students that the world is inherently meaningless has the effect of destroying the concept of virtue. . . . In reducing humanity to mere biological and chemical causal processes, we reduce humanity to just another natural by-product. . . . In attempting to conquer nature, Nature has conquered man.[14]

And Lewis's worst fears regarding the implications of this Newtonian dissection of education, the control exercised by the scientific class over the *hoi polloi*, became evident for all to see in 2020 when the world followed the dictates of a man who claimed to embody science and be the ultimate arbiter of truth.[15]

The society we live in today reflects what I consider to be the unintentional ruin of education. The destruction was unintentional in that modernists presumed to promote learning by elevating reason and individualism, but what they achieved instead was a system increasingly intolerant of views contrary to accepted "truth." They ruined education, true education understood holistically, because without virtue or character, the end result has been blind adherence to impersonal science and perceived fact. Today, we have more knowledge but less wisdom.

Modern society has more knowledge but less wisdom.

The Grand Narrative in Western Civilization

—Professor Mattias Desmet, psychoanalyst and clinical consultant at Ghent University (Belgium)[16]

From the Enlightenment forward, mechanistic thinking provided the Grand Narrative in Western civilization. According to that story, it begins with a big bang that sets an expanding universe in motion . . . From here, guided by natural selection, simple forms of life gradually give way to more complex forms until, at long last, man emerges—the provisional end point of evolution. In this way, the scientific discourse spun its own creation myth. . . .

At its birth, science was synonymous with open-mindedness, with a way of thinking that banished dogmas and questioned beliefs. As it evolved, however, it also turned itself into ideology, belief, and prejudice.

A Deliberate Agenda

The product of Newtonian thinking, the Enlightenment, and the modernist movement is an educational system concerned entirely with scientific reason and devoid of virtue. If we accept Lewis's analysis, this was perhaps inevitable once school began to focus exclusively on rational knowledge. And despite the tremendous advances in science and technology, a majority, in the US at least, now agrees education has gone off track.[17] But to ask whether there was a deliberate agenda is to take the debate a step further. It is to suggest that there was intent, that there has been a deliberate attempt to use education to impose an alternative ideology upon children.

Do I believe there has been an intentional plan to use the public school system to advance a humanist agenda? Yes, I do. Let me explain why.

Impressionable Minds

The importance of education has long been recognized. King Solomon said, "Train up a child in the way he should go: and when he is old, he

51

will not depart from it" (Proverbs 22:6). A famous maxim, purported to have originated with Aristotle and echoed by St. Ignatius Loyola, states, *"Give me a child until he is seven and I will show you the man."*

It is therefore no surprise that those who seek to change culture often focus on teaching the young. And this leads us to another German connection beyond the concept of education for the masses. As we noted in Chapter Two, Plato and Rousseau both advocated state-run schools, with Rousseau being an enthusiastic supporter of the Platonic ideal of comprehensive social control through mass schooling.[18] The ideology of Prussian education, which emphasized government control and was developed on a foundation of the utopian philosophies of Immanuel Kant (1724–1804), Georg Wilhelm Friedrich Hegel, (1770–1831), Jean Jacques Rousseau (1712–1778), Karl Marx (1818–1883) and Friedrich Nietzsche (1844–1900),[19] heavily influenced early American progressive educators such as Mann and Dewey.

Prior to the early 1800s, school in America was the domain of the family and the church. During the last two centuries, however, there has been a struggle to control the structure and content of education, because he who controls the education of the young will shape the future.

The Prussian Connection

—Kevin Swanson[20]

In 1806, a Prussian philosopher, Johann Fichte, gave a landmark speech called "An Address to the German Nation" in which he suggested that children ought to be turned over to the state and subjected to compulsory education. Fichte's point was that "through forced schooling, everyone would learn that 'work makes free,' and working for the State, even laying down one's life to its commands, was the greatest freedom of all."

Later, Karl Marx honed Fichte's ideas, recommending the complete abolishment of both home education and the family in his Communist Manifesto. Yes. Those are his words. He certainly knew that family control over the education of their own children, or a family-based economy, would never allow for the centralizing of power in the state.

The Communist Manifesto

—Karl Marx and Friedrich Engels[21]

Abolition of the family! . . . The bourgeois family will vanish as a matter of course. . . . We destroy the most hallowed of relations, when we replace home education by social. . . .
The Communists have not invented the intervention of society in education; they do but seek to alter the character of that intervention, and to rescue education from the influence of the ruling class.
The bourgeois clap-trap about the family and education, about the hallowed co-relation of parent and child, becomes all the more disgusting. (pp.239-240)
But Communism abolishes eternal truths, it abolishes all religion, and all morality, instead of constituting them on a new basis; it therefore acts in contradiction to all past historical experience. (p.242)
The proletariat will use its political supremacy to wrest, by degrees, all capital from the bourgeoisie, to centralize all instruments of production in the hands of the State . . . the following will be pretty generally applicable: . . .
10. Free education for all children in public schools. (p.243)
But these Socialist and Communist publications contain also a critical element. They attack every principle of existing society. . . . The practical measures proposed in them—such as the abolition . . . of the family. (p.255)
The Communists disdain to conceal their views and aims. They openly declare that their ends can be attained only by the forcible overthrow of all existing social conditions. (p.258)

The Foundations of Public Schooling

The goal of government schools from the late nineteenth century was not to create the independent, self-governing citizens that so impressed de Tocqueville, but to reverse Western Christian tradition and produce a compliant population easy to govern. The word "socialization" was introduced to describe this ideology.[22] The authority that government wished to exert was made clear when the Wisconsin Teachers Association claimed in 1865 that *"children are a property of the state."*[23]

John Dewey touted schools as a tool for social manipulation and progress.[24] In 1897, he wrote, *"every teacher should realize the dignity of his calling; that he is a social servant set apart for the maintenance of the proper social order and the securing of the right social growth."*[25] As the first president of the American Humanist Association, he felt Christianity was the principal problem that needed to be solved by the public education system.[26] In a similar vein, the first National Commissioner of Education, William Harris (1835-1909), wrote in *Philosophy of Education* (1906) that the purpose of school was to cause students to reject the teachings of parents, churches, and traditions.[27]

The Dewey Connection

In his book, *The Right Side of History*, Ben Shapiro describes how continental progressivism, based upon the philosophy of Hegel and Comte, was brought to the United States by John Dewey. Dewey, described by Professor Robert Horwitz as *"the foremost American philosopher of democracy in the twentieth century,"* believed that the application of social science could engineer a new world and humanity; that we could resolve all of our problems if we were just intelligent enough.

But Shapiro highlights the issue of consent. What if we don't wish to grow in the way Dewey thought we should? The response, according to the Progressives, is that we lack intelligence. We're simply not smart enough to understand what's best for society. The state, through people of superior intellect, should be entitled to scientifically investigate any aspect of the democratic system, and favor those associations that are the most valuable for the flourishing of society. In addition, according to progressive ideology, the state ought to educate children in the manner of thinking endorsed by bureaucratic experts.

Shapiro says:[28]

Children are, in effect, the property of the state. . . .

The philosophy of scientifically based expertise proposed by Hegel and Comte and espoused by Dewey came to fruition in the administration of Woodrow Wilson. . . . And he thought that the American Founding Fathers had been wrong—that the social contract theory and inalienable rights of John Locke and Thomas Jefferson were a load of bunk. . . .

In Wilson's vision, the community always took precedence over the individual; scientifically minded experts could best run the country; and the president—you know, someone like Woodrow Wilson—could act as the repository of the Rousseauian general will. . . .

From now on, American government would no longer base itself on the Declaration of Independence and the Constitution of the United States. It would base itself on the pragmatic progressivism of Dewey and Wilson—an ever-growing bureaucracy, self-assured and confident in its own scientific expertise, and aware of its own authority to help shape the formation of the American people from the top down. . . .

If we wish for our civilization to survive, however, we must be willing to teach our children. The only way to protect their children is to make warriors of our own children. We must make of our children messengers for the truths that matter.

The struggle for control of education has escalated since the early 1960s,[29] when liberals were emboldened by Supreme Court rulings that declared school-sponsored prayer and Bible readings unconstitutional. It became more obvious in 2020 as schools sent their children home and resorted to online instruction—and parents saw firsthand what was being taught in the classroom. The efforts to impose an ideology are being exposed. In August 2022, Project Veritas released a video in which a Connecticut school assistant principal states:

> *It's subtle. They* [teachers I hire] *will never say, "Oh, this is* [a] *liberal or a Democratic way of doing this." They'll just make that the norm—and this is how we handle things, it's subtle. . . . That's how you get away with it. . . . The conservative* [teacher], *who is stuck in her ways. I'll never be able to fire her, and I'll never be able to change her. So, I make an impact with the next teacher I hire.*[30]

Soon, the subtle action of the past may become codified in law. The US state of Minnesota is poised to approve licensing regulations requiring teachers to publicly affirm critical race theory and transgender ideology. If enacted, teachers will be required to reject traditional values and endorse progressive dogma—in effect, as the Federalist notes, Christian, Jewish, and Muslim teachers will need to either renounce their faith or their teaching license.[31]

Without a Fight

As far back as 1890, A.A. Hodge of Princeton Theological Seminary predicted the outcome of this agenda: "*A comprehensive and centralized system of national education, separated from religion . . . will prove the most appalling enginery for the propagation of anti-Christian and atheistic unbelief, and of anti-social nihilistic ethics, individual, social and political.*"[32]

Unfortunately, the church ceded this ground without a fight. Following the Second Great Awakening of the early nineteenth century, Christians dominated US cultural institutions including schools and universities. However, evangelical churches made the saving of souls their primary purpose and retreated from involvement in society and government. By treating sin and salvation as the extent of the Gospel message, interpreting "the Kingdom of God" in a purely spiritual sense and fixating on the afterlife, they became focused on evangelism and allowed the broader mandate of the church, "Thy Kingdom come on earth as it is in heaven," to be turned over to the government—first education, and then progressively care for widows, orphans, the sick, the elderly, and the poor.[33,34]

Impact on Society

We need virtuous teachers in our public schools, just as we need servant-hearted politicians and moral filmmakers and compassionate business leaders. To be clear, not all schools have embraced a progressive or woke ideology. But the issue runs deeper. The foundation of public education is scientific rationalism that rejects objective moral values and separates virtue from knowledge. Whether or not a school is teaching a progressive agenda, the seeds of this ideology are contained within the worldview forming the basis of Modern Education.

A person's world view is the collection of his presuppositions or convictions about reality, which represent his total outlook on life.

—W. Andrew Hoffecker[35]

We have all heard horror stories about public schools. And while anecdotes do not prove an argument, there is plenty of solid evidence to suggest there has been a deliberate attempt to entice children to reject the values of their parents and ensure they are inculcated with a humanist worldview, teaching them they are simply products of nature unencumbered by a moral center and subject to the superior intellect of a benevolent (and governing) elite. Mann and Dewey were quite open about their agenda to introduce humanist philosophy in place of the traditional Christian foundation of education. They **intended** to replace Christianity with the religion of scientism.

There will always be a small minority holding extreme positions on both ends of the spectrum. One could argue the examples given are simply outliers. And in any case, how is that different from Christians who wish to impose their values on the educational system? I think these are both fair points, but there comes a time when we need to take an honest look at the outcomes.

> *Education is thus a most powerful ally of Humanism, and every American public school is a school of Humanism. What can the theistic Sunday-schools, meeting for an hour once a week, and teaching only a fraction of the children, do to stem the tide of a five-day program of humanistic teaching?*
>
> —Charles Potter, signer of the first Humanist Manifesto[36]

Ideas have consequences.

I for one do not like what I see happening in public schools or the flow-on impact in society today.

The consequences of a changing culture are evident all around us, from attacks on conservative values, to openly socialist activism, to unquestioning obedience by the masses to the scientific elite, to governments removing basic freedoms "for your safety." The issue is not simply curriculum, which could be solved by parental involvement and the election of conservative school board members. Ron Paul comments that parents have been trying to reform local public schools since 1840 with little success,[38]

> *The education system is broken, and it's up to us as parents to instill the mindsets and values for our kids.*
>
> —Peter Diamandis[37]

and John Taylor Gatto concludes that *"mass compulsion schooling is unreformable."*[39] The problem is the foundation of the system itself.

It is time for an alternative.

Worldview Matters

The clash between Christianity and secular humanism is not simply an intellectual debate. What's at stake when discussing the philosophical foundation of education is not merely a matter of who wins the argument, or whose paradigm takes the popularity vote in society. We live with the consequences of our culture's dominant assumptions.

Ideas have consequences.

At a very basic level, Christians believe that all people are created in the image of God with an immortal soul; in contrast, humanists declare that we are the natural byproduct of time and chance and have no higher purpose. As society becomes increasingly secular, the impact of this worldview becomes evident. Here are a few examples.

- Marriage and family have become social constructs that may be dispensed with if inconvenient.
- Society lacks the cohesion provided by strong family structures and a unifying faith.
- Trust in media and government are around all-time lows.
- Life has diminished in value. "Useless eater" has entered the lexicon, New Zealanders voted in a public referendum to allow euthanasia, and assisted suicide is a leading cause of death in Canada.
- Suicide rates are steadily increasing; in the USA, it is the second-leading cause of death among young people, while New Zealand has the highest youth suicide rate in the developed world.
- Gender has become a personal preference rather than a biological fact.
- The state has assumed the role of provider, leading to dependency.

Worldview Terminology

The Enlightenment

Also known as the Age of Reason, the Enlightenment was a European intellectual movement of the late seventeenth and eighteenth centuries emphasizing reason and individualism rather than tradition, having at its core a belief in reason as the key to human knowledge and progress.

Humanism

This term in philosophy has encompassed systems of thought stressing rational enquiry and human experience over abstract theorizing or orthodox religion.

Progressivism

Progressive ideology arose during the Age of Enlightenment and asserts it is possible to improve society through political action and social reform based on advancements in science, technology, economic development, and social organization.

Scientism

An excessive belief in the power of scientific knowledge and techniques. Scientism is the opinion that science and the scientific method are the best or only way to render truth about the world and reality. It has been used (particularly by critics) to describe the dogmatic endorsement of scientific methods and the reduction of all knowledge to only that which is either true by definition or empirically verifiable.[40]

Culture War

A conflict between social groups, especially liberal and conservative groups, and the struggle for dominance of their values, beliefs, and philosophies.

Woke Ideology

The term "woke" was originally popularized by progressive activists who saw themselves as having awakened to the effects of oppression and social injustice. It has come to encompass a broader awareness of social concerns such as sexism and homosexual rights and has also been used as shorthand for American Left ideas involving identity politics and social justice.

In Summary

My conclusion is that there is an agenda in modern schooling which is antagonistic toward both the Christian worldview and parental involvement in their children's education. The concept of education as the raising of a child and instruction in religious, moral, social, and intellectual matters came under threat following the Enlightenment, when education was broken into constituent parts and intellectual instruction became the domain of schools. Public schooling was then deliberately appropriated to train children in a humanistic ideology devoid of religion, morality, and virtue. This by necessity entailed a rejection of the Judeo-Christian understanding of the world.

But although Modern Education is built on a flawed foundation, there is an alternative, a light in the distance, a beacon of hope. Ron Paul asserts that *"We will win this battle for the minds of men and women. We will win it student by student."*[41] Parents now have an unprecedented opportunity to reaffirm their responsibility and reclaim their right to educate their children in the home.

Additional Perspectives

IndoctriNation: *Public Schools and the Decline of Christianity*
Colin Gunn and Joaquin Fernandez (2011). Documentary film and book.

Summary: Public schooling is unnatural, weird, and outdated.
Look behind the comfortable myths to see an educational system actively at work to alter your child's moral values, worldview, and religious beliefs. Learn the history and philosophy of public-school education—and discover it is based on neither Christian nor American values. Explore the Biblical principles regarding education, and who is ultimately responsible for our children's future.
Solution according to Gunn and Fernandez: Personal parent-to-child discipleship.

The School Revolution: *A New Answer for Our Broken Education System*
Ron Paul (2013)

Summary: Most people can agree that education is vital to the prosperity and future of our society. Yet our current system simply doesn't work. Parents feel increasingly powerless, and nearly half of all Americans give our schools a grade of C. This book provides a focused solution that centers on strong support for homeschooling and the application of free-market principles to the American education system.

Solution according to Paul: The restoration of family-based education, the restoration of open competition in education, and the development of educational programs that are strong on leadership development and rely on self-teaching and student-run tutorials.

Education: Does God Have an Opinion? *A Biblical Apologetic for Christian Education & Homeschooling*
Israel Wayne (2017)

Summary: Since the beginning of the twentieth century, most Christians have embraced the idea that it is a proper role and function of the civil government to control and guide the education of children. This book provides a Biblical basis for arguing that God cares about how our children are schooled.

Solution according to Wayne: A Biblically-based homeschool program.

The Underground History of American Education: *An Intimate Investigation into the Prison of Modern Schooling*
John Taylor Gatto (2017)

Summary: A thirty-year veteran public-school teacher who was twice named the New York State Teacher of the Year, Gatto condemns government-monopoly compulsory schooling. He describes the school system's goal as "social efficiency" which inhibits children's ability to learn, and believes that mass compulsion schooling is unreformable. His own teaching experience shows that children flourish when they are given the freedom to learn.

Young children can acquire the basics of literacy before they are teenagers: reading, writing, and arithmetic. Parents can teach these skills to their children. Once children have these basic skills, they are ready for serious reading and self-education.

Solution according to Gatto: Families should take charge of their children's education, whether at home or in small schools created by communities.

Battle for the American Mind: *Uprooting a Century of Miseducation*
Pete Hegseth and David Goodwin (2022)

Summary: This book is the story of the progressive plan to neutralize the basis of the American Republic by removing the Western Christian *paidaeia* (meaning "enculturation"). Progressives are winning the war and controlling the supply lines of future citizens. Reversing this reality will require parents to radically reorient their children's education; even most homeschooling and Christian school programs are infused with progressive assumptions.
Solution according to Hegseth and Goodwin: Classical Christian Education based on the Greek academy merged with Christianity.

NOTES

1. Paul, *The School Revolution*, p. 14. Used with permission.
2. Florida House Bill HB1557 (2022): *Parental Rights in Education* says that it is "*An act relating to parental rights in education . . . requiring district school boards to adopt procedures that comport with certain provisions of law for notifying a student's parent of specified information; requiring such procedures to reinforce the fundamental right of parents to make decisions regarding upbringing and control of their children.*"
The text of the relevant portion reads: "*Classroom instruction by school personnel or third parties on sexual orientation or gender identity may not occur in kindergarten through grade 3 or in a manner that is not age-appropriate or developmentally appropriate for students.*"
3. David Ng, "Tim Allen Says He Fought to Put Christ Back into Christmas for Disney+ Series 'The Santa Clauses,'" *Breitbart* (23 November 2022), https://www.breitbart.com/entertainment/2022/11/23/tim-allen-says-he-fought-to-put-christ-back-into-christmas-for-disney-series-the-santa-clauses.
4. Turley, *Classical vs. Modern Education*, p. 13.
5. Kennedy and Newcombe, *What if Jesus Had Never Been Born?*, p. 43.
6. Kennedy and Newcombe, *What if Jesus Had Never Been Born?*, p. 45.
7. Kennedy and Newcombe, *What if Jesus Had Never Been Born?*, p. 49.
8. Lawrence A. Cremin, "Horace Mann," in *Encyclopaedia Britannica* (23 February 2023). https://www.britannica.com/biography/Horace-Mann.
9. James S. Gouinlock, "John Dewey," in *Encyclopaedia Britannica* (17 March 2023). https://www.britannica.com/biography/John-Dewey.
10. New Zealand Department of Conservation, https://www.doc.govt.nz.
11. Ronald Nash, "The Myth of a Value-Free Education," *Acton Institute*, https://www.acton.org/node/6421.
12. Lewis, *Abolition of Man*, p. 35.
13. Lewis, *Abolition of Man*, p. 37.
14. Stephen R. Turley, *The Abolition of Sanity: C.S. Lewis on the Consequences of Modernism* (2019), pp. v, 8, 22.
15. Tim Hains, "Fauci: Attacking Me Is Attacking Science," *RealClear Politics* (9 June 2021), https://www.realclearpolitics.com/video/2021/06/09/fauci_attacking_me_is_attacking_science.html, accessed 4 April 2023.
16. Mattias Desmet, *The Psychology of Totalitarianism* (London: Chelsea Green Publishing, 2022), pp. 16-18.
17. Saad, "Satisfaction with K-12 Education."
18. John Taylor Gatto, *The Underground History of American Education: An Intimate Investigation into the Prison of Modern Schooling*, vol. 1 (New York: Oxford Scholars Press, 2017), p. 66.
19. Hegseth and Goodwin, *Battle for the American Mind*, pp. 69-70.
20. Kevin Swanson, *The Second Mayflower*, 3rd ed. (Parker, CO: Generations with Vision, 2008), p. 58.
21. Karl Marx and Friedrich Engels, *The Communist Manifesto* (London: Penguin Books, 2002).

22. Davis and Rachael Carman, "Micro-Schools: An Interview with David Hazel of My Father's World," *Let's Talk Homeschool* (Apologia Educational Ministries, 18 July 2022). Podcast audio. https://anchor.fm/letstalkhomeschool/episodes/128-Micro-Schools–an-Interview-with-David-Hazel-of-My-Fathers-World-e1je708.

23. Carman, "Micro-Schools".

24. Hegseth and Goodwin, *Battle for the American Mind*, pp. 79-80.

25. John Dewey, "My Pedagogic Creed," *School Journal* 54 (January 1897), http://dewey.pragmatism.org/creed.htm.

26. Kennedy and Newcombe, *What if Jesus Had Never Been Born?*, p. 54.

27. Gatto, *The Underground History of American Education*, vol. 1, p. 256.

28. Shapiro, *The Right Side of History*, pp. 143-144, 214.

29. Paul, *The School Revolution*, p. 54.

30. Project Veritas, "Part 1: Connecticut Public School Asst. Principal Admits Discrimination against Catholic Candidates," (YouTube, 30 August 2022). https://youtu.be/AD2kM39S4d4.

    In another video, Project Veritas records a New York City School Activities Director talking about how she sneaks her political agenda into the classroom: Project Veritas, "Trinity School NYC Director of Student Activities Touts Sneaking Political Agenda into Classrooms," (YouTube, 1 September 2022). https://youtu.be/N3_5KEfc3Zc.

31. Joy Pullmann, "Minnesota Poised to Ban Christians, Muslims, and Jews from Teaching in Public Schools," *The Federalist* (12 January 2023), https://thefederalist.com/2023/01/12/minnesota-poised-to-ban-christians-muslims-and-jews-from-teaching-in-public-schools.

32. Archibald Alexander Hodge, *Popular Lectures on Theological Themes* (Philadelphia, PA: Presbyterian Board of Publication, 1887), pp. 283-284.

33. Hegseth and Goodwin, *Battle for the American Mind*, p. 73.

34. Wiley, *The Household and the War for the Cosmos*, p. xi.

35. *Building a Christian World View: God, Man and Knowledge*, vol. 1, ed. W. Andrew Hoffecker (Phillipsburg, NJ: Presbyterian and Reformed Publishing Company, 1986), p. ix.

36. Charles Francis Potter, *Humanism: A New Religion* (New York: Simon & Schuster, 1930), p. 128.

37. Peter Diamandis, "How to Raise Giants: Parenting as an Entrepreneur," *Abundance360*, 8 March 2023.

38. Paul, *The School Revolution*, pp. 190-191.

39. Gatto, *The Underground History of American Education*, vol. 1, p. 43.

40. These two conditions are together known as the principle of empirical verifiability, a principle that forms the foundation of Logical Positivism and is based on the work of David Hume: Norman L. Geisler and Frank Turek, *I Don't Have Enough Faith to Be an Atheist* (Wheaton, IL: Crossway, 2004), pp. 57-59.

41. Paul, *The School Revolution*, p. 8. Used with permission.

THE CONCLUSION

Think Like a Scientist

What if you have made it this far and don't agree with me? You don't believe government schools are trying to steal our children. You hold a different view about Classical Education. Maybe you have an alternative interpretation of the Biblical passages about training a child. Good. If you disagree with me, then you're thinking like a scientist.

Remember, scientists question things. They repeat someone else's research to see if they get the same result. Maybe they develop a different experiment to test the hypothesis. So please, read my sources for yourself. Study what the Bible says. Talk to teachers and home-schoolers and people in education. Read books with alternative views. Proverbs 14:15 (NLT) which says, "Only simpletons believe everything they're told! The prudent carefully consider their steps," applies as much to what I say as to what the government says!

There is a limitation though in thinking about this question like a scientist. Science can never prove anything to be true. However, I believe the Bible to be God's revealed word and therefore objectively true. My interpretation may be faulty, but the Bible itself is correct.

Teaching without a Teacher

In Isaac Asimov's 1958 short story, *The Feeling of Power*, humans live in a computer-aided society and have forgotten the fundamentals of mathematics, even the rudimentary skill of counting. One day, a lowly technician is discovered who can do calculations without the use of a calculator, using only his mind and a pencil. Authorities are initially skeptical. *"'Computing without a computer,' said the President impatiently, 'is a contradiction in terms.'*[1] However, as this lost art continues to be rediscovered and developed, and progress is made beyond addition and multiplication to calculating square and cube roots manually, an exciting future is envisioned in which a ship can navigate space without computers. The story ends as follows:

> *Nine times seven, thought Shuman with deep satisfaction, is sixty-three, and I don't need a computer to tell me so. The computer is in my own head. And it was amazing the feeling of power that gave him.*[2]

Over the course of the last two centuries, we have become conditioned to believe that schooling without a school, or teaching without a teacher, is an oxymoron, a contradiction in terms. We now have the opportunity to envision a future in which we rediscover the lost art of educating our own children and take it far beyond the practices of our ancestors. And as we claim this opportunity, we will be amazed at the feeling of power it gives us.

Individual Instruction

—Murray Rothbard[3]

Since each person is a unique individual, it is clear that the best type of formal instruction is that type which is suited to his own particular individuality. Each child has different intelligence, aptitudes, and interests. Therefore, the best choice of pace, timing, variety, and manner, and of the courses of instruction will differ widely from one child to another. . . . It is obvious, therefore, that the best type of instruction is individual instruction. A course where one teacher instructs one pupil is clearly by far the best type of course. It is only under such conditions that human potentialities can develop to their greatest degree. It is clear that the formal school, characterized by classes in which one teacher instructs many children, is an immensely inferior system. Since each child differs from the other in interest and ability, and the teacher can only teach one thing at a time, it is evident that every school class must cast all the instruction into one uniform mold. Regardless how the teacher instructs, at what pace, timing, or variety, he is doing violence to each and every one of the children. Any schooling involves misfitting each child into a Procrustean bed of unsuitable uniformity.

All Education is Ethical

In 1967, cigarette manufacturer R.J. Reynolds funded a new program in schools on the West Coast of the USA. The goal of the project was to introduce a value-less curriculum focused on feelings. Over the following years, value-free education programs proliferated in public schools throughout all fifty states.[5] But it is a myth to believe anything can be taught without values.[6] Everyone is ethical, every teacher has beliefs, every subject conveys what is right and wrong, what is important and unimportant. Home education and classical schooling may be overt about teaching virtue, but values are learned in every classroom irrespective of whether they are taught intentionally, even if the claim is that they are simply teaching facts. This is another case of Newtonian mechanics gone awry. It is simply not possible to separate the two. Margit Sutrop at the Centre for Ethics, University of Tartu, Estonia states, *"values permeate every aspect of education and . . . value-free education is impossible."*[7]

To my mind the nature of education is deeply ethical, since it is founded on an understanding of what a human being is and how he or she should live.

—Margit Sutrop[4]

The question is not whether your children are learning a worldview at school. They are, whether the school is public, private, classical, or at home. The question to ask is—are my children being taught the values I want them to acquire? But if morality and virtue are not taught explicitly in the classroom, then how can we identify what students are learning?

One way would be to look at their teachers. Author and speaker Heidi St. John quotes Luke 6:40, "Everyone who is fully trained will be like their teacher," and asks, *"Who is the teacher that my child will become like?"*[8] What is the moral code of those in authority over your children, not only their teacher but also school

There is no such thing as a neutral education. . . . Every education, every curriculum, has a viewpoint. That viewpoint either considers God in it or it does not. To teach children about life and the world in which they live without reference to God is to make a statement about God.

—R.C. Sproul[9]

> *There is no such thing as a non-religious education, because all knowledge involves values.*
>
> —Tony Evans[10]

authorities who direct the lesson content?

Another way would be to look at the values of young people coming out of public schools and universities. As C.S. Lewis argues, teaching our students that the world is knowable only through facts has the effect of destroying the concept of virtue,[11] while *"A dogmatic belief in objective value is necessary to the very idea of a rule which is not tyranny or an obedience which is not slavery."*[12] To identify the values being taught in our schools, we may ask: *"Are rulers becoming tyrants, and the 'educated' population obedient slaves?"*

> *But the great danger is that Satan seeks to deceive us. And this he does when we forget that Christ's kingdom is radically opposed to his at every point. We have an example of this deception in the sphere of education. For many years Christian people have imagined that there could be a neutral system of education. But Satan is not neutral, and neither are his servants. Thus we have seen one restriction after another placed upon Christians in what was supposed to be a neutral system of education. Christians should have realized that this would not work. They should have been the ones who pressed the antithesis, by demanding an education for their children that is only and entirely Christian.*
>
> —Gerald Williamson[14]

It is easy to interpret this question to mean that religious people want to teach their children religious principles. Yes, for many, that would be very much their concern. But there are other values which we might want to pass on. For Ron Paul, the key issues are freedom and personal liberty.[13] You might be more concerned about independent thought and self-determination. Or hard work and perseverance. Maybe you don't want your child to ever succumb to feelings of victimhood or entitlement. Perhaps you wish to pass on cultural values related to your family's ethnic origins. Whatever they are, we all have values, and we should know which ones are being taught to our children.

Rightly Ordering Our Loves

If all education, even that claiming to be "value-free," teaches a worldview—that is, the values and priorities of a culture—then we need to think about what worldview our children are being taught. But does it matter?

In *The Abolition of Man*, Lewis discusses how both Augustine and Aristotle were concerned about the "right ordering of loves," or teaching a student to *"like and dislike what he ought."*[16]

> *Parents should make up their minds what kind of children they want, and what sacrifices they are willing to make. They should be aware of what they can do that teachers never can provide. They should consider carefully how much they risk when they place their children in environments over which they have little control.*
>
> —Raymond Moore[15]

Jordan Peterson speaks about needing a hierarchy of values, without which we are unable to act.[17] If we have learned all the knowledge the scientific, rational world can teach us, but we do not know what we **ought** to do, then our lives will descend into chaos. We won't know whether it's better to do one thing or another. You could say we should act in the best interests of society. Well, that is a value. Who is to say that it is a better value than acting in the best interests of myself? If there is no objective basis for deciding on the higher value, or rightly ordering our loves, then it becomes an arbitrary choice. Life itself becomes a series of arbitrary choices, and society descends into madness.

By taking responsibility for our children's education, we can teach them our priorities, our values, our worldview, and give them the moral compass they need to navigate through the world.

Mindset

It has been suggested that homeschooling is only an option for educated and affluent families. In today's world, most cannot survive on one income. And what about single parents? Hasn't homeschooling become a symbol of the elite?

CHAPTER SIX

I don't believe this is the case at all. I know many families face greater difficulties than we do, and I cannot appreciate all they are going through. Nevertheless, I am convinced the determining factor is attitude. Gerald Bradley was fond of saying *"It is your attitude, not your aptitude that will determine your altitude."*[18]

Let me take you back to my story.

When our eldest was four, we visited the local elementary school which was about a ten-minute walk away. We met the teachers, they provided a list of classroom supplies, and we expected he would begin there next fall. A friend taught at another school nearby, and we would have loved it if our son were in his class. But my biggest concern was the distance to his school. The walk would have been about half an hour. You see, we didn't own a car, and I would be walking my son to and from class each day. Yes, I know your grandfather walked three miles to school. Each way. By himself. In the snow. Without shoes. But I wasn't looking forward to doing that through the Minnesota winter, even though I had shoes.

At that time, we lived with my mother-in-law in her apartment. My wife was trying to get a business underway, but we didn't have any income apart from occasional contracting work. The expense of the classroom supplies list felt daunting.

So when we made the decision to educate our son at home, it wasn't because we were well-off, enjoying a large salary, living in a spacious house in the suburbs. Yes, we are very grateful that our situation has improved since then. But I truly believe we need to start with the attitude, the mind-set, the decision that this is right for our family. Giving up a second salary will impact your lifestyle. But so did having children. We know people who made a deliberate choice to start a family before buying a house. It took them decades of paying rent before they were able to purchase their own home. There was significant financial cost to them, but what price do you place on the love of family? They never regretted their choice to value children above assets.

We should count the cost before making the decision, and maybe it will prove unworkable. But if we have the right mindset, if we genuinely believe home education is the right choice for our children and family, then we might find solutions to what we thought were insurmountable problems. Maybe a grandparent can teach. Maybe you can set up a family business to allow you the flexibility of working from home. Home

School Legal Defense Association (HSLDA) offers compassion grants to families who are struggling financially, and curriculum providers may have payment plans or hardship grants.

I don't believe my statement, *"for perhaps the first time in modern history, almost without exception, every family has the potential to return to the Hebraic Model of education in the home,"* is elitist or a consequence of my own privileged position. I don't mean to diminish the hardship anyone else is facing, but I do believe homeschooling is possible for almost everyone. Certainly, it's not always easy, and maybe not practical, but definitely possible if there is the determination to do so. Financial barriers may be difficult to overcome. The more significant challenges will be faced by those who live in countries where home education is not legal, such as Germany, Costa Rica, and South Korea.[19] For them, the cost is less about finances and more about legal consequences.

The School Revolution: A New Answer for Our Broken Education System

—Ron Paul[20]

The fundamental principle of education is this: families have the final say in the content and structure of education for their children. . . . There is only one way that parents can gain authority over the structure and content of education for their children. They must pay for it. Any attempt to transfer the funding of education to some other institution is by necessity a call for the transfer of some authority over that education to that agency. . . .

I am calling for educational reform based on parents returning to the field of education, money in hand, and demanding the right to educate their children in the way they see fit. The cost of educating the children is not just the cost of buying materials, however. It is also the cost in forfeited time and forfeited money: the parents, or [at] least one of the parents (usually the mother), must devote time to educating the children. . . .

Parents should exercise their legal authority to establish whatever kind of curriculum and structured environment they deem appropriate for their children. This assertion of authority is deeply resented by the states' educational bureaucrats, who for more than 150 years have waged a war against parental authority in the field of education in the United States. . . .

The moral environment is far more important than the academic environment. . . .

Governments and politicians are the problem, not the solution.

Sturdy individuals, stable families, vital communities, limited government, and faith in a transcendent God who provides for us through the natural order and the bounties of nature—these alone can break the grip of the idea [quoting Clarence Carson writing about socialism in *The World in the Grip of an Idea*].

Conclusion

Arthur Bloch said, *"A conclusion is the place where you get tired of thinking."* I've reached that point. There is much more to research and write and reflect upon with regard to the rationale for home education. But it is time to wrap up this section.

So what have we discovered in our look under the hood of education? We have identified education as the raising of a child and instruction in religious, moral, social, and intellectual issues. We have seen that the modern school system with its focus on objective knowledge is built on a foundation of humanism and is antithetical to Judeo-Christian values. And we have argued in favor of withdrawing from public school and building a lighthouse.

How do we do this? Well, obviously in a book about home education, the solution is going to be home education.

Parents Are Responsible

To educate our children—that is, to raise them well and instruct them in religion, morality, culture, and academic knowledge—we need to do the following:

1. Parents need to reclaim their right to determine the best method of educating their children, so they can educate the whole child in the way they think best.

2. Parents need to use an educational program built on a moral foundation which aligns with their values. As a Christian, this means a program based on Biblical principles.

Notice that neither point **requires** you to homeschool. The main assertion is that you should be in control of your children's education. **You** should determine the content and the worldview you wish to transmit, whether that be Christian, classical, modern, or post-modern.

Of course, this is much easier if you are the teacher. But home education by itself is not sufficient if the curriculum you use does not align with your worldview. Whichever option you choose, whether public, private, Christian, classical, or home school, I believe parents should be responsible for their children's education and in charge of what they are taught, particularly with regards to culture, character, and values.

> The fundamental theory of liberty upon which all governments in this Union repose excludes any general power of the State to standardize its children by forcing them to accept instruction from public teachers only. The child is not the mere creature of the State; those who nurture him and direct his destiny have the right, coupled with the high duty, to recognize and prepare him for additional obligations.
>
> —US Supreme Court, 1925[21]

Parents should be responsible for their children's education.

Your Country Needs Your Family

In addition to parents taking responsibility for the content being taught, I believe that education within the family setting is the best way for children to learn. And I think parents prefer it too, despite the effort and sacrifice involved. The time spent growing and learning together fosters strong family bonds. And there's an even bigger picture than yourself or your children. Stable families are the nucleus of a flourishing community. Government policy is not the answer to a society falling apart. Educational institutions cannot counteract the impact on young people of a dysfunctional family. If we want our nation to be reformed and our culture transformed, we need to begin with the foundation.[22] Strong families create strong communities, and strong communities create strong nations.

Your country needs you!

Family and Civilization

—William Federer[23]

In 1934, Oxford anthropologist J.D. Unwin published his book Sex and Culture, *which confirmed the trend described by Plato.*
After studying 86 different tribes and civilizations over 5,000 years, including Sumerians, Babylonians, Greeks, Romans, Teutons, and Anglo-Saxons, Unwin found that sexual promiscuity always preceded the decline of a civilization.
In contrast, his research also showed a 100 percent correlation between monogamous heterosexual marriage and cultural advancement.

For the Good of Society

—Sir Paul Coleridge, former UK High Court judge and founder of Marriage Foundation[24]

In 2012 after forty-three years in the family justice system (fourteen sitting as a judge) watching the inexorable and seemingly unstoppable rise in family breakdown, I began to talk publicly about the scale and depth of the problem.
I was not popular. But I was driven by three motives. Firstly a desire to challenge the entrenched belief that nothing could be done to stop the rot, secondly, a conviction, having watched the fallout for so long in the Family Courts, that our children were the sector of the population most adversely affected by the epidemic; and thirdly, that the remedies had to be applied not only to the amelioration of the problem but its entrenched causes. In short, our children's life chances were being seriously and permanently damaged and we had to do something to publicise the scale of the problem and suggest solutions. . . .

The campaign must go on for "the good of society, especially our children."

Stronger Families, Stronger Societies

—William Bennett, writing in The Opinion Pages of *The New York Times*[25]

I am the product of divorce and several stepfathers, but I still believe in the importance of the traditional family . . . because of the facts and the record.
The family is the nucleus of civilization and the basic social unit of society. . . . Research clearly shows that the institution of the family is the first form of community and government and . . . the first, best and original Department of Health, Education and Welfare.
For a civilization to succeed, the family must succeed.

Three Reasons for Home Education

There are many reasons why I now believe that home education is the best choice for our family, and why I think it's also best for your children. Many benefits are practical, such as the flexibility it affords and the ability to provide each child with individual attention and a customized learning program. But for me, there are fundamental factors that are more significant. Here are my three leading arguments for why you should educate your children.

1. **The Hebraic Model**
   The first argument is that education is better undertaken in the home where parents can mentor and disciple their children.
   This is the model described in the Bible. For Christians, that observation should deserve serious reflection. But even if you are not a Christian, consider the difference between family and state, between home and institution. Your child cannot be separated into intellectual and moral components. He or she is a complete person, and you as parents are the only ones who can offer a complete education. I truly believe that home education will provide your child with the best opportunity to thrive. Yes, it does cost in time, finances, and career prospects. But there are wonderful benefits to spending these formative years with your

children. They grow up so fast, and keeping your children together during the school years is a great basis for a strong family unit that will be a blessing your entire life.

2. The Availability of Resources

The second argument is that the resources needed to educate children in the home are now readily accessible and affordable.

Any academic limitations that may have previously existed are no longer a barrier. Resources are available for all subject areas and for all approaches. You can adopt a classical program, a literature-based curriculum, or any other mode of instruction that you want. There are computer-based courses, online classes in specialist subjects, and co-ops to support you and cover those tricky subjects like science and art. There are organizations to help with what you don't know how to do. Today, a comprehensive, quality education is available to any family who wishes to educate their children at home.

3. The Worldview

The third argument recognizes the parents' right to determine the ethical worldview transmitted to their children.

It is difficult to think of anything that will impact a child's life more than the values they learn. As parents, we should be deliberate about the worldview they are taught and protect them from being inculcated with ethics that do not align with our own. Home education provides us with the greatest opportunity to train our children in the values and cultural norms that we believe are best for them and their future.

> I do believe, however, if we abdicate our God-given role to instruct our children, and hand them over to someone else to be educated, we are missing out on many of the wonderful blessings that God has for us.
>
> —Israel Wayne[26]

NOTES

1. Isaac Asimov, "The Feeling of Power," in *Robot Dreams* (New York: Berkley Books, 1986), p. 244.
2. Asimov, "The Feeling of Power," p. 250.
3. Murray Rothbard, *Education: Free & Compulsory* (Auburn, AL: Ludwig von Mises Institute, 1999), pp. 6-7.
4. Sutrop, "Can Values Be Taught?," p. 190.
5. "Value Free Education "Bankrupt" Says Educator," Jay Rogers ed. *The Forerunner*, 2 May 1989, https://www.forerunner.com/forerunner/X0122_Value_Free_Education.
6. Nash, "The Myth of a Value-Free Education".
7. Margit Sutrop, "Can Values Be Taught? The Myth of Value-Free Education," *Trames. A Journal of the Humanities and Social Sciences* 19, no. 2 (2015): p. 189, https://doi.org/10.3176/tr.2015.2.06.
8. Garritt Hampton, "Schoolhouse Rocked: The Homeschool Revolution," (Vision Video, 2021). DVD.
9. R.C. Sproul, *The Myth of Neutral Education, Christian Education* (Ligonier Ministries).
10. Tony Evans, *The Kingdom Agenda* (Nashville, TN: W Publishing, 1999), p. 391.
11. Turley, *The Abolition of Sanity*, p. 8.
12. Lewis, *Abolition of Man*, p. 46.
13. Ron Paul Curriculum, https://www.ronpaulcurriculum.com.
14. Williamson, *The Westminster Shorter Catechism*, p. 334.
15. Moore, Moore, and Moore, *Better Late than Early*, p. 24.
16. Lewis, *Abolition of Man*, p. 10.
17. Jordan Peterson, *12 Rules for Life: An Antidote to Chaos* (Toronto: Random House, 2018), p. 198.
18. Gerald H. Bradley, *Powerful Inspirational Motivation* (Kuala Lumpur: Vinlin Press, 1993), p. 25.
19. Homeschool Legal Defense Association, https://hslda.org/legal/international, accessed 31 December 2022.
20. Paul, *The School Revolution*, pp. 69, 76, 91, 188, 196. Used with permission.
21. U.S. Supreme Court, "Pierce v. Society of Sisters," in *268 U.S. 510* (1925). https://supreme.justia.com/cases/federal/us/268/510.
22. Israel Wayne, *Revival in the Home* (1 September 2014).
23. Federer, *Socialism*, p. 14.
24. Marriage Foundation, https://marriagefoundation.org.uk/about-us, accessed 9 January 2023.
25. William Bennett, "Stronger Families, Stronger Societies," *The New York Times* 24 April 2012, https://www.nytimes.com/roomfordebate/2012/04/24/are-family-values-outdated/stronger-families-stronger-societies.
26. Wayne, *Education: Does God Have an Opinion?*, p. 60.

PART 2

ABOUT FATHERS

Exploring the challenges
of transitioning from a career to a calling
as the full-time educator of one's children.

WHEN DAD IS THE TEACHER

The Elephant in the Room

The average cost of raising a child in the USA, from birth to age eighteen and excluding savings for tertiary education, is reported to be $310,605.[1] Whether or not you spend that much, we are all aware that having children means investing in what benefits our family. As parents, we know the feeling of sacrificing for our children and relinquishing personal ambitions for the sake of others. Family is all about self-sacrifice, with marriage being the first step in really understanding this process by transitioning from "I" to "we."

When I was newly married, back before I had children of my own and so naturally knew everything about raising them, people would tell me and my wife that we needed to enjoy life as a couple before starting a family. The unspoken implication was—before we became burdened with kids, and they cramped our lifestyle. The years before children were supposedly the time to travel, live in the city, drive a nice car, and develop our careers. Once kids arrived, it would be all over.

In my great wisdom, I would respond to this advice by saying that life with children wouldn't be worse, it would just be different. It wasn't a case of one lifestyle being better than the other. My philosophy was to make the most of every season—to enjoy life as a single, then to enjoy life as a couple, and then to enjoy life with children.

A similar mindset applies to living in a different country. Being a foreigner, I am frequently asked: "Which is better—living in the USA or in New Zealand? Do you miss your homeland?" I always reply that I make a point of appreciating what's great about my current location, because if I were to spend my time thinking about what's better elsewhere, I would miss that which is wonderful about where I live today.

CHAPTER SEVEN

Those of us who homeschool have chosen to do so for the benefit of our children. We know this involves sacrifice, not only of finances and time but also of careers. And it's a price we are willing to pay because we understand the tremendous blessings and benefits in doing so. Our focus is on what's best for our children. And the focus of this book is our children, and the thoughts and ideas about home education I have developed as a result of coming into this role from an engineering background. My goal is to inspire and encourage and help you on your journey.

It is about foundational principles, with the starting point being the values underpinning choices and decisions. Understanding the "why" is necessary before deciding on the "how." From this source flow the every-day decisions, both the longer-term choices affecting an entire school year and beyond as well as the daily decisions made in the moment.

It is about how, as an engineer, I have gone about educating my sons. What difference does it make that I have an analytical mindset? That my *modus operandi* is to experiment and test and try things out? That I view the challenges we face in life, even the people challenges, as simply problems to be solved? What have I learned and observed and tried out while on this journey?

But first, I will address the elephant in the room—the bull elephant. That would be me. I'm going to talk about being a man. What difference does it make when the teacher is the father, rather than the mother? What impact does this have on dad? This book doesn't focus on fathers exclusively, but it may very well be the reason you picked it up. As a man, I have wrestled with this role over the years, so let's take some time to explore the topic together.

I don't think men and women are the same. I believe that husbands and wives have different and complementary roles in the family, and I am not suggesting there should be more men taking primary responsibility for their children.

But sometimes, things just work out that way. Sometimes, circumstances leave no other choice.

When dad looks after the children and becomes their teacher, he can do the job and do it well. It isn't a neutral decision though, and both parents should be aware of the implications, of the long-term challenges he faces: spiritually, socially, psychologically, and emotionally. As with the rest of this book, this part is directed toward both parents. However, where the father is the teacher, it is really important that their wives read this chapter also. Men tend to set aside, or bottle up, their emotions and get on with the job at hand. I have talked very little to anyone about my struggle to embrace this role, and my wife may learn more from this chapter than she has from me directly in the last eight years!

A Career Forfeited

Much of what I reflect on in Part 2 is related to a loss of identity and purpose experienced through giving up aspirations for a career. I can only speak from my perspective as a man, but many of these struggles may be shared by women who have relinquished their career goals to become a full-time mom. Being at home with the children is a sacrifice made for the benefit of the family, whether or not homeschooling is involved. I can imagine many women will also identify with the challenges I have faced, particularly in the emotional and psychological areas. I hope moms also find encouragement and insight from what I have to share.

Ladies, this is for you too.

The Homeschool Dad

The Hidden Minority

In homeschool circles, fathers are usually mentioned in the context of how he can share his wife's workload, typically by tutoring mathematics and helping with science experiments and field trips in the evenings or on weekends when he is home from work. Homeschool conferences have sessions with titles such as "Help, I'm Married to a Homeschool Mom!" and "How to Get Dads Involved in Homeschooling." They discuss how dad is like the school principal while mom is the classroom teacher.

When fathers are acknowledged as the teacher, it is usually mentioned as an afterthought to cover the bases. Because, you know, there may be the odd man out there who is actually doing the homeschooling. So I come across somewhat patronizing lines like "when Mom is teaching—or it could even be Dad . . ."

How many of us are there? I couldn't find any hard data regarding the number of dads who are teaching their children full-time. Many people have told me that they've heard of a homeschooling father, but

I have never met or spoken with one. Very little has been written for or about us. In my research, I unearthed only one podcast addressing this topic[2] and nothing written for or by a homeschooling dad.

It would be safe to assume we are a small percentage, yet if the ratio is only one in a hundred, that is still many thousands of homeschooling dads in the USA alone.

How Many Homeschool Dads?

The most recent Household Pulse Survey covering the 2020–21 academic year indicates that 11.1 percent of the 32.2 million households in the US with school-age children include at least one homeschool child.[3] This amounts to over three and a half million parents teaching their children.

Studies have shown that at least 90 percent of homeschooled children are taught by their mother.[4] This does not mean 10 percent are taught by their father, as grandparents or other relatives are likely to play a role, and many couples may share the responsibility. But if 1 percent of the teachers were fathers, that is still over 35,000 homeschool dads in the USA.[5]

Men Without (Paid) Work

In 2016, Dr. Nicholas Eberstadt published a study entitled "Men Without Work"[6] which highlighted an overlooked crisis: depression-era work rates for American men of *"prime working age"* (25–54 years). This work rate had been steadily decreasing for half a century, until by 2016 in the USA, nearly one in six prime working-age men had no paid employment at all—and nearly one in eight were out of the labor force entirely, neither working nor even looking for work. The *New York Times* described this as *"an unsettling portrait not just of male unemployment, but also of lives deeply alienated from civil society."*[7]

Combined with the growth of the homeschool movement, this trend toward more men being without work means, undoubtedly, the number of homeschool dads is increasing. The pressures they face are not unique to homeschooling but are part of a broader societal trend, a trend which even the *New York Times* recognizes is alienating for the men involved.

Homeschool Dad: A father whose primary responsibility is the education of his children.

While there are many ways to understand the term "homeschool dad," this book uses it exclusively to indicate a father whose primary family role is raising and teaching his children. I am not referring to a dad who shares teaching responsibilities with his wife, or who fits homeschooling duties around full-time or part-time paid employment or self-employment. Typically, his wife would be earning the sole family income. In this book, a homeschool dad is one whose primary role is teaching his children.

Let me clarify a couple of points.

First, by homeschool dad I mean a father who is at home with the children all day and is not working at another job, whether full-time, part-time, or self-employed. Homeschooling affords great flexibility, and many families take advantage of this, leading to considerable variation in family dynamics. There are plenty of cases where the parents share responsibilities for childcare and education and earning income, or where the father is self-employed or works from home and is closely involved with his children's education. In some families, both parents work full-time but, because of flexible hours, are able to fit homeschooling around work.

It is great if families can adapt and have the father involved. However, there is a significant difference between being involved and taking sole responsibility for something. In my view, when it concerns childcare, this difference constitutes a quantum leap rather than a matter of degree. Much of the distinction may be in the mind of the father, but I think the difference between "a homeschool dad" and "a dad who homeschools" is far more profound than merely a variation in terminology.

There is a fundamental difference between being involved and taking full responsibility.

The issues raised in the following chapters are far more easily resolved or may not even be relevant if the father is working to support his family and partnering with his wife in the educational endeavor. By contrast, in this book, the term "homeschool dad" refers to the father who has taken primary responsibility for educating his children and sees this as his essential role. In this family dynamic, the wife is the principal income generator.

Second, having said that, I am not advocating for more representation of fathers in this role. I am not calling for support groups for homeschool dads or saying the homeschool community needs to be more inclusive in recognizing men as home educators. What I **do** intend is to bring a greater awareness of the particular needs of homeschool dads, because they are different.

The vast majority of homeschool teachers are moms, so it's appropriate that homeschool conferences and organizations and curriculum companies focus on them. They are entirely justified in assuming their target audience is women. I am reminded of this every time a supplier sends me an encouraging email on Mother's Day! I understand completely that the support group at my church, "Homeschool Mamas," was hesitant to allow me to attend because my presence would change the dynamic and might mean moms wouldn't feel as free to share openly. Would I want to reveal my struggles at a women's group? Not in a million years! (Although, given my temperament, I wouldn't be likely to share at a men's group either!)

And yet, I know I am not the only homeschool dad. For me, it has been a long and lonely journey. Part of that is self-inflicted. I have never attended a homeschool conference. I have never tried to become involved in a homeschool support group or co-op or forum. I have never talked to anyone about what it's like being a stay-at-home dad educating my children. And although I have known in the back of my mind that this is an important subject to grapple with, I have never deliberately reflected on my journey. Until now. The process of writing this section has been cathartic. And as you read, I hope you will be informed and encouraged as we explore the implications of being a papa in a homeschool mama's world.

The Good

There are some great benefits to being a stay-at-home dad, and a male teacher in the classroom is something to celebrate.

In my small hometown, the chair of the primary school board was a member of our church. She once told me that if two similarly qualified teachers applied at her school and one was male, she would hire him every time. She wasn't sexist and didn't believe men were better at the job. But she knew that teachers are predominantly women, and that many children progress through their entire primary school education without a single male teacher. She also knew that a male figure in the classroom would be beneficial for the large number of fatherless children. In her view, male teachers were a more valuable asset to the school because they were male, not because they were better teachers.

Women make up 76 percent of all teachers at public and private schools. At the elementary school level, women comprise 89 percent of teachers.

—2017–18 National Teacher and Principal Survey[8]

According to the US Census Bureau, based on 2019 figures, 73 percent of all STEM workers were men. Men comprised 52 percent of all US workers.[9]

Having a father as the teacher is therefore a great thing. Both sons and daughters benefit from the presence of a committed male figure in the home. Even in well-functioning families, the father may spend long hours at work and have limited day-to-day involvement with his children. Dad being at home and actively involved is a blessing, as it gives him more opportunity to be a role model to his children.[10]

In generations past, the father would naturally be a mentor by teaching practical skills on the farm or in a trade. But today, many children never see their father at work. Since the industrial revolution moved occupations out of the home, fathers have had less chance to spend time with their children and pass on their wisdom, knowledge, and skills.

Dad as the teacher provides a wonderful opportunity for this to occur. In addition, learning about the outdoors, embracing adventure, taking risks, playing sports, and being competitive are inherently on the syllabus. Men have the potential to be excellent instructors, and children are likely to thrive just as much if they are taught by their father as by their mother.

This part of the book, however, is not about whether men are **able** to perform the role of teacher. It's not about whether the children will survive being taught by their dad. It's about whether their dad will survive. It's whether he can, as Chris Boyer says, *"move on from mere survival to a place of 'Thrival.'"*

We turn next to the impact on dad when he is the stay-at-home teacher.

The Bad & the Ugly

For all the good about having a homeschool dad, there are also downsides.

Raising children is not for the faint-hearted. Yes, it's wonderful, but it is also hard work. Adding home education to the equation multiplies the amount of work. Not many women are prepared to take on this task, and even fewer men.

Let's say you are convinced as parents that the education of your children is your responsibility. If that is your conviction, as it is mine, then you should find a way to make it happen if it's within your power to do so. And if that means dad needs to be the teacher, then dad should be the teacher. But there are implications. Along with the good, there is the bad and the ugly. There are psychological and emotional challenges dad will face, along with social pressures. There are spiritual dynamics that come into play. He may feel isolated, undervalued, and inadequate for the role. Women may experience similar feelings when they become stay-at-home moms, but that's little comfort to the man taking on this task.

It won't help either the husband or wife to sugar-coat the down-sides, but we can more easily avoid misery if we understand what we are facing. It will help you to be aware of what follows, to understand there is hope, and to know that both you and your children are worth it.

NOTES

1. Maryalene LaPonsie, "How Much Does It Cost to Raise a Child?," *U.S. News* (7 September 2022), https://money.usnews.com/money/personal-finance/articles/how-much-does-it-cost-to-raise-a-child.
2. Hal and Melanie Young, "When DAD Is the Teacher," *Making Biblical Family Life Practical*, episode MBFLP 204 (13 June 2018). Podcast audio. https://ultimateradioshow.com/when-dad-is-the-teacher-mbflp-204.
   The podcast did not interview a homeschool dad, and most of the episode was spent talking about other topics.
3. *What Is Homeschooling?*, HSLDA Action (Purcellville, VA, 2022).
4. Lines, "Home Instruction: The Size and Growth of the Movement."
5. A 2023 *Washington Post* survey suggests that the number of dads who are the primary homeschool educator has increased from 5 percent in 2019 to 40 percent in 2023. Suzanne Blake, "Dads Homeschooling Children Surges," *Newsweek* (28 September 2023), https://www.newsweek.com/dads-homeschooling-increase-pandemic-remote-work-1830730.
   The figure of 40 percent is certainly not accurate, although the number of dads involved in their children's homeschooling activities is undoubtedly increasing as more are working from home.
6. Nicholas Eberstadt, *Men Without Work: America's Invisible Crisis*, New Threats to Freedom, (West Conshohocken, PA: Templeton Press, 2016).
7. American Enterprise Institute, https://www.aei.org/research-products/book/men-without-work-2, accessed 3 January 2023.
8. S. Taie and R. Goldring, *Characteristics of Public and Private Elementary and Secondary School Teachers in the United States: Results from the 2017–18 National Teacher and Principal Survey*, National Center for Education Statistics (Washington, DC: U.S. Department of Education, 2020), https://nces.ed.gov/pubsearch/pubsinfo.asp?pubid=2020142rev.
9. Anthony Martinez and Cheridan Christnacht, "Women Making Gains in STEM Occupations but Still Underrepresented," *United States Census Bureau* (26 January 2021), https://www.census.gov/library/stories/2021/01/women-making-gains-in-stem-occupations-but-still-underrepresented.html.
10. Farrington cites numerous references that highlight the benefits to children of their father's involvement, and says *"many articles have been written showing consistent results with father involvement: increased levels of father involvement have positive impacts on student performance, disciplinary issues, and positive outcomes for children."* Farrington, "The Lived Experience of Evangelical Christian Homeschooling Fathers," p. 194.

THE SPIRITUAL MAN

Spiritual Considerations

A Biblical Model

As a Christian, the starting point for any question in life is this: what does God say about it in the Bible? We are created in the image of God; we are spiritual beings. For me, then, the starting point for understanding homeschool dads is the spiritual perspective. And some clear Biblical principles need to be considered when thinking about the role of fathers in the family.

> "So God created man in his own image, in the image of God he created him; male and female he created them" (Genesis 1:27).
>
> "Therefore a man shall leave his father and his mother and hold fast to his wife, and they shall become one flesh" (Genesis 2:24).
>
> "The Lord God took the man and put him in the garden of Eden to work it and keep it" (Genesis 2:15).
>
> "For I have chosen him, that he may command his children and his household after him to keep the way of the Lord by doing righteousness and justice" (Genesis 18:19).
>
> "But if anyone does not provide for his relatives, and especially for members of his household, he has denied the faith and is worse than an unbeliever" (1 Timothy 5:8).
>
> "Likewise, husbands, live with your wives in an understanding way, showing honor to the woman as the weaker vessel, since they are heirs with you of the grace of life, so that your prayers may not be hindered" (1 Peter 3:7).

"Children are a heritage from the LORD, the fruit of the womb a reward. Like arrows in the hand of a warrior are the children of one's youth. Blessed is the man who fills his quiver with them!" (Psalm 127:3-5).

"But I want you to understand that the head of every man is Christ, the head of a wife is her husband, and the head of Christ is God" (1 Corinthians 11:3).

"She looks well to the ways of her household and does not eat the bread of idleness. Her children rise up and call her blessed; her husband also, and he praises her" (Proverbs 31:27-28).

"Older women likewise are to be reverent in behavior, not slanderers or slaves to much wine. They are to teach what is good, and so train the young women to love their husbands and children, to be self-controlled, pure, working at home, kind, and submissive to their own husbands, that the word of God may not be reviled" (Titus 2:3-5).

There is something deep within the heart of a man that makes him want to protect his family and provide for them financially. He just **knows** he is supposed to be the breadwinner. For the Christian, 1 Timothy 5:8 provides confirmation that this is the role of a worthy husband.

I sensed there must be more to it. That as a homeschool dad, I wasn't breaking the law of God. That I wasn't failing my family. But it took me a long time to face this issue head-on and reach an understanding that teaching my children was what God had called me to do, rather than it being a failure on my part. Eventually, I came to the realization that protection and provision should be understood more broadly than simply earning money. We are protecting our children and providing for them in a much more profound way by teaching, mentoring, and discipling them, and this is entirely consistent with what the Bible teaches.

Later in this chapter, I will look further at the theology of a father's role in the family and talk about the solutions I have found to give homeschool dads hope. But for now, let's go back to where I was when I first took on this role of stay-at-home dad.

The Role of Provider: Part 1

My belief about what the Bible said went something like this.

> *God created family, and He created us to be in a family. His model is for children to be raised in a Godly home with two parents—a father and a mother. The father's role is to be the head of the household and provide for his wife and children, both protection and provision. The mother's role is to manage the home and care for their children. Together, the parents raise their children in the fear and knowledge of the* LORD.

But we live in a fallen world. Sin has impacted every aspect of our lives, including our families. There is no such thing as the perfect family, and so in our world today we are familiar with broken people and broken homes. Thankfully, God extends grace to us and is able to take our broken lives and use them for His glory; thus, His purposes can still be fulfilled through imperfect people and families.

However, that does not mean His ideal is no longer relevant. As Jordan Peterson observed, we shouldn't sacrifice the ideal simply because we know we can never attain it. We should still strive to follow the Biblical example as closely as we can, and that includes the husband's role as provider.

This, I think, was the biggest struggle I faced—believing that I was not providing for my family.

I started off well. By the age of thirty I had a well-paid job, was financially secure, owned a house and a car and a motorbike, and had saved $30,000 to fund the process of finding, courting, and marrying a woman. I paid off my fiancée's student debt and covered most of the cost of our wedding. I was a Bible College student when we married, and my wife was a consultant. For our entire married life, she has earned more than me. It didn't bother me in those newlywed days because I had brought significant financial assets into our marriage. And by the time I finished my MBA, I knew a lucrative corporate job was just around the corner.

Except it wasn't.

And when I thought about this Biblical model of a husband and father and of the role of a provider, I felt acutely aware of how I failed to measure up.

2 Thessalonians 3:10 says that if we do not work, then we should not eat. Of course, we know childcare counts. Work in the home may be under-appreciated, but honorable men affirm the vital contribution their wives make to the household. My wife has consistently and vociferously affirmed my role in the home, and has often taken me to task for replying *"Nothing"* when I'm asked, *"What do you do?"* But I can tell you, as a father it was not very satisfying to admit I was a stay-at-home dad. I felt I was not providing for my household as commanded in 1 Timothy 5:8.

Your Job Is Not Who You Are

In today's world, as it has been for millennia, our identity is often indistinguishable from our jobs. We respond to the question *"What do you do?"* by saying *"I am . . ."* rather than *"I do . . ."* Many surnames such as Cooper, Smith, and Baker are simply an ancestor's trade.

I hate being asked *"What do you do?"* Even worse, someone recently used the phrase, *"Obviously you work . . ."* Every time I hear that, I die a little inside. Sure, I could come up with some clever comeback: *"I'm socializing two* Homo sapiens *into the dominant values of the Judeo-Christian tradition,"* but that merely feels like glossing over the issue.

I was once asked at church whether I had found work, and replied, *"Yes! I'm a private tutor to two gifted children!"* The woman who asked was delighted; she knew I had been job-hunting for a long time. But then I watched the joy in her face fade as the penny dropped, and she realized I meant I was actually "just teaching my children." To avoid any misrepresentation, I absolutely affirm that teaching your children is one of the most worthwhile activities in which you could invest your time. And the person at church would agree. But in that moment, her unguarded reaction encapsulated my pain.

It wasn't an issue of whether I could competently answer the question, *"What do you do?"* It didn't matter if I rejected society's error in conflating work with identity. The issue for me was that my task as a father was to be the provider. How could I be the leader of my household when I was not providing for them?

This is something every homeschool dad faces. It's something they and their wives need to consider together and appreciate that it goes deeper than our culture's tendency to equate identity with paid employment. There is a spiritual element as well.

> *I am socialising two* Homo sapiens *into the dominant values of the Judeo-Christian tradition in order that they might be instruments for the transformation of the social order into the kind of eschatological utopia that God willed from the beginning of creation. And what do you do?*
>
> —Peggy Campolo, a full-time mother, responding to the question, "*What do you do?*"[1]

And it's something for which I initially had no solutions. I knew there would be answers to the social, psychological, and emotional aspects of being a stay-at-home father. But until writing this book, I didn't know what to say about the spiritual side of the equation, except that we live in a fallen world and that's how it is.

To be clear, I don't believe it is breaking God's law for the wife to be the provider and the husband to educate his children. However, I believe God has laid out in the Bible the principles for living a life of abundance, because He created not only the universe but also the laws of the universe. He knows best how life works. The wisdom contained in the Bible is for our benefit. We should do our utmost to follow these patterns as closely as we can and be cautious if our circumstances are pushing us in a different direction. We should always seek God's direction, trust Him to correct us if we step to the right or to the left (Isaiah 30:21), and then ask Him to bless the decision we have made to the best of our abilities, knowing we are always dependent on His provision and strength in every situation.

Theological Correction

It will come as no surprise that when you scrape away the theories and explanations and excuses, when you look for what underpins the spiritual, social, psychological, and emotional struggles, when you get beyond the disillusionment and frustration and helplessness, the heart of all my issues was pride. I **wanted** to have a rewarding career. I **wanted** to be the breadwinner. I **wanted** to be seen as successful. And when that didn't happen, I tried to blame something or someone other than myself. Life was not fair. American companies were stupid for ignoring my talent. It was God's fault.

Walking through the Valley

My wife's father was a Bible teacher passionate about sound theology. Sitting with his family in the pews listening to a speaker, he would at times whisper to his children, *"Theological correction coming."* They knew that once home, their dad was going to correct the errant theology of the preacher!

And so it's time to correct my interpretation of the Biblical imperative to provide for my household. It's essential, however, to understand why I didn't simply begin this section with sound theology.

During the years of feeling inadequate and a failure, it wasn't a solution I needed. Being given a theological kick in the pants would not fix the problem. I deliberately didn't want to understand the truth so that I had an excuse to avoid dealing with my pride.

What I needed was someone to understand my pain and walk with me anyway. I would sit in church and listen to testimonies of people who have struggled and overcome, and now want to share what helped them. Rather than being encouraged, I would feel even more despondent and think, *"Why don't they ask me for my testimony? I'd say, 'I'm struggling through the dark, deep in the valley, and I can't see any way out. But God is still God.'"* That's it. That's all I had.

So if you are a dad who is feeling the pain of not providing for your family, I know what that's like. Even if you have accepted your role, that doesn't mean the struggle is over. Offering solutions is not the same as identifying with your battle. I want you to know I feel for you and know what it's like. In many ways, I'm still going through the valley myself. But I now have a perspective that has helped me better understand my journey and begin to come to terms with my situation. I hope this will help you also.

The Dark Night of the Soul

"The Dark Night of the Soul" is a title given to a poem by the sixteenth century Spanish mystic St. John of the Cross. This expression signifies the beginning of a shift in perspective from our ego to our soul. According to Eckhart Tolle, it describes a collapse of perceived meaning in life when an identity derived from our career, wealth, relationships, or roles is challenged. What dies, in essence, is the egotistic sense of self.

CHAPTER EIGHT

What to Do During the Dark Night of the Soul

—Yong Kang Chan, "The Emotional Gift"[2]

Embrace it instead of resisting it.
First, you have to realize that the Dark Night of the Soul is not some-thing that you have to fix. Fixing is what the mind wants and is familiar with. Our mind is problem-focused. Sometimes, our mind creates a problem so that it has something to fix.
However, the Dark Night of the Soul is a process initiated by the soul. The soul desires growth and expansion. It pulls you towards a direction of love, joy, and peace because the soul knows that you are ready for growth.

The process cannot be rushed, but if we allow God to do His work, we will emerge with our identity defined by the value God places on us, rather than that which we create based on our achievements. We are not what we do; we are who God says we are.

And that is why I didn't want to jump too quickly to solutions. I want you to understand the valley's depths before we climb back up to the mountaintop.

But now, let's correct that theology!

The Role of Provider: Part 2

Central to my struggles was the belief that I should protect and provide for my family: "If anyone does not provide for his relatives, and especially for members of his household, he has denied the faith and is worse than an unbeliever" (1 Timothy 5:8). The modern man, reading this verse in English, immediately equates "provide" with finances. But the Greek term *pronoéō*, translated "provide" in most English translations but "care for" in the New Living Translation, has the following definition: *to consider in advance, to look out for beforehand, to provide (for)*. We shouldn't think of this verse exclusively in terms of finances or even material assets. Looking after and caring for our family involves much more than earning an income, and 1 Timothy 5:8 conveys this broad meaning rather than a narrow understanding of "provide (money)." In addition, this verse employs the Greek indefinite pronoun. The use of "he" in most English translations refers to any person, male or female.[3]

If 1 Timothy 5:8 doesn't say that the husband should be the financial breadwinner, then is there any other Biblical support for this position? Or is this interpretation a result of ego and culture? Although Scripture clearly assigns different roles to husbands and wives, I don't see any indication that this difference relates to employment. Both husbands and wives are described as earning income, and in fact, Proverbs 31:10–31 specifically praises the noble wife who has a successful business and provides food for her household, while her husband volunteers his time in leading the city.

Furthermore, while there is no Scriptural justification for saying that earning the money is dad's job, there **is** plenty to suggest the father has primary responsibility for his children's education. This doesn't mean he is instructed to do all of the teaching, as the Bible clearly gives this role to both parents. But he is explicitly responsible for discipling his children.[4,5] Ephesians 6:4, which talks about instructing children, is specifically directed to the father rather than generically referring to the husband or wife.

"Fathers, do not exasperate your children; instead, bring them up in the training and instruction of the Lord" (Ephesians 6:4 NIV).

"Hear, O sons, a father's instruction, and be attentive, that you may gain insight" (Proverbs 4:1).

"And he will turn the hearts of fathers to their children and the hearts of children to their fathers, lest I come and strike the land with a decree of utter destruction" (Malachi 4:6).

In Genesis 2:15, God put man in the garden to tend it. After the Fall, as a consequence of sin entering the world, Adam's work became difficult. This suggests it is the Biblical norm for men to undertake physical work. In the agrarian world of the Bible, providing for a family usually involved hard manual labor. Since men are generally physically stronger than women, husbands would be expected to take on this manual role in order to honor their wife as the weaker partner (1 Peter 3:7) while still acknowledging her equality before God. To complement this, women tend to be more nurturing, making up an estimated 94 percent of pre-school teachers in the USA[6] and 90 percent of nurses globally.[7] Wives would generally raise the children and maintain the home.

But this distinction between the **roles** of husband and wife is not mandated in the Bible. It is descriptive, rather than prescriptive.

Where does that leave us, then? The culmination of these insights is an updated Biblical model of the family.

God created family, and He created us to be in family. His model is for children to be raised in a Godly home with two parents—a father and a mother. The husband's role is to be the head of the household and to protect and care for his wife and children. The husband and wife, as one flesh and equal partners before God, work within their respective areas of gifting to manage the household and care for their children. Together, the parents raise their children in the fear and knowledge of the LORD.

A Comprehensive Examination of 1 Timothy 5:8

—Dr. George Wieland,[8] former Research Fellow and New Testament Lecturer, Carey Baptist College

"But if anyone does not provide for his relatives, and especially for members of his household, he has denied the faith and is worse than an unbeliever" (1 Timothy 5:8).

The word "provide" (Greek: pronoeō) is understood in a much broader sense than making financial provision. The term comprises "pro" (beforehand) and "noeō" (think, perceive, intend). So its basic sense is of taking thought for. This sense is demonstrated by the two other instances in the New Testament where pronoeō is used, Romans 12:17 (taking into consideration, planning, intending good) and 2 Corinthians 8:21 (again, giving thought to what is good). In each case, Paul is urging the Christians to give thought to how they behave and respond to others, considering what is good both in God's eyes and in the eyes of other people. The implicit framing is the dual responsibility that Paul sees, to the Lord in worship and obedience and to people in the witness of their lives.

In 1 Timothy 5, the immediate context is the question of the provision for the widows in the Christian community. "Widows and orphans" were among the most vulnerable groups in society, and both the

Old and New Testaments reveal God as one who cares particularly for them, and instructs communities of people who worship God to give special attention to include them in the festivals, help them out practically in whatever ways were required (food, money, housing), and stand up for them when they were being treated unjustly or ignored by the authorities because of their poverty. The first generations of Christian believers also found themselves with a large number of widows among them and the practical provision for those widows was a major activity (Acts 6). 1 Timothy reflects that reality.

Provision for someone often took the form of taking them into a household. For those widows who were not included within the life and care of a household, life was precarious and the church as a community had to consider becoming the substitute family or household for them. Paul sees it as a basic duty of worshippers of God to make that kind of provision, which would involve all that is included in sharing life, not only providing somewhere to sleep and a meal a day.

In verse 8, the subject of the verb pronoeō is the indefinite pronoun "tis." It's in the masculine form by default, but the usage is general—"If anyone/someone/one does not . . ." It is anyone in the position to provide the necessary care. Most often that would be the patriarch of the household but there were examples of women heading households (for example, Lydia in Acts 16). It seems that Paul is not concerned here with the gender of the provider, but the responsibilities of people with resources towards those—especially those of their own families—who are in need.

There is one further point to note: the particular issue here is not parents failing to provide for their children, but adult children failing to provide for their parents (verse 4). Paul's concern in Romans and Corinthians about Christians not doing what is recognized as good or virtuous by people generally resonates with the concern of many Asian Christians that they could be shamed in their societies if they do not demonstrate the level of respect and care for parents that their societies regard as virtuous. The perception that Christianity makes people disregard their parents is a major challenge in many cultures.

CHAPTER EIGHT

Spiritual Solutions

We'll finish this chapter by focusing on solutions.

Not every father will go through the same struggles I did. I'm sure many of you will cope much better! I do believe, however, that the issues I am discussing in the current and subsequent chapters will be relevant to most men. At the very least, being aware of them is the first line of defense in ensuring they do not derail your endeavors to educate your children. In each chapter, I will talk about what I faced and try to understand the root causes but will end with solutions and practical ideas for helping fathers embrace their manhood while teaching their children.

Spiritual Solution 1:
Affirm your God-given calling.

For years, men of the patriarchy have lauded the critical role that mothers play in the home. And rightly so. We can cheerfully claim that while we are providing for and building the present, mothers are raising the next generation who will shape our future. Now, if we find the shoe on the other foot, it's time to dispel any doubt that our words were empty platitudes masking a secret conviction that our careers were the superior calling. It's time to honestly believe what we've been saying.

As a parent, there is nothing more important than investing in your children. You can consider being a homeschool dad as a higher calling than being the breadwinner. Money is temporal, but the impact of nurturing a young life in the knowledge and fear of the LORD has eternal consequences.

It may be tempting to think that a solution is for the husband and wife to share roles, affording your family the best of both worlds. In some situations, this might be an effective compromise. However, in general I believe our children need one of their parents to focus on them and to accept raising and educating them as their vocation. If circumstances dictate that this parent is the father, then that is what God has called you to do. You are protecting and caring for your family in a far more meaningful way than by providing income.

Spiritual Solution 2: Answer the question.

If the first solution to the spiritual challenge is to affirm your God-given calling, then the second is to respond on this basis when asked, *"What do you do?"* Come up with something that makes you feel good about yourself. Something that would make a VP in a Fortune 500 company embarrassed to answer your follow-up question, *"And what do you do?"* If Peggy Campolo's response is too much for you, try something more straight forward: *"I'm investing in the future of our family by providing my children with the best education they can possibly receive."* Or maybe you could say something like this:

> *I am a full-time homeschool dad, and it is the most challenging and rewarding role I've ever had. It's taken immense work to get to this point and many sacrifices as a family. Still, it's all been worth it for our children's academic and emotional gains.*

NOTES

1. *NZ Baptist*, June 2006, p. 15.
2. Yong Kang Chan, "How to Get Through the Dark Night of the Soul," *Nerdy Creator*, 31 March 2020, https://www.nerdycreator.com/blog/dark-night-of-the-soul.
3. Dr. Malcolm Elliot-Hogg, PhD in Semitic studies and lecturer in Greek, 12 December 2022. Personal correspondence.
4. Wayne, *Is Homeschooling Just for Women?*
5. Young, "When DAD Is the Teacher".
6. "Preschool Teacher Demographics and Statistics in the US," *Zippia* (9 September 2022), https://www.zippia.com/preschool-teacher-jobs/demographics, accessed 23 November 2022.
7. "ICN Celebrates International Women's Day." Press release, 8 March 2021, https://www.icn.ch/news/icn-celebrates-international-womens-day.
8. Dr. George Wieland, Former Research Fellow and New Testament Lecturer, Carey Baptist College (Auckland, NZ), 17 December 2022. Personal correspondence. Used with permission.

THE SOCIAL MAN

Social Considerations

As important as it is to be aware of the spiritual aspects of deciding to become a homeschool dad, we know God is gracious. But people are less so. Part of what I have wrestled with are the expectations of others. I don't care much about other people's opinions, but I do care about my wider family.

Setting an Example

My Dad was not much of a talker, but his actions spoke louder than words. He never once discussed finances with me, yet his example of wise stewardship put me on solid financial ground. He worked hard, serving the LORD as the director of a camping and conference center. My siblings and I saw the long hours of ministry and physical labor, took part in plenty of it ourselves, and were involved in all that happened at the camp. Even though he was never well-paid, Dad provided for his family. I know he loved me, but he never did understand why I spent so much time at university. He was waiting for me to put that learning to good use and do something more worthwhile with my life than simply collect degrees.

When my wife and I moved to the USA, my career as a business consultant was poised to take off. I knew what I wanted and how to get it, and just needed that one opportunity at a big consulting firm to prove to my Dad that all the training was justified. All I needed was that job.

Mum would have been proud of me teaching my boys, but I always felt like a disappointment to my Dad. He wouldn't have minded if I were flipping burgers, as long as I were working hard. I started Uber driving before Dad passed away in 2019. I wish I had told him about it;

he would have been pleased I was earning income. It's too late for me to talk to him now, but he invested his life in children's ministry; I hope he wouldn't be disappointed that I am investing my life in my children.

Thinking about my Dad and the example of hard work he set for me raises the question: how do I ensure I am setting an example for *my* children?

Men at Work

Family businesses frequently follow a well-studied path. The founder starts a venture and works hard to make it a success. His children see his example of dedicated commitment and long hours of toil as the enterprise begins to flourish, and they emulate these traits as they follow their father into the business. With more hard work and a solid foundation in place, the second generation of the family grows the company to the point where they can enjoy the fruits of their labor. They become wealthy and ensure their families have the luxuries they missed out on when they were young. And that is why family businesses often fail in the third generation. The founder's grandchildren have grown up knowing abundance but not being exposed to the hard work that earned it. Family businesses often struggle when handed over to the third generation and usually require external management to maintain the success.[1]

The work habits that a father models for his children are essential. Although everyone is capable of rising above adversity and breaking the constraints imposed by their environment, as fathers we should also keep in mind that our actions and habits may have a limiting effect on our children. It is certainly something that has concerned me.

> Hard times create strong men, strong men create good times, good times create weak men, and weak men create hard times.
>
> —G. Michael Hopf

If my children don't see me working hard, then how can I expect them to work hard? That is one of the reasons I started Uber driving—I wanted my children to see me working. The money it brought in was pretty insignificant. Still, it felt satisfying to be actually contributing to the household finances, and it got me out of the house and provided interaction with other adults (some of whom were very interesting; some less mature than my pre-teen boys). But the primary benefit was that for a couple of years, my boys saw me heading out to work for a few hours. At times I would drive all night, and they would be awake by the time I got home to bed.

We all know children follow our example more than our instruction. Dads, if your primary focus is educating your children, then think through the example you wish to set and consider whether there is anything different you want to model. I do believe that if our role is to focus on our children, they **should** be our focus. But perhaps there is something else you feel should be modeled, whether ministry involvement, a side hustle, or a productive hobby such as gardening or woodworking. Where possible, involve your children in these activities so they can learn new skills and see you at work.

After I finished with Uber in 2020, I attempted day trading in the stock market. That has been less successful financially than Uber driving, but my boys know I am doing it to contribute to the household. They have picked out a few shares themselves, and even made a small profit!

How's the Weather?

In the previous chapter, I discussed the identity we derive from our careers. This was relevant to "The Spiritual Man" because it related to my role as provider for my family. It is also a factor in the struggles I faced socially, feeling awkward and out of place as others were talking about their work. I have experienced other men attempting to include me in their conversation with an innocent question, and hearing dead silence after my response as they realize my world has nothing in common with theirs, then listening to trite platitudes before they return to the important topics of their working lives. This disconnect with other men is not only about work—the entire family dynamic is different with a working wife and a stay-at-home dad.

Whenever I met someone new, I would never ask them about their job because I dreaded that question myself. And if you're not talking about work, once you've finished with the weather there's not much left to say!

Some of you may have a more active social life than I do and might experience greater cultural stress from being without paid employment. There could be pressure from friends, perhaps well-meaning but discouraging nonetheless. While I was able to ignore this to a large extent, mostly by simply not talking to people, you might have to find ways to deal with the expectations of others.

For me, the two areas of social significance are my wife and children, and my immediate family, and ignoring or not talking to them is not an option. When dad is the homeschool teacher, both the husband and wife must consider the social implications.

Perspectives in Film
Wild Hogs (2007)
In the adventure-comedy film *Wild Hogs*, the character Bobby, played by Martin Lawrence, has taken a year off work to write a book. As he struggles to control his children, his mother-in-law reinforces societal stereotypes by declaring, *"It's hard for kids to respect the man that don't do none of the providin'. In my day, the ladies stayed home, not the lazy men."*

Home Improvement: Ye Olde Shoppe Teacher
The American sitcom *Home Improvement* starring Tim Allen provides a more helpful perspective. In the episode titled "Ye Olde Shoppe Teacher" which aired in 1994, Tim is struggling with how to affirm his school workshop teacher whose arthritis prevents him from working in the shop like he used to. Tim talks over the problem with Wilson, a neighbor and confidant who serves as an all-wise sage in the show, doling out advice and always providing the right counsel to solve a problem.

[Tim]   *Hey Wilson, lemme ask you a question.*
[Wilson]   *Sure.*
[Tim]   *If a boulder fell on you, . . . Wouldn't you be too proud to ask for my help?*
[Wilson]   *Why would I be too proud?*
[Tim]   *Because you're a, 'cos you're a man. . . . Let's say you couldn't use your hands real well anymore, and I tried to help you out. It'd make you feel like you had no dignity left.*
[Wilson]   *Balderdash!*
[Tim]   *Well, it, it would if you were a tool man like my old shop teacher and me. When we lose our hands, we lose everything.*

[Wilson]	*Tim, there's a lot more to a man than just his hands. You have to look at his gestalt. . . . Gestalt is a psychological term meaning that the whole is more than the sum of the parts. I mean, take you for an example. You're a heck of a lot more than just Tim the Tool Man.*
[Tim]	*Yeah, but you know for guys, what we do is what we are.*
[Wilson]	*Well unfortunately sometimes society pressures men to define themselves in terms of their work.*
[Tim]	*I don't feel any pressure. I like being Tim the Tool Man.*
[Wilson]	*Yeah, what happens when someday you're no longer able to be Tim the Tool Man?*
[Tim]	*Oh oh oh. Oh man, that'd be horrible. I'd feel useless. I wouldn't be myself anymore.*
[Wilson]	*Tim, you are also a great husband, you're a great father, you're a, a great neighbor. I think you might find your true happiness lies in being Tim the Man.*

Social Solutions

Social Solution 1:
Recognize that your identity is not your job.

We must reject the cultural expectation that our job defines our identity. This assumption is reinforced every time someone says, "I *am a plumber*" or "*I am a salesman*" or even "*I am a teacher.*" Even the most demanding career will only take part of our time and isn't who we are; it is just what we do.

Even if you choose to answer the question, "*What do you do?*" by saying, "*I'm a stay-at-home dad educating my children,*" be very clear in your mind that your identity is not defined by what you do.

Social Solution 2: Talk to your family.

Your wider family is family, and if you care at all about what they think of you, then I'm pretty sure they will care about your journey and offer you their support and encouragement. But for them to do so, they need to understand what you are going through. You need to talk with them.

Social Solution 3:
Model hard work to your children.

If you have a job outside the home, your children will not see how you work. Therefore, homeschool dads have a better opportunity than many employed fathers to model good work habits to their children.

As a homeschool dad, then, make a point of working around the house and using your time productively. Don't wait until the kids are asleep before catching up on projects and chores. Let your children see you working hard and using your time well, whether it's a hobby, household task, or some freelance work. As your children mature, you may find you have more time to put into a side hustle or activities outside the home.

Whatever you do, ensure that your children are still your number one responsibility, but be deliberate about modeling a strong work ethic.

NOTES

1.   Scott McCollum, "Why the 3rd Generation Always Destroys a Family Business," LinkedIn (8 September 2016), https://www.linkedin.com/pulse/keeping-wealth-past-3rd-generation -scott-mccollum.
     An article published by the Harvard Business Review claims that this "*three-generation rule . . . could not be further from the truth*": Josh Baron and Rob Lachenauer, "Do Most Family Businesses Really Fail by the Third Generation?," Harvard Business Review (19 July 2021), https://hbr.org/2021/07/do-most-family-businesses-really-fail -by-the-third-generation.
     But even if the "evidence" for the three-generation rule is more anecdotal than real, we all recognize the impact on children of the example set by fathers.

CHAPTER TEN

THE PSYCHOLOGICAL MAN

Psychological Considerations

In the 1990s sitcom *Married with Children*, Jefferson D'Arcy is the toy-boy husband of the liberated career woman, Marcy. Jefferson is a happy-go-lucky opportunist who exploits his good looks by marrying a woman of means, leaving him free to enjoy a life of leisure. He adds comic relief by portraying a character who is satisfied with being a kept man and doesn't care that he is unemployed. But the show hints there is more to Jefferson than this shallow persona. In the 1994 episode "The D'Arcy Files," viewers are teased by the suggestion that Jefferson may have a secret life as a CIA operative.

Men have a thirst for danger and excitement that is more than mere bravado. It is a deep psychological need to display courage and prove their manhood.

The Four Cardinal Virtues

—Steve Turley[1]

In the ancient world, there were four cardinal virtues that every man was expected to cultivate in his life. Wisdom, justice, moderation, and courage. Which of those four did they believe was the most important? . . . Courage, because without courage you don't have the fortitude to fight for the other three.

Slaying the Corporate Dragon

A feature of many cultures throughout history has been a rite of passage in which boys prove their worth before being accepted as men. In past centuries, war provided a chance to display courage. This compulsion to prove one's manhood has not disappeared, even though the opportunities to do so have diminished. Nowadays, I often think that men express this need to show courage by driving too fast and taking risks on the road—contributing to their far higher road fatality rate.[2] Young men have the highest accident rate and pay an average of 14 percent more for their vehicle insurance than young women.[3] Maybe I did drive a little too fast when I was younger! And I did ride a motorbike. But I think I proved my manhood in my twenties by skiing down a 100m cliff and kayaking over a 10m waterfall.

In *Wild at Heart*, John Eldredge expresses this psychological need by claiming that *"In the heart of every man is a desperate desire for a battle to fight, an adventure to live, and a beauty to rescue."*[4] We see this theme expressed time and again in literature and fairy tales.

But modern man is frustrated in these endeavors. There are no giants left to battle. So he turns his face toward slaying the corporate dragon. His sense of fulfillment as a man comes from his career.

Dragons, Monsters, and Men

—Jordan Peterson

Where do you find a sustaining meaning to take you through the difficult times? In [your] responsibility to yourself and to other people.[5]

One of the things I tell young men . . . you want to fight the dragons that guard the gates of the treasure that you wish to attain. That willingness to make sacrifices which is the hallmark of maturity in the service of a higher goal. It orients you solidly in the world if you do that, and it gives you a dragon to fight. You have to say to yourself, "I will do good nonetheless." Everyone great makes that decision. Make that decision, because maybe you're great.[6]

As the idea of this book began forming in my mind, I reached out to a contact in the publishing industry. He was happy to meet with me, and I was pretty much free any time. But he was really busy with work, and then he had a scheduling conflict, and then travel got in the way. It took over four months to finally meet for a twenty-minute conversation.

What struck me the most was how this process made me feel. Work is the modern-day arena, and this husband and father was out battling each day to provide for his family. He was doing what all strong men were supposed to do.

Where did that leave me? Defeated. I wasn't fighting the corporate monster. I wasn't battling the tyrant of time. Worse than defeated, I wasn't even in the fight. Of course, it's easy to point out the many positives of not being caught up in the corporate rat race and being flexible with my time. However, that doesn't address the deep-felt need to slay the dragon, much less the supposed spiritual imperative to provide for my family. And it was hard to avoid the conclusion that I wasn't a real man.

But confronting the corporate dragon is commonplace these days, whereas you as a homeschool dad are far from ordinary. As a man, you are taking on a battle far more significant; you are facing a dragon far more powerful. You are forgoing your own ambitions for the sake of your children; you are putting the welfare of your family above your personal need to find fulfillment in a career. What could be a more powerful demonstration of how you are providing for your family than by sacrificing the very thing most men see as their identity and highest achievement? Your children are worth fighting for, and you are battling a formidable opponent—your ambition, your pride, your own desire for recognition and achievement in a career, in order to give your family what is best for them. Recognize you have gone to war to protect them, and your dragon is sacrifice.

> **Homeschool dads forgo their own ambitions for the sake of their children.**

Financial Decisions

Another psychological factor derives from the role of the provider. Men feel this burden and responsibility deeply, even if we understand that it is not a Biblical imperative. In his doctoral dissertation, William

Farrington highlights that fathers feel it is their responsibility to be the main breadwinner for the family unit.[7] In today's world, provision for a family's basic needs of food and shelter is primarily a function of income. It makes sense, therefore, that the one who earns the most should continue in their career while the lesser-earning spouse forfeits his or her lower earning potential to care for and educate their children. And in cases where the wife has the greater salary, the husband may feel obliged to swallow his pride and become the domestic partner.

We have already thought about provision in terms of the father's spiritual role in the family. But there is another aspect to this, one which can be ignored or more easily brushed aside when both husband and wife are earning. Income brings into focus the question of who makes the financial decisions. Who has the final say regarding spending?

Money is frequently a contentious issue in a marriage. It's easy to say that a married couple should reach a mutual agreement on such issues. But sometimes, a decision needs to be made even though both parties are not in full agreement. In these cases, if the husband and wife are Christians, they might accept the Biblical pattern of 1 Corinthians 11:3 in which the wife defers to the husband. If the husband is earning a steady income, even if he is earning less than his wife, we can accept he has an equal voice in the discussion and even that he is entitled to cast the deciding vote when there is a deadlock.

But think about the situation of the homeschool dad where the wife is the only breadwinner. Does it make a difference if she earns **all** the income? Is there now pressure for the husband to defer to the wife on important financial matters?

I have noticed in our marriage that there is a tendency for my wife as the income-earner to be the financial decision-maker. In fact, I tested it twice. On two occasions when discussing a potential purchase, I told my wife no, I didn't think we should spend the money. I didn't have any good reason to object, but did so deliberately to see what would happen. On both occasions, my wife chose to spend the money regardless.

There is a psychological element to being the financial provider for the family. If the husband is to become a homeschool dad, both parents must be aware that this impacts decision-making. It may be subtle and difficult to detect, and is most likely unconscious and unintentional, but it is there. By being aware of the existence of this tension between earning income and ultimate authority, we can first talk about it openly, and second, agree on where the burden of final decision-making should lie: whether it should be completely mutual (which I think in practice will ultimately be challenged;) whether it should be the husband; or whether it should be the financial provider.

Psychological: *of or pertaining to the mind.*
The word derives from the Greek *psyche* meaning "mind" or "soul," and *logos* meaning "the study of." Psychology is a science, as it follows the scientific method and deals with empirical evidence. It is a practical science, rather than a theoretical science derived mathematically.

Emotional: *of or pertaining to feelings or emotions.*
Emotions are instinctive or intuitive feelings as distinguished from reasoning or knowledge. They are reactions that we experience in response to events or situations.

Psychological Solutions

Psychological Solution 1:
Recognize that your dragon is sacrifice.

As a homeschool dad, you fight the battle by being willing to sacrifice for your family. You are forfeiting the opportunity to slay the corporate dragon and are taking on a more powerful giant—that of for-going your own ambitions for the sake of your children; that of putting your family above your career.

Your children are worth fighting for. Recognize that you have gone to war to protect them, and that your dragon is sacrifice.

Psychological Solution 2:
Talk with your wife.

If you haven't talked with your wife about all of this, and specifi-cally about financial decision-making, then it is time to do so. Here are some suggestions to get you started.

Finances
- Who should manage the finances?
- How should decisions be made? What will you do if you can't reach an agreement?
- What are your long-term financial goals?

Discipline
- How is discipline of your children working? Any changes or improvements needed?
- Who is the ultimate authority? Does *"Wait until your mother gets home"* work?

Affirmation
- Talk about your need for affirmation as husband and your wife's need for affection.
- What about your needs for intimacy?
- What does your wife require when she finishes work each day? What do you need after a hard day with the kids?
- How do you like to be affirmed and encouraged?

Domestic Duties
- Who is going to take care of meals? Cleaning? Putting the children in bed?
- How are things going on the home front? Does anything need to be done differently?

Home Education Duties
- What role does your wife want to play in your children's education? Does she want to be involved a lot, or a little, or not at all?
- What are your respective interests and skills? How can you use them in the homeschool program?
- Who does the planning? Who decides on the curriculum? What about grading assignments and keeping records?

Social & Ministry Activities
- Are you doing too much or too little in terms of social and ministry activities?

- What kind of social activities do you want to plan, and how is the family calendar managed?
- How's it going with getting time to yourself, whether as a couple or as an individual? Do you need to create a plan to give yourself space and time?

Reflections

- What is going well? What is not going well? What are you thankful for?
- What is one thing you would change if you could?
- Dream a little. Think about your hopes and aspirations for the future.

NOTES

1. Stephen R. Turley, "Is America Turning More Red than Ever in History?," (YouTube, 27 September 2022). https://youtu.be/mpM6rw8ksb4.
2. "Car Accident Statistics on Male vs. Female: Who Causes More Car Accidents?," *The Patel Firm* (18 April 2022), https://thepatelfirm.com/car-accident-statistics-male-vs-female, accessed 2 January 2023.
3. Ava Lynch, "Who Pays More for Car Insurance: Men or Women?," *The Zebra*, https://www.thezebra.com/auto-insurance/driver/other-factors/male-vs-female-car-insurance-rates, accessed 2 January 2023.
4. John Eldredge, *Wild at Heart: Discovering the Secret of a Man's Soul* (Nashville, TN: Thomas Nelson, 2001), pp. 9-10.
5. Jordan Peterson, "You Have to Slay the Dragon," (YouTube, 16 June 2021). https://youtu.be/FYNgq-8-p8w.
6. Jordan Peterson, "Jordan Peterson's 'Dragons, Monsters, and Men'," (YouTube, 30 June 2022). https://youtu.be/UGT5mauvaUg.
7. Farrington, "The Lived Experience of Evangelical Christian Homeschooling Fathers," pp. 162, 198-199.

THE EMOTIONAL MAN

Emotional Considerations

I began the journey of a homeschool dad emotionally shattered by my unsuccessful job search and believing myself a total loser. In five years of seeking employment, not a single company thought I had anything worthwhile to offer them. I wrestled with impatience, reflective of my own feelings of inadequacy. I felt like I was letting down my wife and children, that I was a disappointment to my parents, that I had failed God, that God had failed me. I felt I was wasting the talents, training, and opportunities I had been given.

As disheartening as it was to recognize my inability to fulfill what I thought was a spiritual obligation to provide for my family, as discouraging as it was to feel I had disappointed my father and was setting a poor example to my children, as demoralizing as it was to have people ask me what I did for a living, the most challenging part of this journey for me has been my own emotional struggle over the sense of failure at being unable to find work.

Searching for Meaning

Zig Ziglar highlights the importance of self-esteem by saying that the feeling of our own worth influences every facet of our life.[1] When we lose that sense of our own worth, we will struggle. In his 1944 play *Caligula*, Albert Camus writes *"What's intolerable is to see one's life being drained of meaning. . . . A man can't live without some reason for living."*[2]

Gratitude

But there was hope for me, and there is hope for you. It is a tremendous privilege to be spending these formative years with our children. Time is the rarest commodity, and the fact that we are able to devote it to our children is the biggest gift we can give them. This is our legacy, one which few other men have the opportunity to leave in quite the same way.

It took me years to come to terms with my emotional rollercoaster, and I'm still a work in progress. But in my experience, the first key to dealing with my feelings of disillusionment was to change my focus from myself to God and others, particularly my boys during day-to-day lessons. That is easier said than done, of course. But it works. Gratitude is a great way to shift our attention outward and is a well-established method for improving our emotional state.

Gratitude Improves Your Health

Expressing gratitude is associated with a host of mental and physical benefits. Studies have shown that feeling thankful can improve sleep, mood and immunity. Gratitude can decrease depression, anxiety, difficulties with chronic pain and risk of disease.[3]

Personal Reflections

The husband who sacrifices his career to allow his wife to pursue hers displays a sense of *noblesse oblige*. And I could imagine a feeling of achievement for the man who has already enjoyed a fulfilling career, has sold his business, and is retired by the age of thirty! Some men are naturally gifted at teaching, and such a husband might feel right at home educating his children. None of these situations applied to me. I did not give up my job to serve my family. Becoming a teacher was the last thing I wanted to do. Even now, I pray daily that God will provide a career for me in some way.

So it's been a long, hard road.

But God is still God.

Noblesse oblige: the obligation of the nobility to go beyond the requirements of their duty

I can only tell you what I have learned from my own pilgrimage. Your challenges and struggles will be unique, your temperament and circumstances will be different, but there may be shared experiences helpful to you. With my engineering background, I tend to be fairly analytical even when it comes to emotions. But whether or not you identify with my journey, I think you'll find the solutions encouraging. Two points to keep in mind, though.

First, while I believe these solutions are effective, to me that was never the issue. I knew how to solve the problem; what I lacked was the resolve to take the necessary steps. Maybe we are waiting for others to do something, or God to show up and take care of it all. Yes, we need God's help, but we might need to take the first step.

Second, you matter to God. What you are doing is **very** important to Him, and He wants you to succeed. He has a purpose for your life, and He has a reason for taking you through this experience.

"For the sake of Christ, then, I am content with weaknesses, insults, hardships, persecutions, and calamities. For when I am weak, then I am strong" (2 Corinthians 12:10).

"For we are God's masterpiece. He has created us anew in Christ Jesus, so we can do the good things he planned for us long ago" (Ephesians 2:10 NLT).

"Let us run with endurance the race that is set before us, looking to Jesus, the founder and perfecter of our faith" (Hebrews 12:1-2).

We Can Choose Our Response

I am a firm believer in the following principle:

Between stimulus and response, there is a space. In that space lies our power to choose our response. In that choice lies our growth and freedom.

What sets us apart as humans is our ability to choose our response to stimuli. We do not need to be slaves to our reactions.

Between stimulus and response, there is a space.

This insight was made famous in Stephen Covey's writings and is often attributed to Holocaust survivor Victor Frankl although it does not appear in Frankl's writings. Covey tells the story:[4]

While on a writing sabbatical in Hawaii and in a very reflective state of mind, I was wandering through the stacks of a university library and picked up a book. I read the following three lines, which literally staggered me and again reaffirmed Frankl's essential teachings:

Between stimulus and response, there is a space.
In that space lies our freedom and our power to choose our response.
In our response lies our growth and our happiness.

I did not note the name of the author, so I've never been able to give proper attribution. On a later trip to Hawaii I even went back to find the source and found the library building itself was no longer present. The space between what happens to us and our response, our freedom to choose that response and the impact it can have upon our lives, beautifully illustrate that we can become a product of our decisions, not our conditions.

Victor Frankl's first core principle is:
Exercise the freedom to choose your attitude. *In all situations, no matter how desperate they may appear or actually be, you always have the ultimate freedom to choose your attitude.*[5]

I discovered this principle for myself before I had heard of Stephen Covey or Victor Frankl. That moment is still vividly etched in my mind. I was a shy and insecure teenager, attending a youth group event but feeling lonely and left out. So I went home and planned to head to bed and cry myself to sleep. But then a thought struck me: *"I can choose my reaction to my circumstances! I can decide whether or not to feel lonely!"* I returned to the event and, somewhat to my surprise, discovered that when I **chose** to be happy, I actually **felt** happy!

"For as he thinks in his heart, so is he" (Proverbs 23:7 NKJV).

"Be careful how you think; your life is shaped by your thoughts" (Proverbs 4:23 GNT).

Fooling No One

My Mum used to encourage me to stay out of the Canyon of Inferiority. But three decades later, after years of fruitless job hunting, I was deep in the pit of despair wallowing in self-pity. Yet I knew there was a space between stimulus and response. That this was my choice. I could choose at any moment to stop feeling sorry for myself, pack up the violins, and shut down the pity-party. I could choose to focus on the blessings of my situation. Like Jefferson D'Arcy, I was a kept man, and I could enjoy it.

Even in the valley, I knew the reason I didn't want to give up the self-pity was that it was the only thing left I could control. Giving that up would mean relinquishing my last vestige of authority and accepting my fate.

The impact of this emotional state was of course fairly predictable. Homeschool parents need to be aware that their emotions impact their behavior, and their behavior impacts their children. It is undoubtedly easier for schoolteachers to compartmentalize their lives into professional and private realms and behave professionally in the classroom while expressing their emotions at home. Parents don't have this luxury. Our children see us the way we are, and how we feel impacts their behavior and learning.

It was a big struggle knowing that my sense of inadequacy was impacting my children. I could see it. I even tested it (depressed engineers are still engineers!) My children's behavior was noticeably better if I portrayed a positive outlook. And when I was grumpy, they were fighting. I soon learned that their behavior was linked to how I was going to respond. My attitude had to improve before theirs would. When I was determined to react with kindness and love, their behavior would be better. And when I was patient and relaxed, they were as well.

But think about what this understanding meant to me. It wasn't a solution or a way out of the struggle, it was merely more condemnation, more guilt. When my children misbehaved, it was **my** fault. In other words, not only had I failed to find work and provide for my family, but I was also accountable for my emotional state and culpable for my children's behavior.

A Companion on the Journey

I'm sure homeschool moms never struggle with their emotions! Men, however, are less likely to admit their emotional fragility, share their feelings, and seek support. I sure didn't. I didn't need anyone to tell me the solutions—I already knew them.

And that is why homeschool dads and their wives need to be aware of the emotional implications of being the primary educator for their children. As with the spiritual, social, and psychological aspects, being prepared for the emotional impact and having open and honest conversations with your wife is important for getting through this successfully.

Spiritual, social, and psychological factors are essentially rational, and we can think through them and talk about them and seek solutions. In many ways though, the emotional impact of being a homeschool dad may be harder to deal with because it is, well, emotional. It is about feelings, and each person will be dealing with different feelings and emotions. And feelings aren't resolved by logic. So I wouldn't try to offer any kind of generic, universal solution. But for me, the answer was fairly straightforward.

At one of my darkest moments, my wife was in tears and said to me, *"I just don't know how to solve this!"* It kind of shocked me, because I didn't need a solution. I knew how to fix it. There is a space between stimulus and response, and in that space is my power to choose. I simply needed to swallow my pride, accept that this was God's best for my life, and choose to have a positive frame of mind. I already knew the solution. What I needed was for someone to walk with me on the journey.

I wouldn't call it a silver bullet, but I know it will help you to have the encouragement and backing of your wife. You might also find support from close friends, a fellowship group, or a homeschool support network.

In John Bunyan's *Pilgrim's Progress*, Christian enters the Valley of the Shadow of Death alone, but there encounters a fellow pilgrim, Faithful. Faithful encourages Christian, and they continue on the path together. After Faithful's execution at the town of Vanity, Christian is joined by Hopeful with whom he journeys the remainder of the way to the Celestial City. Psalm 23 tells us that God is with us in the Valley of the Shadow of Death, but He also knows we need human companions.

It seems obvious, but we shouldn't reject help when it is offered. Yet that is easy to do. I found that when times were tough, when I was feeling disillusioned and a failure, I didn't want to accept people's support. It seemed that if they helped me, then I would have no excuse for being angry about my life. And I had a right to be angry, didn't I? Those close to us need to understand this dynamic and support us even if rebuffed. I had one elderly friend who made a point of catching up with me regularly. He had been through depression—in fact, he had grown up during The Great Depression—and he knew that I needed a fellow pilgrim. I will always be grateful for his companionship.

Emotional Solutions

Emotional Solution 1: Embrace the space between stimulus and response.

Between stimulus and response, there is a space. In that space lies our power to choose our response. In that choice lies our growth and freedom.

You have more power than you might think to choose your attitude and your emotions. You may find that books or podcasts or seminars help you understand and embrace this principle. I have been impacted over the years by the work of authors such as Zig Ziglar, Gerald Bradley, and Stephen Covey, and I encourage you to look for resources that will help you learn to choose a positive response to whatever life throws at you.

Emotional Solution 2: Find companions on the journey.

You need someone to walk the road with you. Your wife is obviously key, but for additional companionship, find family members or friends who will support and encourage you.

Emotional Solution 3:
Don't reject the support that is offered.

Those close to you need to understand that they must stand with you whether you accept their help or not. But for your part, don't reject their support when they offer it.

Emotional Solution 4:
Keep your focus outward.

Emotional struggles are not overcome by focusing on ourselves. If you are a believer, then look to Jesus. Focus on others rather than yourself—especially your wife and children. The more time you spend thinking about your role in relation to others you love, the less time you will expend on self-pity.

Emotional Solution 5: Be grateful.

There are many ways to be deliberate about gratitude. Write thank you notes. Keep a gratitude journal. Write down three things each day for which you're grateful. Count your blessings. Laugh at funny stories. Watch memes.[6] However you do it, these positive thoughts will release hormones like dopamine, serotonin, and oxytocin that are beneficial emotionally and physically.

Emotional Solution 6: Keep a journal.

I was sure that writing about my experiences would help me to process them, and for a number of years I tried to get into journaling. I could never turn it into a habit, but writing this book has helped me tremendously. I am confident that writing will help you also, so maybe keeping a journal, writing letters, or even writing a book will work for you.

The Silver Bullet

There is no silver bullet, no panacea that will solve all of the difficulties that the homeschool dad will face. But I expect that talking over how you're feeling with your wife would come pretty close.

When moms are the stay-at-home parent, they need their husbands to appreciate the challenges they face and affirm the critical role they play in their family. I would say it's even more important for the wives of stay-at-home dads to consistently appreciate and affirm their husbands, because men tend to have a greater need for respect and may feel more keenly a sense of inadequacy. Men in this role may face greater spiritual, social, and psychological pressure than women would.

> Women need love and men need respect.
>
> —Emerson Eggerichs[7]

The task of home education requires a team effort. And even if the husband, being a stubborn male, thinks he can handle the teaching all by himself, he still needs emotional support and undoubtedly help with tasks around the house. Whatever the challenge, honest communication between husband and wife is one of the key solutions.

Closure

I mentioned earlier that writing this section has been helpful to me as I have taken the opportunity to think through and accept my role as a homeschool dad. In many ways, the writing has provided a degree of closure to the most difficult chapter in my life. I want to acknowledge my wife, who has loved and supported me throughout this journey. I never fooled her into giving me the pity I craved but didn't need. When she read the first draft of this book, her response was, *"I always knew you'd get through this. It took longer than I expected, though!"*

In 2017, I visited New Zealand with my boys after being in the USA for seven years. The primary reason for deciding to educate our children at home was so we would have the flexibility to travel. I took advantage of this by taking lessons with us, and we spent almost four months with my family.

While in New Zealand, I caught up with a friend. Although we'd had very little contact over the previous decade, I had supported him through some critical moments in his life. After our visit, this friend sent me an email. I knew what he was going to say and couldn't face what I was sure would be a healthy dose of honesty. But I knew the day would eventually come when I could handle the truth.

Five years later, while preparing this chapter, I read his email for the first time, and he had it completely right. It is well worth sharing and is copied in full, edited slightly for clarity.

Hi Craig

It was great to see you the other day. I couldn't help but notice the tone in your voice; that while you're holding the fort and doing what you feel you should to support the family, you're also feeling depressed with the strain of two young boys and also feeling in some way a failure with not being able to find a job or support your family in the way that maybe traditionally a male would.

Firstly, I want you to know I am reaching out in love for a brother whom I care for, and am willing to give you a little piece of brotherly advice. These thoughts that you are maybe having are quite frankly a load of rubbish. It is the devil's trick to pull us down, especially if we are raising a younger generation with Godly values. He will come like a thief in the night to steal the joy, and when he does this, he knows the battle is already half won.

Also, never, never underestimate the power of the time that you spend with your two sons. Time is the rarest commodity, and the fact that you get to spend that with your sons is the biggest gift you can give them!!!

Finally, do not ever, ever lose hope. God says very clearly in the Bible "I know the plans I have for you . . ." (Jeremiah 29:11) and they are plans for good and for fortune, filled with God's blessing. Sometimes He takes us through some really hard times to build our faith, for without faith we are worthless. Remember, life is a refining process and God is always trying to refine us for His glory. Even Abraham's wife was old before she gave birth. Think of the years she had to go through of heartache and pain with not having a child. God will give you the desires of your heart, Craig, just make sure you're chasing His desires. Don't listen to what the world says and burden yourself with what may or may not happen in the future.

I believe that God will put the right desires in our hearts if we ask Him, and give us peace in our hearts if we place our trust in Him. Do not fear what your boys may think when they get older about you staying home to look after them. Do not worry about not working right now. God will open the right door when the time comes. He knows you want to work. But instead, praise Him each day and thank Him for giving you this amazing opportunity to be at home with two amazing boys, to be a true father and be at their side, to grow them in love and knowledge.

It is for such a short, short time in our lives that we have the opportunity to invest in turning these gifts, these precious young lives that God has given us, into great men. This is the legacy that you have the opportunity to leave behind, and something that is passed on from generation to generation. This is far, far better than earning some money or having a "job." The Craig I know is an amazing guy and has a lot to share with two young boys, so take some time to really see through God's eyes how lucky you are!!!

The rest, leave up to God to fill in the gaps in HIS time, as you don't need to know what His plan is right now. Focus on the things He has given you to do now, and do them with passion and to the best of your ability so that He will reward you with even more.

Take care Craig and keep in contact!!! We are on this road together :-)

NOTES

1. Zig Ziglar, "The Many Attitudes of Life," *Creators Syndicate* (28 September 2022), https://www.creators.com/read/classic-zig-ziglar/09/22/the-many-attitudes-of-life-7628f, accessed 7 April 2023.
2. John Blanchard, *Why Are You Here? Searching for the Meaning of Life* (Darlington, England: EP Books, 2014), p. 116.
3. Amanda Logan, "Can Expressing Gratitude Improve Your Mental, Physical Health?," *Mayo Clinic Health System* (6 December 2022), https://www.mayoclinichealthsystem.org/hometown-health/speaking-of-health/can-expressing-gratitude-improve-health.
4. Alex Pattakos, *Prisoners of Our Thoughts: Viktor Frankl's Principles for Discovering Meaning in Life and Work*, 2nd ed. (San Francisco, CA: Berrett-Koehler, 2010), pp. vi-vii. Excerpt available at https://www.viktorfrankl.org/assets/pdf/Covey_Intro_to_Pattakos_Prisoners.pdf.
5. Pattakos, *Prisoners of Our Thoughts*, p. iv.
6. I highly recommend Tyler Zed's channel Zeducation: https://zedmedia.substack.com.
7. Emerson Eggerichs, *Love & Respect: The Love She Most Desires; The Respect He Desperately Needs* (Nashville, TN: Thomas Nelson, 2004), p. 47.

PART 3

ABOUT FOUNDATIONS

As we begin on more practical matters related to home education,

I discuss some fundamental issues such as

purpose, priorities, program, and assessment.

CHAPTER TWELVE

ESTABLISHING YOUR FOUNDATION

Of Greatest Importance

Creating Options

Being a scientist, I abhor assumptions. Have you heard the saying, "'assume' makes an 'ass' out of 'u' and 'me'"? That's my attitude. So I don't want to assume, but it's probably a safe bet that you love your children and want the best for them.

This book is about home education, but let's take a step back. Why do our children need to learn? What is the purpose of education? Why is there so much emphasis on academics? I wonder if we sometimes make schooling out to be more important than it actually is. Maybe it's worth pausing and thinking about what we're really trying to achieve. Is the end goal a high school diploma? Is it a university degree? Many people focus on these milestones, but that's not why we make the effort to study. For some, they might just enjoy learning. That's great, but it isn't the ultimate objective either.

A sound educational program prepares a person to succeed in life. Being well-educated affords them options. If they are competent in multiple areas, they will have more possibilities for work and occupation. People who want to advance their career or change track know the importance of professional development. Competence in multiple areas isn't only relevant to

> The goal of education is to increase human freedom and the ability to make reasonable choices.
>
> —Margit Sutrop[1]

academic subjects; it applies to trades as well. If you learn two trades, you will have twice as many options as someone skilled in one trade. And it isn't only work-related. It can apply to music, sport, and leisure activities also. If you know how to play Go Fish, Spades, War, Solitaire, and Old Maid, then a deck of cards offers you more options than if you only know Pickup 52. (Not familiar with this one? You throw the entire deck of fifty-two cards up in the air and yell at your opponent, "Pickup 52!")

> *Perhaps the most significant tool I received from home education was the ability to learn. If a child has the ability to learn, he can achieve virtually anything. My mother's philosophy was, "Teach your children how to read, how to reason, and how to research, and they will know how to succeed in life."*
>
> —Israel Wayne[2]

The value of education, then, is to expand the opportunities for your children in life. This encompasses the broad definition of "education" used in this book, because instruction in religious, moral, and social matters will also increase their options. Not everyone is capable of achieving great academic results, but whether or not you are intellectually gifted, education including moral and social instruction will enhance your chances of success. A disciplined young person who is thoughtful, well-presented, and well-spoken will be valued by employers more than one who is slovenly and unreliable.

Being Loved

There is something more important than being well-educated. Not every child will complete the training we would hope for them. For a variety of reasons outside of our control, some will have very few options in life. But there's something even more meaningful that we can do for them. A quality education is not the most important thing. As humans, we strive to be successful and are easily distracted by wealth and careers, but most of us would admit that relationships impact us more than jobs or income. We crave love more than success. In fact, our reason for desiring success is likely so that people will acknowledge and appreciate us. We long to feel wanted and special. More significant than giving your children a good education is providing them with a caring home.

Now being poor does not necessarily mean you are happy. But I suspect that being in a loving family has greater impact on a child's happiness and development than living in a wealthy household. If we love our children, then we're doing more for them than we would by merely providing them with an excellent education. It's more important for children to know they are loved; that they are part of a family that loves them. Not only will they be happy, which is what we all ultimately desire, but it will give them the confidence and security to achieve their best in life regardless of their abilities or the path they choose.

Preparing for Eternity

A high standard of education is no substitute for a loving family because at heart, we simply want to be happy. But C.S. Lewis says that *"Human history is the long terrible story of man trying to find something other than God which will make him happy."* Augustine talked about a God-shaped hole in our hearts that only He can fill. We will never be truly happy without a relationship with God.

And so, there is something even more important than giving our children a loving home. As important as family is, it isn't the **most** important. For Christian parents, our greatest task is to pass on our faith. Our ultimate objective in education is to know our Creator. This is what gives us purpose during our time on Earth, and it also has eternal consequences. Our faith is what will last for eternity and is what matters the most.

> *What is the one thing we should do to prepare future generations for success? Teach your family the message of life.*
>
> —Gary Ezzo[3]

The Harrison Shorter Catechism

During the daily grind of lessons and life, it can be hard to think beyond what needs to be done each day. It's important, however, to keep the end in mind, not only for parents but also for children. They need to know why they are doing their lessons; what's the point of it all. I talk about this frequently with my boys and it has become like a catechism.

> *The purpose of education is to provide you with opportunities and prepare you to succeed in life. More important than being well-educated, however, is for you to know you are loved; that you are part of a family that loves you. But the MOST important thing is that you walk closely with Jesus for your entire life.*

Truth for Christ and the Church

Harvard University's "Rules and Precepts" adopted in 1646 state:

Let every Student be plainly instructed, and earnestly pressed to consider well, the maine end of his life and studies is, to know God and Jesus Christ which is eternal life (John 17:3) and therefore to lay Christ in the bottome, as the only foundation of all sound knowledge and Learning. And seeing the Lord only giveth wisedome, Let every one seriously set himself by prayer in secret to seeke it of him. (Prov. 2:3) The motto of the University adopted in 1692 was "Veritas Christo et Ecclesiae" which translated from Latin means "Truth for Christ and the Church."[4]

The Harrison Shorter Catechism

What is the goal of education?
The goal of education is to prepare you to succeed in life.

What is more important than education?
It is more important for you to know that we love you.

What is most important?
It is of greatest importance that you follow Jesus closely.

The Family

Central to our thinking about education is our view of family. Families have long been acknowledged as the cornerstone of a flourishing culture, and home education plays an important role in building strong families and nurturing traditional values.

Family and State

The globalist and humanist ideologies dominating Western culture hate the traditional family and are actively trying to redefine the concept of marriage and destroy the conservative family unit. This animosity has come about because families provide identity independent of the state and therefore enable children to flourish without being dependent on government, thereby lessening authoritarian control over the population. Families preserve culture and tradition while liberal democracy and global control require the relinquishing of customs, culture, and historical norms. As government control has grown, traditional morals and customs have given way to lifestyle values where each individual creates his or her own belief system, including religion, gender identity, and marriage.[5]

The Family and the Totalitarian State

In *Live Not By Lies: A Manual for Christian Dissidents*, Rod Dreher discusses the insights of Václav Benda, a Czech human rights activist under communism. Benda wrote an article in 1988 entitled *"The Family and the Totalitarian State"* in which he explained how the family could endure in the face of a government and society seeking its destruction. Benda believed that the bedrock of civilization is the family, which must be nurtured and defended at any price. He related how the family came under concerted attack by the communist government, which viewed family sovereignty as a threat to state control over individuals. Dreher writes:[6]

Strong families produced citizens capable of building strong civil societies. . . .

Traditional families, Christian and otherwise, living in the postcommunist liberal capitalism of today know all too well that the left-wing assault on traditional marriage and family commenced in the West with the sexual revolution in the 1960s.

It continues today in the form of direct attacks by the woke Left, including law professors advocating legal structures that dismantle the traditional family as an oppressive institution. More ominously, it comes from policies, laws, and court decisions that diminish or sever parental rights in cases involving transgender minors. . . .

Benda said that . . . the loving, secure Christian home is a place that forms children who are capable of loving and serving others within the family, the church, the neighborhood, and indeed the nation. The family does not exist for itself alone, but first for God, and then for the sake of the broader community—a family of families.

When that nation and its people are held captive by a totalitarian order, then Christians and their families must push as hard against the totalitarian world as it pushes against them. . . .

"It's no accident that every dictatorship always tries to break down the family, because it's in the family that you get the strength to be able to fight," says María Komáromi, a Catholic teacher in Budapest. . . . "It's just as true today as it was under communism." . . .

Christian parents must be intentionally countercultural in their approach to family dynamics.

Despite the onslaught against families in the West, there are glimmers of hope. I believe that over the coming years, traditional conservative values recognizing the foundational importance of family and also the role of faith and national culture will experience a resurgence. Signs of this renaissance are already evident in Hungary, Georgia, and Russia.[7]

The Georgian and Russian Orthodox Churches have both been making efforts to support and revitalize the family, while the Kremlin holds an annual ceremony to publicly honor families with more than eight children.[8] And the Hungarian constitution, adopted in 2011 states, *"We believe that our children and grandchildren will make Hungary great again"* and defends *"the institution of marriage as the union of a man and a woman . . . and the family as the basis of the nation's survival."*[9] When I visited the Hungarian Government website recently, its homepage featured

> *Successful households are the natural reservoir of liberty. They aim at autonomy or independence, enabling their members to resist oppression, survive economic, social, and political turbulence, and renew the world after troubles have passed.*
>
> —Allan Carlson

the graphic of a family along with the message, *"The personal income tax exemption for mothers under 30 begins in January."*

Family Team

Although family has always been important to us, my wife and I held the conventional view of the home being a place of nurture, where children are raised, trained,

> At the end of the day, life is about being happy being who you are, and I feel like we are so blessed to have the support system and the best family to really just support each other no matter what we're going through.
>
> —Kim Kardashian

and cared for until they are old enough to leave the nest and survive on their own. The Bible compares children to arrows in a warrior's quiver, ready to be fired out into the world.

> "Children are a heritage from the LORD, offspring a reward from Him. Like arrows in the hands of a warrior are children born in one's youth. Blessed is the man whose quiver is full of them" (Psalm 127:3-5 NIV).

The home as a nest is an apt metaphor. But family can also be viewed as a team. In this respect, we believe God has a purpose for our family as a whole and has provided children with the skills and abilities necessary to fulfill our collective mission.

Neither metaphor, of family being a nest or a team, is perfect, and the reality will invariably be multifaceted. But my wife and I have sensed a growing conviction over recent years that family is to be our focus and that we are all on this journey together. Although we only came across the terminology of "family team" recently,[10] we can see how this concept has influenced our decisions regarding education over the years.

In order to discover our mission as a family, I created a notebook for each of us which provides space to record our own interests and abilities, to list the strengths we see in each other, to suggest what we think we should be doing together, to put down ideas on funding our mission, and to provide suggestions for a family motto, logo, and emblem. Sample pages from this workbook are provided in Appendix A. Children should be included in this process to the extent that they are able. As they mature and their thinking develops, it would be worth revisiting the family mission to capture their developing insight and contribution.

Nevertheless, it would be a great process to think about and work through before beginning your children's education. Establishing a family team in your home, rather than considering it as a nest or launching pad for your children, will impact the decisions you make concerning education.

Start with Why

It is as true with home education as it is with any other endeavor in life: start with "why." Don't get distracted thinking about "how" before you understand your "why." There will come times when you wonder whether it's all worthwhile, and knowing a clearly articulated purpose can keep you going.

Despite the tremendous growth of homeschooling in the last few years, the default option for children once they reach school age—the easy option—is a public school. There needs to be a specific reason for thinking beyond the status quo for your children's education, whether that be a private school or homeschool. It will be a deliberate choice and require extra work to investigate the alternatives and decide on what's right for your family.

If you embrace home education, both you and your spouse need to be clear about why. And there are many possible motives. In 2016, safety was the primary justification for choosing to homeschool.[11] By 2021, schools closing their doors topped the list.[12] Other major reasons parents choose to educate their children at home rather than send them to traditional schools include concerns about academic quality, a desire for greater flexibility, the cost of private schools, and an ability to give children more one-on-one attention. Wanting to provide religious instruction was cited in 51 percent of the responses in 2016, but had dropped to 43 percent by 2021.

A Positive Reason

As we were considering home education, an experienced friend gave us some excellent advice.

Decide to homeschool because you're FOR something, not because you're AGAINST something.

Sarita Holzmann, CEO of Sonlight Curriculum, echoes this sentiment: homeschooling to escape a negative might be a helpful place to start, but for the long haul, we all need to answer what we are homeschooling *toward*, because positive goals have the power to motivate.[13]

There are many positive motives. A few that resonate with us are:

- To provide an education focused on the individual child, rather than the group average.
- To allow the child to learn in the way that best suits him.
- To cover a broad curriculum which includes subjects such as Bible and world history.
- To ensure mastery of the fundamentals of reading, writing, and arithmetic.
- To teach material from a Christian perspective.
- To provide an environment in which the child is socialized within a multi-generational group (adults and elderly as well as children) rather than spending most of the day with peers.

However, we defined one primary "why."

Our purpose for educating our children at home was to allow the flexibility to travel.

My wife travels frequently for work. Many times, we have driven with her to meetings. We often take a family vacation in May, while school is still in session and before peak season begins. And before peak-season prices! And we have spent four months in New Zealand during the school year. These trips are possible because I can simply collect lesson materials and take them with us. We don't have to fit around a public-school schedule, and our children don't sacrifice lesson time. Travel is part of their learning.

In many circles, homeschooling is still thought of as a fringe activity carried out solely by religious zealots. I have been asked whether we are homeschooling for religious reasons, and it feels gratifying to be able to answer with an emphatic **no**; to explain our "why" and give examples of how we have taken advantage of this flexibility. Ironically, both times I was asked this specific question were while on a family trip during the school year. The freedom to travel is something everyone can appreciate and relate to, irrespective of their religious views or opinion of public education.

Yes, we did want our children to be educated with values aligning to our own. We did want the Bible and Christian faith to be central to our curriculum. We did want to be able to tailor the program to the needs and abilities and interests of our boys.

But it feels good to be able to articulate a clear, positive "why." It's beneficial for us as parents to have this certainty. And I think it's also helpful for those asking, because it contributes to countering the stereotype that homeschooling is merely a marginal anti-cultural reaction. In many ways, I'm very pleased we chose the flexibility to travel as our primary reason, rather than religious education or a concern about bullying or violence in public schools. People could debate the issue of school safety. And they may disagree with our religious position and feel parents shouldn't be free to indoctrinate their children—that that's the prerogative of the school board. But I imagine everyone would see value in being able to travel the country and the world without impacting their children's education.

If you are beginning your journey in home education, start with "why."

A Robust Indoctrination Plan

Dr. Scott Ziegler, Superintendent of Loudoun Public Schools (Virginia, USA), stated at a 28 June 2022 meeting that the school board had a robust "indoctrination" plan in place for students in the upcoming school year. This plan was in response to parents and members of the community who grew vocal in 2021 about their opposition to critical race theory and gender ideology being included in the curriculum. Ziegler appeared to correct himself by saying that it was an "inculturation" plan. Either term should concern parents.[14]

NOTES

1. Sutrop, "Can Values Be Taught?," p. 190.
2. Wayne, *Education: Does God Have an Opinion?*, pp. 69-70.
3. Gary Ezzo, Growing Families International, 29 May 2022. Personal correspondence.
4. "Shield and 'Veritas' History," *Harvard Graduate School Christian Fellowship*, https://hgscf.org/harvard-shield, accessed 6 January 2023.
5. Stephen R. Turley, *The Return of Christendom: Demography, Politics, and the Coming Christian Majority* (2019), p. ix.
6. Rod Dreher, *Live Not by Lies: A Manual for Christian Dissidents* (New York: Sentinel, 2020), pp. 132, 134, 148-149.
7. See for example the following books by Steve Turley:
   Turley, *The Return of Christendom*.
   Stephen R. Turley, *The Coming Rise of Christian Education: How Political and Religious Trends are Fueling a Surge in Christian Schooling* (2019).
8. Turley, *The Return of Christendom*, p. 14.
9. "Hungarian Constitution," https://www.constituteproject.org/constitution/Hungary_2016?lang=en, accessed 7 January 2023.
10. Family Teams, https://familyteams.com.
11. Meghan McQuiggan and Mahi Megra, *Parent and Family Involvement in Education: Results from the National Household Education Surveys Program of 2016*, U.S. Department of Education (Washington, DC: National Center for Education Statistics, 2017), p. 19, http://nces.ed.gov/pubsearch/pubsinfo.asp?pubid=2017102.
12. *Homeschooling Market Survey Analysis*, Hanover Research (March 2021), p. 8.
13. Sarita Holzmann, "Homeschooling Away From a Fear Versus Towards a Goal," *Sarita's Word*, 15 May 2017, https://blog.sonlight.com/homeschooling-goal-fear.html.
14. Joshua Young, "School Superintendent Speaks of 'Indoctrination Plan' for Loudon County Parents, Students," *The Post Millennial* (5 July 2022), https://thepostmillennial.com/school-superintendent-speaks-of-indoctrination-plan-for-loudon-county-parents-students.

SETTING YOUR PRIORITIES

Learning to Learn

At this point, let's say you have decided to educate your own children. You are clear about why you have chosen to do so, which is important because this foundational conviction will sustain you through the years ahead. You have thought about your educational philosophy and goals to help filter through the many options and choices available for resources, curricula, and methodology. Now it's time to redirect the focus from education to teaching.

> *Oxford English Reference Dictionary* 1995
> **teach** *transitive verb*
> 1 **a.** give systematic information to (a person) or about (a subject or skill) . . .
>   **c.** enable (a person) to do something by instruction and training . . .
> 3 **a.** induce (a person) by example or punishment to do or not to do a thing
> **Noah Webster 1828**
> **teach** *transitive verb*
>   **1.** To instruct; to inform; to communicate to another the knowledge of that of which he was before ignorant . . .
>   **10.** To counsel and direct
>
> **The Harrison Parochial Dictionary 2022**
> Teaching is the process of starting from what a student knows and guiding him into a knowledge of new material.

When I worked in research and development, my fellow engineers had graduated from either a university or technical college. Technical college taught students the practical skills of electronics design, and these engineers were at an immediate advantage. They would mock us university types with our theoretical knowledge of physics, because we didn't know the resistor color code or how to program a micro-controller.

However, university taught us how to think and how to learn and how to solve problems. We could always learn to program micros and memorize the resistor chart if needed. Although tech grads were more useful on day one, we held a long-term advantage because if we didn't know something, we knew how to find it out, and we were better equipped to discover solutions to the difficult problems that didn't have textbook answers.

I have applied the same principle to educating my children. From the beginning, I have had in mind the question: what do I need to teach them so that they will become effective life-long learners? I wanted to teach them **how** to think, rather than **what** to think. There is a saying: *"give a man a fish, and you will feed him for a day; teach him how to fish, and you will feed him for a life-time."* Teaching my children how to learn is not like giving a man a fish, or teaching him how to catch one. It's not even giving him a fishing rod. It's teaching a man how to **learn** so that he can **teach himself** how to fish, or make a fishing rod, or hunt, or program a micro-controller.

Teach your children HOW to think, not WHAT to think.

Priority List

Reading is an obvious foundational skill because it enables every other aspect of learning, so this became my first priority. Curiosity about the world also made sense to me, and I included a lot of science in the earlier years. Exploring, experimenting, and using resources such as encyclopedias and reference books were part of our program. Although I left creative writing until later years, my children needed the ability to write. And do mathematics. Math is the language of the universe and needs to be introduced progressively over the years.

You are justified in thinking I am biased toward STEM subjects! You don't need to agree with me, but whatever your particular inclination,

I encourage you to think in terms of teaching your children **how** to be learners, rather than focusing on what specifically they are learning.

> **STEM:** an acronym for Science, Technology, Engineering, and Mathematics
>
> **Parochial:** merely local, narrow, or restricted in scope

A second level of priority was foreign language, logic, and programming. In Part 5: About Subjects, I will cover in more detail how I went about teaching various subjects, but for now let me explain why I consider these ones to be important.

Languages expand a person's horizons. And logic is necessary in order to think critically about the world. I am continually frustrated by the lack of logical thought in the conversations around me. I love the scene from *The Lion, the Witch and the Wardrobe* in which the Professor takes Peter and Susan to task for failing to think logically about whether Lucy is telling the truth and exclaims *"Why don't they teach logic at these schools?"*[1] In my school, we learn logic.

But why programming? While it is related to logic and mathematics, the reason I made it a second-tier priority is that a basic understanding of computer programming will be helpful in almost any career. Computers, technology, and programming are part of modern life, and it is useful to have some background knowledge and skills whether you work as a farmer, an artist, or a mountain climber.

The third level of priority covers music, economics, and apologetics.

Learning Goals
A love of learning.
Curiosity about the world.
Global awareness.
Technical skills to cope in a high-tech world.

Priority Subjects
Level 1: Reading, science, writing, mathematics.
Level 2: Foreign language, logic, programming.
Level 3: Music, economics, apologetics.

To be clear, these aren't the only subjects I taught. We studied history each year, and I consider it important, but it just didn't get onto my Priority List! And although it isn't a discrete subject, written and oral communication is important. So is the ability to listen well. Language furnishes the skills to relate to other people, while mathematics provides the logic for dealing with technology.

I also encouraged music over sport. My expectation was for our sons to receive a solid grounding in piano and then become competent in playing one instrument, because music is something that can be used for an entire lifetime. Not that I discouraged sports and physical activity—that's important too! And leadership . . . we mustn't forget that leadership is a key skill for our children to learn. Plus, speaking of ships, there's entrepreneurship.

And that illustrates the dilemma. When you begin to think through all the various activities, it all seems important. The value of a Priority List is to help keep everything in perspective and identify what you feel is **most** important.

It doesn't mean that I started with Priority 1 subjects before moving on to Priority 2 and 3 later. This was simply a way to organize my thinking, sharpen my focus on those areas I wanted to emphasize, and ensure I didn't miss out any topics I thought were too important to be overlooked.

As with the story about the engineer and the dishwasher, the purpose is not for you to agree with my list of most and least important subjects. The point is that you think about it. Take some time to consider the big picture of your long-term objectives and create an intentional Priority List. Justify it to yourself, and write it down. It probably won't be the same as mine, but it will certainly be useful in your planning and will help you remain focused on the important subjects while avoiding the distraction of lower-priority activities.

> *Don't ask kids what they want to be when they grow up but what problems do they want to solve. This changes the conversation from who do I want to work for, to what do I need to learn to be able to do that.*
>
> —Jaime Casap, Google Global Education Evangelist

The Signs of a Successful Education

—Davis Carman[2]

Rachael and I just finished our 26th and final year of teaching our seven kids at home. Sure we were concerned at times that we weren't "getting it all in." And we were acutely aware of the fact that we wouldn't be able to teach them everything. So we had to prioritize and decide what was of utmost importance. . . .
Here are my top four—what I call the signs of a successful education. In other words, when any student graduates from high school, if the following is true for them, then I would say they are well educated.

> *A Love of Reading*
> *A Love of Learning*
> *A Love of Wisdom*
> *A Love of God*

It is important to teach our children to become lifelong learners, curious and inquisitive. Equally important is to instill in children a sense of play, that thinking isn't just serious, it can be fun. This entails giving them the freedom to make mistakes, to explore new thoughts and ideas outside of the ordinary—divergent thinking will be increasingly necessary to solve some of the biggest problems facing the world today. Benjamin Zander, conductor of the Boston Philharmonic, teaches young musicians that self-criticism is the enemy of creativity: "When you make a mistake say to yourself 'how interesting!' A mistake is an opportunity to learn!"

—Daniel Levitin, The Organized Mind[5]

Feel free to update your list over time, but do so thoughtfully and be sure you convince yourself of the reasons for any change. Limit the number of subjects in each level to three or four, because if everything is important, then nothing is important. And make sure your Priority List respects its status in your homeschool world as a servant, not a master.

One final caution. I am aware that children learn at different rates and stages. Classical programs generally won't begin logic until students are about ten years old, when their minds begin to think more analytically. Dr. Raymond Moore, one of the early homeschooling pioneers and author of *Better Late than Early*, believes that children aren't ready for formal learning until age eight to ten.[3] He suggests that boys in particular are often not ready to read until they are seven or older.[4] We can be flexible and adapt to each child's unique needs. Again, the Priority List isn't supposed to be the order in which subjects should be taught, and if a child isn't reading yet, there is still plenty of good stuff to be done. We can read lots of books to him, try plenty of science experiments, play with math manipulatives and do coloring to build fine motor skills in preparation for writing later. Just be sensitive to what works best for your child.

> *The art of teaching is the art of assisting discovery.*
>
> —Mark Van Doren

NOTES

1. C.S. Lewis, *The Lion, the Witch and the Wardrobe* (New York: HarperTrophy, 1950), p. 48.
2. Davis Carman, "Four Signs of a Successful Education," *Apologia*, 19 August 2022, https://www.apologia.com/four-signs-of-a-successful-education.
3. Moore, Moore, and Moore, *Better Late than Early*, p. xvi.
4. Moore, Moore, and Moore, *Better Late than Early*, p. 207.
5. Daniel J. Levitin, *The Organized Mind: Thinking Straight in the Age of Information Overload* (New York: Dutton, 2014), p. 365.

A FRAMEWORK &
TWO MODELS

Consultants love coming up with conceptual models, particularly those with four quadrants or clever alliteration, and particularly, **particularly** models they can publish and trademark and make money from. In many cases, what a consultant will call a "model" or a "tool" is just plain common sense. Often, they have appropriated the idea from elsewhere. A consultant has been described as someone who will borrow your watch, tell you the time, and then charge you $100 for the service. I contend that if someone owns a watch but is too busy to look at it, or doesn't know how to tell the time, then the consultant's services are necessary, and the fees justified.

Being a former aspiring consultant, I have developed some models for home education. You may already be familiar with the ideas or think they are common sense. Even so, it can be helpful to formalize common sense into a model in order to bring ideas into focus, to understand them explicitly rather than implicitly, and to give them a name.

I use a framework to keep the big picture in mind, and two fundamental models to guide my thinking about how to approach individual subjects: the Fencepost Model, which I have applied since my early days of home education; and the Competency Model, which took shape over the last few years. I will be referring to these models when discussing specific subjects.

As with the Priority List, these tools are useful servants but terrible masters. Use them if they are helpful; discard them if they're not. And keep in mind that a model is an ideal representation of a world which is anything but perfect. While they can be useful for thinking about different learning situations, don't expect everything to work flawlessly.

Our Education Framework

It's always helpful to know where you are heading. We kick off each academic year by reviewing the big picture of what we are aiming for in education. To make this easy to understand, I put together a framework dubbed OEF (Our Education Framework).

Focus	Level	Teaching Mode	Classical *Trivium*	Responsibility
Contributing knowledge	Research + Life	Advising		Independence
Exploring ideas	Tertiary (University)	Supporting	Rhetoric (self-expression)	
Understanding concepts	Secondary (High School)	Discussing	Dialectic (argumentation)	
Learning facts	Primary (Elementary)	Instructing	Grammar (memorization)	Dependence

(Wisdom — vertical axis)

Figure 4. Our Education Framework

This framework is fairly self-explanatory, but some points of clarification:

- Our goal is to develop independent learners who are contributing knowledge to the world. But more important than knowledge is that we want our children to increase in wisdom.

- The teaching mode at primary and secondary level also includes a lot of assisting. This should reduce significantly during high school, as the student's level of responsibility for their own learning moves from dependence toward independence.

- Classical educators will argue that all three stages of the *trivium* are completed by the end of secondary school. Perhaps this is the case in classical schools, but I think most students are still mastering dialectic in high school. In fact, I bet most university undergraduates have, like, limited rhetorical ability. Mostly though, I structured the *trivium* in this way because it fitted nicely into the framework!

As with any other model, feel free to modify this framework to suit your own situation.

Wisdom
—*the right use or exercise of knowledge* (Noah Webster 1828)
—*experience and knowledge together with the power of applying them critically or practically* (*Oxford English Reference Dictionary* 1995)
—*knowledge of what is true or right coupled with just judgement as to action* (dictionary.com)

The Fencepost Model

Let's say you live in the frozen north, maybe in Canada or Scandinavia. Imagine it's winter, and you want to build a fence. You have two choices. The first is to put on your winter gear, go outside with a pickaxe, and chip away at the frozen ground until you have made a hole deep enough for the first post. Then you move on to the second post. Maybe you build a fire to help thaw out the ground and make the digging easier. It might take weeks to finish the job, or all winter, but if you persevere, you will eventually have enough holes to put in all your posts and build the fence.

Your second choice is to wait until summer. Let the temperature rise and the ground thaw. Once it's nice and warm, you can go out in shorts and a t-shirt and dig the post holes with a shovel. In a few hours, perhaps a couple of days at most, you will have your fence finished. The job could have been completed before summer started if you had begun during winter, but it was much easier and took a lot less of your time to wait until the ground had thawed.[1]

Summer or Winter?

When I contemplate different subjects, and learning opportunities more broadly, I am thinking to myself, *"Is this a winter job, or a summer job? Would I be better to chip away at teaching this subject a little at a time over the long-haul? Or should I wait until my boys are older and more capable of learning it quickly?"*

On 2 February 1813, General William Henry Harrison ordered his American troops to build Fort Meigs in Ohio in order to protect the

Northwest Territory from British attacks. For the next three months, professional soldiers and militiamen alike persevered through cold winter weather and mud that would at times be knee-deep. The fort was completed a mere days before the British launched an attack, and General Harrison's men survived two sieges.

The Fencepost Model is not meant to suggest that it is always better to wait until summer. As the attack on Fort Meigs illustrates, sometimes the fence needs to be built in winter. And some subjects need to be taught little by little over the years. Mathematics would be an obvious candidate. Nevertheless, there are limited hours in the day, and we all need to prioritize what we think is most important to teach. As home-school parents, we are bombarded with advice about subjects critical to our children's healthy development. We can't cover everything, and often default to what is taught in public schools (because, you know, they are the professionals). The Fencepost Model, along with our Priority List, gives us a framework for thinking critically about the choices we make. How do we choose between Latin and logic and literature? Should we teach a little bit of everything? Could we free up time by leaving some subjects until later years? What works better if done a little at a time, consistently over many years, and what can wait until the student is more capable of learning the topic quickly?

Coercion

We should also be conscious of our children's temperament and adjust accordingly. My oldest son loves reading. When he was six, I decided I could encourage him to engage more critically with literature and develop his writing skills by having him complete a book report each week. He did well with the first one, but it went downhill from there and soon reached the point at which getting a report out of him was like trying to squeeze blood from a stone. Figure 5 shows his final effort.

After pushing him to produce book reports for a year, I finally realized that if I kept this up, I was not only going to make him hate writing but I would also sabotage his love of reading. He had already devoured *The Lord of the Rings* and his current favorite was Jules Verne's *The Mysterious Island*. Did I want to spoil his obvious love of reading by hanging the cloud of a book report over his head? So I dropped this requirement and simply let him enjoy reading.

Book Report

by Ethan Harrison

| Book Details | Title: *The JUNGLE Book* |
| | Author: *Rudyard Kipling* |

| Written Report | Date: *14 June 2016* |
| | Favourite Word: *Mowgli* |

I like The Jungle Book. It is about a boy named Mowgli. He is brave, good and explorer.

Mera

Figure 5. Book Report

Along the same lines as making a child do written assignments, a question I've asked myself many times is, "*Should a child be forced to take music lessons?*" It is true that early exposure to a subject may help a child develop a love for it in a way that would not happen if they only encountered that subject when they were older. But maybe it will also put them off for life.

While there are genuine nuances to consider, I do believe it is never too late to learn. If your curriculum doesn't include a particular subject, your children are not deprived forever. If they are interested enough, they can always pick it up later.

The Competency Model

The second tool which I have found helpful is the Competency Model. There are two competing methods for attaining competency in a skill: the Incremental Approach and the Apprenticeship Approach.

Most academic learning employs what I call the Incremental Approach. This suits a classroom setting in which the teacher needs all students to be at the same or similar level. Using this strategy, children begin by learning the basics of a subject at a novice level. Beginner's books, for example, use simple words and a limited vocabulary. Dr. Seuss was the master of this approach. As beginners grasp the basics, they move up a step to the next level. Over time, like climbing a staircase, they progress to a higher and higher level of competency.

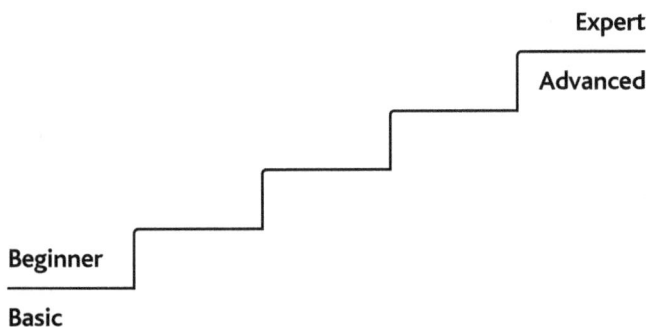

Figure 6. The Incremental Approach

While developing skills over time is the only way to advance from beginner to expert, climbing the stairs of the Incremental Approach is not the only way to achieve this.

Building a House

Imagine your dream home is being built. You have hired a master builder to take on the project, and he has an apprentice. The apprentice is a novice, but you're not concerned because the master builder came highly recommended. You trust him to oversee the work of the apprentice and ensure it is up to standard. The trainee won't be left by himself to just work to the best of his ability. Not on your house! It would not comfort you to know that he expects to gradually improve over time. Instead, the master builder is going to show his apprentice how a task is performed to a professional standard and will assist him until he can do the job correctly by himself. You wouldn't settle for a house half-built to a beginner's level and half-built to an expert level. You want the entire house constructed to an expert level, even though the apprentice needs assistance to meet this standard.

Building Mastery

Using the Apprenticeship Approach, a child masters a subject in a similar manner. As a beginner, the student receives a lot of assistance from the teacher in order to produce work to a high standard. Over time, while maintaining the same expectations for the quality of the work, the student receives less and less help as he becomes more competent, until he is able to produce masterful work by himself.

Apprentice		Master
High Assistance	Low Assistance	No Assistance

Figure 7. The Apprenticeship Approach

Benjamin Franklin used this method to teach himself to write elegantly and expressively. He found examples of excellent writing, and copied and rewrote the articles until he could achieve that same standard of written expression.

> **The Franklin Method**
>
> In his autobiography, Benjamin Franklin relates how he taught himself to write expertly after his father had pointed out his lack of "elegance of expression."
>
> *"About this time I met with an odd volume of the* Spectator*. . . . I thought the writing excellent, and wished if possible to imitate it. With that view I took some of the papers, and making short hints of the sentiments in each sentence, laid them by a few days, and then, without looking at the book, tried to complete the papers again, by expressing each hinted sentiment at length, and as fully as it had been expressed before, in any suitable words that should occur to me. Then I compared my "Spectator" with the original, discovered some of my faults, and corrected them."*[2]

This will not work for all subjects. In fact, it probably won't work for most subjects. We wouldn't begin math with calculus or ask a novice piano student to play Rachmaninoff, no matter how much support we provided. But for some subjects, it makes little sense in my view to teach my children to do something to a poor standard, grade them based on low expectations, and expect them to gradually step up their game and improve over time. Written work is the main area to which I have applied this approach. I think they will learn to write well by writing well, even if I am initially providing a huge amount of assistance. I would rather they learn what excellent writing is by doing excellent writing than by writing poorly and having the faults corrected out of them.

The Apprenticeship Approach is an unconventional method that I have used successfully in appropriate situations. I will talk more about it in relation to assessment in Chapter Sixteen.

NOTES

1. I came across this story years ago, but unfortunately did not note the source and have been unable to track it down. If any reader knows where this Fencepost Model originated, please contact me as I would be happy to give credit to the author for what has been a very helpful idea.
2. Benjamin Franklin, *The Autobiography of Benjamin Franklin* (New York: Barnes & Noble, 2005), pp. 11-12.

PROGRAM BASICS

What's a Grade between Friends?

When we began our homeschooling journey, we did not make a commitment "'til death do us part." Our intention was to take it a year at a time and see how it went. My boys made rapid progress, and within a few years, I knew it would be difficult for them to enter a classroom. They would either be significantly ahead academically if they joined a class based on their age or far behind physically at their grade level.

One aspect of life in the USA that confuses me is how children's activities are based on grade rather than age. In eight years of education, I have still not found the correct answer to the question, *"What grade is your son in?"* I could say what grade lessons he is doing, but that is usually not what is being asked. It's kind of like when your wife asks you a question, and you're trying to figure out the correct answer.

I remember registering one child for a church activity, and the online form required me to choose a grade. Back then, I had not worked out that I needed to mislead my church when answering this question. I wanted him with an appropriate age group, but after I entered the grade of his lessons, the children's ministries director contacted me to suggest my child should be placed in a younger group. They knew the age was what mattered, even though they'd asked for his grade. Another time, I was trying to find the appropriate room for him and asked one of the leaders, *"Which group has seven-year-olds?"* He answered, *"What grade is he in?"* I said, *"He's seven years old. What age is this group?"* The leader didn't know. All he knew was the grade; he had no idea how old the children were.

As homeschoolers, we can be flexible with the level of work we are teaching. We can adapt courses to the right level for our child, whether that is above or below their "grade level." There's no need to move a child on if they require more time to master the topic, and it's not necessary to hold them back if they have already grasped it. Our determining factor should be what will best help our child learn, not what age he is or what grade he's in.

The curriculum we used recognizes this dynamic and labels the programs by letter rather than grade. And the boys take their annual external exam a couple of levels ahead of their age.

Another feature of home education is that multiple ages can be taught using the same material. Some subjects have very distinct levels—particularly mathematics—which require your children to work separately. But many topics can be taught to multiple ages at once, including history, science, and literature. My boys are a little over two years apart in age but have been taught using the same curriculum. The standard of work expected from the elder is greater than that of the younger, and their mathematics courses are different. Apart from that, they've been learning together since the youngest began formal lessons.

> The age-segregated, peer-group schooling model was fatally flawed from the beginning, and when you add in government control and bureaucracy, you have [a] recipe for educational disaster, which is what we are seeing today. . . .
> A one-size-fits-all model of learning negatively impacts both the challenged learner (special needs), the accelerated learner, and any other student that has any substantial variance from average.
> —Dr. Douglas Pietersma[1]

Curriculum

Unlike institutional schools, which must standardize to cater for a large group of students, there are as many different ways of implementing home education as there are homeschoolers. Even children in the same family could use completely different programs. And during the last decade, curriculum companies have proliferated to meet the varied and growing demand. The resources available today are numerous and comprehensive. I find myself looking through catalogues thinking, *"I would love to include this"* but knowing that we simply don't have enough hours in the day or weeks in the year to fit it all in.

Some parents put together their own program, which is a great way to ensure you are covering exactly what you wish to prioritize. But when I started out, I didn't want to have to figure everything out myself, and so I chose a complete curriculum.

The Teacher Matters

Choosing resources, courses, and programs is very important. Some resources are specific to one discipline, such as science, mathematics, or history, while others are comprehensive and encompass all the subjects expected to be covered in a year. For those new to home education, I would suggest you pick a complete curriculum. Why reinvent the wheel? There are plenty of options for a full program, so you might as well let someone else do the work and buy one that covers all the bases.

The plethora of choices feels overwhelming, but don't be too concerned about whether or not you're making the right call. While most programs will do an excellent job of assisting you to educate your children, you won't know whether it works for you until you try it. So check out the options, but don't succumb to analysis paralysis—just pick one and go for it.

There is value in persisting with the same curriculum in order to be consistent over the years, to systematically cover all of the recommended topics, and to allow your children to become familiar with a regular pattern of learning. Each curriculum has its own particular approach, and continuity may be helpful for their learning. However, choosing a curriculum is not an immutable decision. You can change it. And you can certainly adapt, add, and remove elements when you see what is working well and what isn't.

My best piece of advice in this area is something we heard as we began to look into homeschooling. A friend told us to choose a curriculum that **we** wanted to teach. This was an excellent tip, one every parent should know and put into practice.

**Choose a curriculum that
you are excited to teach.**

Or putting it another way, the curriculum or program needs to work for the parents as much as for the children.

Of course, a particular learning style may suit one child and not another, and this needs to be considered. You naturally want your children to do as well as they can. But it's easy to overlook the fact that the teacher needs to do well also. Enthusiasm is contagious, and your attitude toward the material will be noticed by your students. If you love the teaching style, you will love teaching. And if you love teaching, your children will learn. Period. End of story.

I can't promise that if you love a subject, your children will love it too. But I can almost guarantee they will not like something you dislike. I'm afraid our attitudes as parents are more influential in the negative than the positive!

Making It Your Own

My wife and I love reading. And when we came across the Sonlight curriculum, we knew this was for us. It caught our eye as it was a comprehensive literature-based program. We were excited by a curriculum that included lots of stories rather than textbooks. We also appreciated their global perspective, with world history being taught before US history.

And it has worked very well for us over the years. With time and experience, I have customized the program to suit our needs. I have adjusted and adapted and added to and taken away. I have used very little of the language arts program, as I will explain in Chapter Twenty. And I've added many additional topics like foreign language and logic. The curriculum is flexible enough to form the basis of an educational program meeting the needs of multiple ages and teaching approaches. Typically, we spend about $1,000 each year for the curriculum, additional courses, materials, and resources. As this is shared between both boys, the cost is about $500 per child per year.[2]

When adding subjects and adapting a curriculum, keep in mind that you don't need to complete everything in a particular program.

- Some subjects build on skills year on year—for example, mathematics. If you don't get through it all, you'll probably come back to it next year.

- Some subjects are too vast to cover completely. History is like that. No matter how much time you spend on it, you're not going to teach all there is to know.

- Some subjects may be left out completely. Your children will learn them if they have enough interest. I didn't teach a formal course in typing and computer use, but that didn't stop my son from figuring out video editing when he wanted to put together a film.

- Some subjects can be left until later. Civics and government might be understood better when your children are in high school.

- Some subjects may be useful as an introduction, but mastery is not needed during primary or secondary education. As much as I love physics, an introduction will be fine for most students.

The Benefit of Hindsight

In the last year, I have shifted to a course-based approach more suitable for high school and leading toward university. I'm picking material from multiple vendors as well as creating my own courses, such as in New Zealand politics, to suit my boys' emerging interests.

With the benefit of hindsight, if I were to start over I wonder whether I would have chosen a classical curriculum or at least taught using a classical framework. I did some of this instinctually, such as introducing logic and incorporating public speaking, but without the understanding and structure of the *trivium*. I might have needed to shoehorn the classical approach into my preferred science-heavy primary program. But the classical model of knowledge, logic, and expression fits in well with what I wanted to achieve. And I am very attracted to programs such as Generations[3] that have a foundation of discipleship and Biblical studies. The Moore Formula devised by child development specialist and homeschool pioneer Dr. Raymond Moore is also intriguing: limited formal study beginning at age eight to ten; as much manual work as academic study; and daily home and community service.[4]

When you're starting out, experienced homeschoolers will be happy to give you advice on curricula! Check out a co-op or support group, visit a curriculum fair, or attend a homeschool conference. You might feel overwhelmed, but remember to look for something that makes sense for you as well as your children. Don't feel nervous about making a decision. Try it and see how it works. You can always choose a different one next year, or sooner if it's really not working. But don't switch for the sake of change, particularly as your children get older. Within a few years, you'll be one of the experienced professionals handing out advice to the newcomers!

High School

It was easy enough to adapt an entire curriculum to both the level and the age difference of my boys. But with high school looming, I knew I had to get to grips with the next few years.

The first question was whether to continue teaching through high school. I understand that this is seen as a barrier for many parents. Primary or elementary education appears easy enough, but high school might be daunting. How will we provide the resources? Do I know enough to be able to teach the subjects? What about sports, or driver's ed., or prom? In my case though, I felt no qualms about teaching at secondary level, and as the time drew closer, the answer became obvious. We would be continuing through high school.

There were some details I needed to understand first. What was different about secondary education? What were the requirements for graduating and receiving a high school diploma? I spent an entire summer figuring this out, researching and reading and preparing for the academic year. And in the end, I completely changed our approach. We have recently begun our second year of the high school program, so it remains a work in progress and will no doubt be adjusted along the way.

Individual Courses

Here's what we are doing.

Rather than teaching a range of different activities as part of a single, integrated curriculum, our secondary-level program consists of individual one-credit courses. As I understand it, this matches the usual distinction between primary (elementary) and secondary (high school) education. Primary education is taught by a single teacher covering all disciplines to a fixed group of children in a specific classroom. In contrast, secondary education is taught as individual subjects having specialized instructors, with students moving between classrooms. The increased specialization is perhaps why there is a psychological barrier for some parents to teaching through high school.

I followed this general approach when developing our secondary program. I prepared each course individually and created a syllabus which outlined the work required to complete the course, the assessments, and the marking guide for each assessment. I also included an agreement to be signed by both teacher and student. See Appendix B for a sample course outline.

How to Assess Learning

I have always tried to guard against education being viewed by the metric of time. It's hard to remember this during the daily grind, but sitting in a classroom for five hours a day, 180 days a year does not educate a child. For many students, school means completing activities; for the less-motivated, it is about counting down the hours. One of the beauties of home education is the possibility that you can complete all of the lessons in four days or less per week, or by lunch every day, or finish up the year months before school is out.

Tertiary education (university or college) moves in the direction of learning being assessed by measuring the outcome, rather than the time or activity, but it isn't really until doctoral work that time and activity become irrelevant, and outcome takes center stage as the sole measure of achievement.

Our high school program emphasizes that each course has a required set of activities and assessments which define when the course is completed, whether that takes more or less time than a year. Completing activities such as reading a book, undertaking an experiment, or handing in an assignment is of course not the goal of education either, any more than being present for a prescribed number of hours a day. The goal of education is to learn, and while activities are a helpful tool, they are still a proxy for learning. Assessment is also a proxy for learning and is not necessarily the best way to measure it.

In our current secondary program, we are moving toward the point of judging learning by the outcome rather than elapsed time, completed activities, or graded assessments. But a high school transcript requires these details, and for now in our high school courses, time and activity still play a role while the importance of assessment is increasing. Again, in the home setting, we have greater freedom to determine the form the assessment takes.

When I was at university, I would work on physics assignments with a couple of friends. If we reached an impasse, we would all go together to ask the lecturer for help. A number of times, while walking down the hall and talking over how to articulate our question, one of us would solve the problem before we even reached the professor's office. In a similar way, tutoring and teaching a topic is the best way to learn it. Demme Learning uses this approach to teaching back new material in order to demonstrate learning. To the old adage, *"Tell me and I will forget; show me and I will remember; involve me and I will understand,"* Steve Demme adds, *"Let me teach it and I will have achieved mastery!"*[5] I think that discussing and explaining a topic is a valuable way to reinforce and assess learning, matching the dialectic and rhetoric stages of the classical *trivium*. I may shift more in this direction and away from written assignments with future courses.

However, working under pressure, completing required assignments, and being evaluated on the results are beneficial life skills. It is valuable for my children to have experience at writing papers and learning how to take tests. For the last two years, I have used assignments as the primary means of grading courses. This may change in the future, but I feel it's useful for now.

High School Objectives

Our educational goals go beyond simply completing the school district's requirements. The objectives guiding our secondary program are:

1. To satisfy the legal graduation requirement;
2. To create a compelling College Admission Transcript;
3. To meet our personal expectations for a well-rounded educational program.

State Requirements

Regulations will vary depending on where you live, but in our state, homeschool students do not need to meet graduation requirements. However, we are using our state's legal requirements as the lowest level goal for completing high school. In our case, this comprises 21½ credits with 14½ of those being specified subjects.

Neither our state nor our school district provides a clear definition of what constitutes a credit. Unless your jurisdiction stipulates otherwise, you are free to use common sense. A general guide is that a one-credit course is about equivalent to 120 hours of work.

College Admission Transcript

From an academic perspective, our objective is for our children to create a compelling college admission transcript. In saying this, we are not assuming they will attend university. There may be better alternatives depending on what they wish to pursue. Nevertheless, this goal keeps our sights set on a challenging and worthy target. Advanced mathematics and foreign languages are added to strengthen the overall program, and extra-curricular activities become important.

My wife volunteered for many years as an interviewer of prospective students for her *alma mater*, Georgetown University. She knows what makes for a strong application, and it isn't simply grades. Service, leadership, entrepreneurship, and other interests are aspects of a student's background that impress college admissions departments. In addition to the course work, we will be looking to add activities such as hands-on business experience and mission trips.

Personal Expectations

Once state and college admissions requirements are under control, our focus will move toward those activities that will develop our children's skills and interests. We want to take full advantage of the freedom afforded by home education to pursue an uncommon approach to learning.

In the next few years, we will be looking to add short courses. Many universities and other organizations offer block courses for teens, particularly over the summer. Leadership, political simulations, engineering, and robotics are some we have noted with interest. There are debate competitions and drama schools. And one which really caught my children's attention was a culinary tour of the world—learning to cook a pizza for each country "visited."

Do Not Be Intimidated!

Secondary school is different from primary, not only due to the academic level but also in the change to individual courses. However, this is also matched by your child's increasing ability to learn independently. Children should be taught, and expected, to learn how to do their work by themselves. If specialist help is needed, for example in mathematics or science, there are online courses, homeschool associations, and co-operatives that can provide assistance.

There is no need for high school to be a barrier to you as a parent teaching your children.[6] You don't need to be the expert, and you don't need to think you're depriving your children if the academic level exceeds your own. You may need some extra support, you may need to find alternative solutions such as online courses for certain subjects, and you may need to teach your children to become independent learners. But you **can** continue home education through high school.

NOTES

1. Douglas J. Pietersma, https://www.facebook.com/HomeEducationDr, accessed 29 December 2022.
2. According to the National Home Education Research Institute, homeschool families in the USA spend an average of $600 per student annually for their education. By comparison, the US Census Bureau in a press release dated 18 May 2021 said that public education spending was $13,187 per pupil in 2019, over $750 billion annually. Homeschooling therefore saves US taxpayers $56 billion each year: Brian Ray, "Homeschooling: The Research," *National Home Education Research Institute* (11 March 2023), https://www.nheri.org/research-facts-on-homeschooling.
3. Generations, https://www.generations.org.
4. Moore Academy, https://www.moorefoundation.com/about/formula.
5. Stephen Demme, *Geometry Instruction Manual* (Lancaster, PA: Demme Learning, 2009), p. 11.
6. Lee Binz (the Homescholar) specializes in helping parents homeschool through high school. She provides useful resources on her website, https://www.homehighschoolhelp.com, as well as paid services such as "The High School Solution."

CHAPTER SIXTEEN

ASSESSMENT

Testing

There are two types of people in this world: those who have studied hard for a exam, achieved a great result, and promptly forgotten what they learned; and those who have never taken a test. And very few people these days fall into the latter category, since assessment and testing are a fact of life.

Tests do make sense in a classroom setting. They provide a simple and consistent way of comparing students. And there are some tests in our program. In general, though, I have avoided them. Apart from mathematics and the annual external test to meet state requirements, my boys completed almost no graded assignments for the first five years of their education. I am increasing the amount of written assessment and testing now as they move into secondary education, more so they learn how to deal with assessment than for me to be able to gauge their progress. But I think it's important to have a clear understanding of the purpose of testing and assessment.

I realize I have frequently mentioned results in this book. A high grade or score is something to celebrate, but it is only one tool in the learning arsenal and should not be thought of as the objective. A more important measure is the amount of effort put into the work. Zig Ziglar says that we should praise children for their effort, rather than their intelligence. *"Results will be better, and lifetime habits will be formed, producing lifetime winners."*[1]

From day one, I have told my children that test results are a reflection of my teaching, rather than of their ability. I have described tests as assessing my success as an instructor and identifying any areas I have failed to teach thoroughly. If a child does well, then I have taught him well. If he gets anything wrong, then it means I need to spend more time with him on that lesson. By taking this approach, it helps avoid unnecessary pressure on my children to perform well. I don't want them to feel nervous about sitting exams.

Is Testing Necessary?

Testing and assessment should not really be needed in home education. It is one of those elements that is easy to transfer across from the school environment, but the reason for using it in a school setting is less relevant in the home. A classroom teacher needs a way to gauge the learning of an entire class full of children. A homeschool parent should be able to assess how well their children are learning by observing them carefully and working with them individually. Are they getting through their math problems easily, or finding them difficult? Do they ask questions about the stories they are hearing or reading? In what subjects are they showing interest? If you are in tune with your child, then you don't need to test them.

And that's the approach I adopted, for the most part, during my boys' primary education. I think it would be fine to do without testing and assessment completely. However, our state mandates an annual external exam, and although I don't like mandates and would not have chosen to do these every year if they weren't required, I'll grudgingly admit that maybe it's perhaps a good thing we did them.

First, it provides a useful confirmation that I am teaching adequately and my children are learning well. The results are a convenient benchmark. Second, it is encouraging for my children when they are successful. They actually look forward to the tests (and to earning a $1 bounty for each perfect score). They can see proof they are excelling and know this is in the context of a nationwide reference point. Third, it gives them practice in the skill of test-taking. They will need to take tests at some point in their lives.

What Is the Point?

But back to my opening comment. What's the deal with acing an exam and promptly forgetting the material? What is the point of a test or assessment? Does a good result mean the student actually understands the subject, or did they simply learn to parrot the correct answers? What does the result reveal? If the student achieves a perfect score, is that a worthwhile result? Or does it mean the work was not challenging enough and therefore of limited learning value?

In my view, the objective of taking a course of study is to gain knowledge, not to achieve a respectable grade. It is learning that I care about, not a GPA. Believe me, I have sat enough tests in my life to know that effective exam technique is as important as knowing the material. And before each external exam, I spend time with my boys teaching them the techniques to do well in the tests, which are all multiple choice. Read the question carefully. Eliminate obviously wrong answers. Watch out for the trick solution. Test each answer choice, even if you think you know the solution. Work backward from the answer to the question.

I learned the hard way. In my first undergraduate degree, I would leave multiple choice questions until the end because if I were running out of time, it would be easier to pick up extra marks in the last minute by ticking a box than by attempting a written answer. In one particular exam, time was almost up and I had ten multi-choice questions left. I randomly picked the answers. And got them all wrong! I did worse than the monkey mark—the number that a monkey should have gotten correct! Since then, I have never picked random answers.

So we know how to work the system. But again, what is the point? Is it to get an acceptable grade, or to learn and understand the material?

The objective is to learn, not to get a satisfactory grade.

The Apprenticeship Approach

There are two specific practices I introduced this year that are unorthodox, and might perhaps be seen by some as wrong. So let me explain my reasoning carefully.

The first is the Apprenticeship Approach. This was introduced in Chapter Fourteen; refer back to Figure 7 on page 152. I will discuss it again, this time specifically with reference to assessment.

Just as the Fencepost Model provides two fundamentally different time-frames for introducing a subject, both of which are valid but dependent on the topic being taught, so the Competency Model provides two fundamentally different approaches for achieving mastery. This thinking can also be applied to tests or assignments. Using the Incremental Approach, an assessment is tailored to the student's level of expertise. You don't want them to get a perfect score, because that means the test is too easy and therefore not challenging. But you don't want it to be too hard, because it will be frustrating and discouraging if the student fails completely. As they continue to learn, however, the assignments will become progressively more challenging until they are submitting high-quality work. That is how most assessments are traditionally structured. And for some subjects, this is completely appropriate. Mathematics, for example, should be assessed using this Incremental Approach. It can be applied even when a piece of work is not graded, like art. You put your child's artwork on the fridge, no matter how good it is.

But in some cases, I think the Apprenticeship Approach is a better way.

Using the Apprenticeship Approach, the standard of work is expected to be at the highest level from the start, and assignments are graded to this standard. What varies is the amount of assistance provided by the teacher.

For some subjects and assessments, I think the Apprenticeship Approach is a better technique for helping a child achieve mastery. I'm specifically applying this method to written essays and reaction papers. In the last year, my boys were assigned eighteen reaction papers and about six essays. I expect these written assessments to be completed to a university undergraduate standard and grade them as such. But I'm not expecting them to write at this level by themselves. So for this past year, I have spent a lot of time helping them brainstorm, research, create outlines, draft, edit, and complete their written assignments. Sometimes the final paper has been much more me than them. But over the next few years, they will contribute increasingly more and I will assist less, until they are completing the assignments entirely by themselves. However, from the very beginning, they will have been producing written work to a high standard.

Clearly this model doesn't work from day one of schooling. A wannabe builder needs some basic skills before receiving an apprenticeship.

So it fits in better with areas like writing essays that I have left until my boys are older. I am specifically using it for written work, but it could no doubt be adapted and applied in other subjects, such as science experiments.

And this is an experiment in progress. I'm pleased with what has been achieved so far and with how much improvement my boys have shown in their written work. I think the quality of the assignments they are producing is excellent, considering the amount of assistance I am giving them and the fact that this is the first year they have written essays.

Signs of Improvement

I mentioned in Chapter Fourteen that I gave up on making my eldest son write book reports. Six years later, after reintroducing written assignments and working with him using the Apprenticeship Approach, he produced the paper in Figure 8 without any of my assistance.

Retests

The second unorthodox approach which I've introduced this year was prompted by a science course. My boys had chosen biology, which was a tenth-grade program and very challenging. They really struggled with the first module test, and it was clear they would be in trouble if I didn't intervene. I thought to myself, *"The test is an indication of how much they remember. But what is the purpose of the course? Is it to get a good grade? Or is it to understand the material?"* I decided that learning biology should be the focus and that being thoroughly familiar with a subsection of the material would be a superior outcome to being unfamiliar with all of it. They are more likely to retain something they understand.

So I introduced a process for them to follow. They studied the entire module and completed all the study problems and other work, as before. However, when they were ready for the module test, they were allowed to preview the test questions. They weren't to look at the solutions, but this gave them an opportunity to thoroughly study what they specifically needed to know for the test, which was only a subset of the material in the module. If their test score was then less than

75 percent, they could retake the same test but first needed to review all of the questions and the model answers, and their final score would be the average of the two results. And once they completed the test satisfactorily, they were required to again review the model answers before moving on to the next module.

Is it cheating to see the questions before sitting the test? Many times, my university professors would tell the class what to expect in the exam so we knew how to focus our study time. For challenging topics with a lot of material, knowing the questions in advance makes it more likely that the student will learn part of the topic comprehensively, rather than all of it superficially. And redoing the same test means the student is going to learn those particular questions much more thoroughly. Maybe he will even remember them after the module is completed!

Of course, these results aren't a fair comparison with students who have taken the test once without knowing the questions in advance. But if you're not comparing results and are more interested in learning, then I think this approach has merit. It has certainly helped my boys grasp the material in the biology course. With this method, I am confident they will have learned more than if they simply sat the test as a one-shot effort at the end of the module.

When my wife attended Georgetown University, her marketing professor allowed students to take one sheet of notes into the final exam. My wife said that her classmates worked intensely to identify the key information and reduce the entire course down to one piece of paper. This marketing professor's plan was for his students to learn the material while focused on creating their cheat sheet. In contrast, my physics exams were open book, meaning we could take our texts into the final exam. This avoided the need to memorize all the formulas but didn't help as much with our preparation. The physical act of writing something down helps us to remember it. Both methods benefited students during the exam, but the marketing professor's approach helped his students learn his course.

In real life, if we don't know something, we look it up. People don't even remember their phone number anymore. So I think in the home learning environment, it's okay to get creative about testing as long as it serves the purpose of helping our children learn.

What Hearts

Ethan Harrison   9/11/2022

What Hearts is a book written by Bruce
Brooks. It is compiled of four short stories
about a boy named Asa. The story seems to
be set in the USA, around 2010, but there are
very few place details. It's more about personal
feelings and circumstances.

Asa appears to lead a troubled life. The first
story starts with him getting all A's on his report
card and coming home to find out that his
parents are getting divorced. Divorce has got to
be one of the hardest things for a kid to go
through. Asa takes it by becoming less out-
going. I think it might have been best for his
situation, but I feel that if he expressed his
feelings into a pillow or with a trusted friend,
that might help him a bit more.

When his mother remarries, things don't improve. His stepfather, Dave, doesn't really like
Asa and on top of that, Asa's family start to
move around. Seven moves in three years.

I didn't enjoy this book. It was written
~~well~~ well, I just didn't enjoy reading
about divorce, a stepfather who is a bully,
and not being able to settle in. I must just

not like reading about hardships that happen in life. I understand kids all over the world are in situations like this, but I wish I could help them without reading about their life.

So, I didn't like this book. I did empathise with his hardships, even though I haven't been through many. If there is anything I've learned from this book, it's that I'm very blessed to have parents who love me and eachother, a wonderful home, and that I matter.

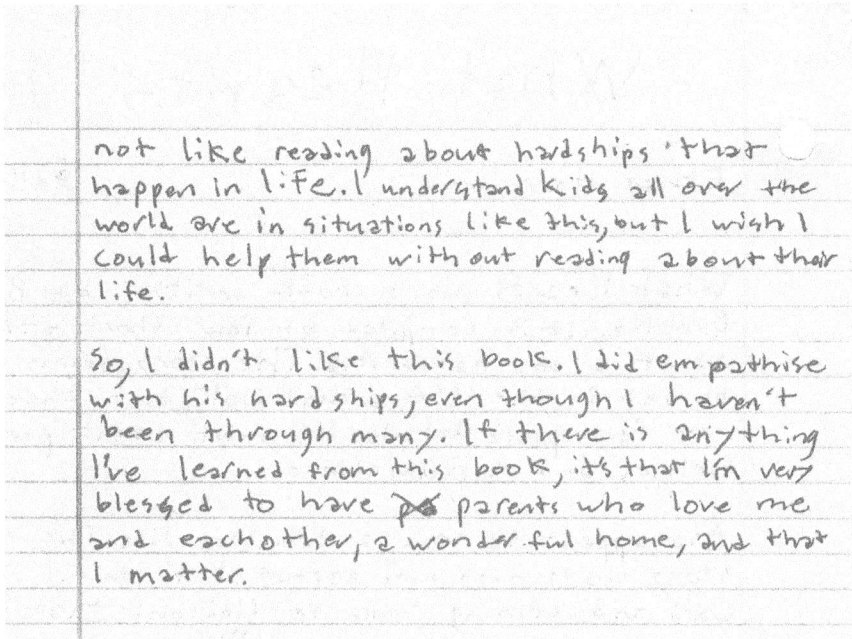

Figure 8. Reaction Paper

Whatever It Takes to Get an A

Nancy Bjorkman provides a refreshing perspective. She reminds us that **everything** is made up. School teachers create their material and decide how to grade their students' work. They determine when it's appropriate to offer a make-up test or an extra credit activity. Curriculum writers put together the resources used by teachers. Examiners write the tests that are taken nationwide. Doctoral examination committees judge whether a thesis contributes a substantial body of original research. There is no absolute standard for any of this. People just make it up. Nancy Bjorkman encourages us to use our best judgement regarding grades and credits, and comments that homeschool parents are usually tougher on their students because we know how hard they have worked.[2]

In practically any course, given enough time, any student should be able to master the material and achieve an A grade. Usually, students don't have the luxury of unlimited time, and it may only be the academically gifted or exceptionally hard-working ones that achieve top

> Success is honest effort,
> fully expended, in quest
> of a worthy ideal.
>
> —Zig Ziglar[3]

marks. I want my boys to work hard at their studies, and they have done very well in many subjects. But there are some in which they have struggled, and my attitude has been that I will provide all the resources they need to learn the topic, and we will keep working at it until they reach an A-grade standard. As homeschoolers, we have the flexibility to do whatever it takes, including investing extra time. The biology course mentioned above is a great case in point, as is their classic literature course. In each of these, they put in between 230–250 hours, more than double the expected amount of time for a one-credit course. They fully deserve their A grades; they earned them.

And to quote Forrest Gump, *"That's about all I have to say about that."*

NOTES

1. Zig Ziglar, "The Proper Way to Praise," *Creators Syndicate* (24 August 2022), https://www.creators.com/read/classic-zig-ziglar/08/22/the-proper-way-to-praise-57851, accessed 24 August 2022.
2. Nancy Bjorkman, *Homeschooling through High School* (Mache Convention 2023: Minnesota Association of Christian Home Educators, 20 May 2023).
3. Zig Ziglar, "It Don't Matter," *Creators Syndicate* (11 January 2023), https://www.creators.com/read/classic-zig-ziglar/01/23/it-dont-matter-6fa74, accessed 11 January 2023.

PART 4

ABOUT TEACHING

Lessons that I learned about teaching boys,
about training children,
and about managing time effectively.

WHAT I LEARNED
THE HARD WAY

According to the Harrison Parochial Dictionary 2022, a child is defined as a human who isn't bothered by making mistakes, while an adult is a human who expresses the desire to avoid the errors of others, but makes them anyway.

I've made plenty of mistakes on this journey, along with successes, and hope you will benefit from both. While others are more knowledgeable about education, and more experienced as teachers, and more abundant in offspring, very few of them will have the same perspective that I have. In fact, I can say with complete certainty that no one else is me. And so, I venture to offer my advice!

In these next sections, Part 4: About Teaching and Part 5: About Subjects, I will be sharing what I've learned the hard way, and offering advice and ideas and thoughts on various topics and subjects. I am not attempting to provide a comprehensive analysis of any of them. Some I have thought about a lot, some I have thought about very little. Hey, I only had two children to practice on! But what I have learned, I am passing on to you.

Every home is different, every situation is different, every child is different, and every parent is different. So what I've concluded may not be applicable in your circumstances. But there are things you will learn, and you can adapt ideas to your unique setting. My experience may help you understand and better deal with something you face. Even if you disagree with me, there's still value to be found as you think about why I am wrong and convince yourself why you are right.

What I Learned about Boys

I was a studious child. While the teacher was occupied with the rest of the class, I learned to block out the noise and work in my own private world. I wasn't naturally gifted and certainly not a genius, but I had a drive to achieve perfection. The workshop teacher described me as "the complete woodworker." I achieved a perfect score in the high school entrance exam. It didn't take me long to realize not all boys were like me. I didn't fit neatly into the box.

Talking about what I've learned teaching boys is therefore a little tricky. My observations may not apply to your boys, and they probably wouldn't have applied to me. Stereotypes may work on average but will allow many to fall through the gaps. However, I think generalizations can provide a useful starting point, as long as we move on from there to treat our children as individuals. A stereotype is a place to begin, not a place to end.

Boys Are Active

In general, boys learn better when they are active.

Although I'd heard this before, I can still remember the feeling of astonishment when I saw it with my own eyes. My oldest was in his first year of formal education, part of which involved memorization. My youngest was three at the time and wanted to join in. He proceeded to run around the room, reciting as he went. My first instinct was to stop him moving and hold him still so that he would concentrate on the memorization. But I'm pleased to say I got it right—I let him run. And for years, whenever he recited from memory, he would move or run or bounce around the room. I realized the purpose of memorization was memorization, not sitting still. And if he were achieving the objective while being active, then why stop him?

Of course, this would never work in a classroom. So in public school, a boy's tendency to be active is suppressed by necessity. But we are not a public school. We have the freedom to help our children learn. So if your children fidget or move around or like to read while hanging backward off the sofa, then watch to see if they are actually doing the work, and if they are, do your best to embrace the activity and accommodate the way they learn.

There is an established connection between physical activity and brain function, and strong evidence that aerobic exercise remodels the brain for peak performance on all fronts.[1] I had heard that jumping on a rebounder aids memorization. Trampoline sellers certainly claim so, though I couldn't find any independent confirmation! However, it can't hurt and rebounding could be incorporated into lessons as a way to allow children to be active while memorizing or listening to stories or watching videos. I always meant to experiment with this but never got around to it.

Ensuring boys get physical activity when they take a break is also highly recommended. Playing computer games does little to recharge the mind and body.

I want to be clear though that a need to be active shouldn't be an excuse for poor self-control. Boys are quite capable of keeping still for long periods, even if it's not their preferred approach. Since birth, we have had our boys sit with us in church, right through the sermon. Whether they are listening or not, I cannot tell you. But we wished to expose them to the life and praxis of the church and wanted them to learn to be attentive and quiet for extended periods. We have no qualms about taking them to an orchestra or play or business meeting because we know they can control themselves, and we expect them to do so.

There is very definitely a place for self-control, and it is a learned behavior which boys are perfectly capable of mastering. But the point is we can help children learn more effectively by taking advantage of, rather than suppressing, their natural tendencies.

And a quick, funny story about hyper-active boys. There's no moral, it just makes me smile whenever I remember it. I was the leader at a boys' camp and sat directly behind a very energetic camper during chapel. For the entire half-hour, he wiggled his way forward to get away from me. As soon as he had escaped an arm's length, I would reach out, grab the waistband of his shorts, and slide him back along the carpet toward me. Every thirty seconds or so, for the whole chapel period. Oh look, there's a cardinal in our apple tree!

Back to the book . . .

Let Boys Be Boys

—Mark Hancock, Trail Life USA[2]

Embrace the difference between boys and girls.

- Boys need variety, both visual and auditory.
- Boys' brains are compartmentalized. They love structure and think in terms of discrete topics.
- Understand and make use of risk and competition.
- Boys want to know: who's with me; who's in charge; and what's our mission.
- Recognize the importance of movement.

Boys Are Competitive and Task-Oriented

Boys also tend to be competitive. Used appropriately, this has proven an effective way to encourage them to finish their work. My oldest became incredibly prolific at completing assignments when he wanted to watch the Star Wars series and was required to hand in a written piece of work for each movie watched. My youngest loves completing challenges, particularly if he can earn a reward.

During their primary education, my boys seemed to be more interested in completing the lessons than savoring the activities. We mixed things up at times by reading books outside, going to museums, and having free learning times when they could study anything they wanted. But they were more interested in checking that activity off the list and being done for the day so they could play. Maybe that is more reflective of my personality or the way I organized the schedule, but I suspect it is a characteristic of many boys. It isn't necessarily a bad thing and can be used as motivation to complete lessons. But it does make it harder to learn through discussion and dialogue. Child-directed or delight-directed learning, where the teacher responds to the interests of the child, would totally not work for us. My boys just want to know what they have to do to get done, and they need specified tasks and activities to keep them on track. I am working hard to introduce more discourse as they grow older, but it's still a work in progress.

And children need lots of affirmation. I'm sure this is equally applicable to girls, but maybe we forget that boys need it too. It is my practice to begin each day by putting my arms around my boys and affirming them and praying a blessing over them.

> **Making Biblical Family Life Practical: When Dad Is the Homeschool Teacher**
>
> —Hal and Melanie Young[3]
>
> *As the dad, you may not be as tuned in to your child's non-verbal and emotional communication. Get your wife's input and trust her instincts. (On the plus side, you are likely to experience less stress and uncertainty over choices and directions for the homeschool. We tell moms to recruit their husbands' decisiveness to break the impasse they experience).*
>
> *Do be sensitive to your children's childhood. We dads get really goal-oriented and sometimes we don't allow for their normal levels of distraction, fatigue, and so forth. They're kids!*
>
> *Understand the learning differences between your sons and your daughters. Boys tend to be noisy, physical, active, and just hard to teach. Moms often don't instinctively get this, and you do. But you might need some insight into what makes your daughters special.*
>
> *For example, our sons like the teaching to be emphatic, confident, engaging, challenging. They like to debate. And they like the room well lit and cold, preferably with a breeze in their faces. We understand this. Our daughters like things more warm and nurturing, affirming, peaceable, gentle rather than stirring. You need to speak both languages, if you have both sons and daughters to teach.*

What I Learned about Personalities

Learning Style

Let me reveal a secret every parent already knows—children have their own individual personality. As the joke goes, you are unique, just like everyone else. Each child has his own interests, preferences, strengths, weaknesses, temperament, and preferred learning style. Some do better in group situations, while others thrive when working individually. One will learn by listening and talking, another by doing, and yet another by reading. While there are those who express themselves easily and simply won't keep quiet, getting a response from others might seem like an uphill battle.

In class-sized groups, learning can at best be designed to suit the majority. And in practice, this means children must conform their learning style to the needs of the group. But you are not teaching a large group of children (not even if you have twelve kids). You are teaching individuals, and home education provides the opportunity to tailor the style of learning to best match your child's personality. What's more, as a parent, you probably know your child better than anyone else.

In the same way as there are characteristics generally common to boys, children can be grouped by different personalities and stages of life. When children are younger, they tend to be inquisitive about the world and learn facts easily. Kinesthetic learners process information through touch and movement. Some thrive on discussion, while others prefer to get on with their work by themselves. We can help children learn more effectively by leveraging their individual characteristics.

Again, as with the previous discussion about boys learning to focus, it's important to avoid making the world revolve around any child. We shouldn't adapt everything to their particular whims; they also need to learn to be flexible and mindful of others. But the point is we have the opportunity to be responsive to our children's individuality and can take advantage of their preferred learning style to enhance their education and make our job as teacher easier.

Motivation

In addition to learning styles, each child is motivated differently. Our oldest gains a lot of satisfaction from accomplishing goals, while our youngest enjoys challenges and competition. Sometimes I think the most important task I face as a parent is to figure out how to motivate my children. I've tried many different techniques to incentivize them over the years, and at times it seems their motivations change daily!

Incentives are clearly a more effective way of encouraging their learning than threats of punishment and make for a far happier lesson time. How do your children respond to rewards? Do they like praise? Having their work displayed on the fridge or wall? Getting stickers?

I have always been motivated by perfection. Eighty percent is not good enough for me. Neither is 95 percent. At one point, I was concerned my boys were not making enough effort to get their math tests correct. I can deal with them being unable to solve a problem, but they gave the impression they just couldn't be bothered. For a time, most of the forfeited marks were either because I couldn't read their writing or because they hadn't even answered the question. So I instituted a $1 bounty for each 100 percent correct test. That has worked marvelously over the years. They don't achieve enough perfect scores to bankrupt me, but it's motivation enough to take the tests seriously.

What has worked well in the last couple of years is that my boys are able to earn computer time by completing their learning goals and chores for the week. They know exactly what they need to do to earn the reward, and there are clear consequences, both positive and negative, for their effort.

Group Work

If your child enjoys working in a group and being with others, then a homeschool co-operative offers this opportunity. However, we can also accommodate students who prefer to work in a quiet place by themselves, something that is limited in a classroom setting. The child that would rather work alone is not forced to remain in a group. Even if you are snow-bound in a small house with brothers and sisters, there are ways to create a quiet space. My mother used to find personal time in a busy home full of kids by locking herself in the bathroom. Maybe this is a hereditary trait, as it came naturally to my boys. They spend hours reading in the bathroom. And sometimes doing lessons there. Our oldest in particular prefers his privacy when working. I know that sometimes this is an excuse and he isn't actually working, so I need to monitor whether he is truly getting through his lessons. But the point is we are able to be flexible, and he has the ability to work by himself, while our youngest who likes company can do his lessons with me.

CHAPTER SEVENTEEN

The Power of Names

I have always been fascinated by people who seem to embody their name. Clearly it isn't always the case—not everyone named Christian or Jesus acts like Jesus Christ. But it seems to me more than coincidence if someone with a perpetual smile is named "Joy," or when you can always count on "Peter."

Is it because their parents had an intuition or divine revelation about their newborn's character? Or did the child develop that affinity as he grew? We were very deliberate in choosing names for our children. The name of our oldest means "strong defender of the people," and he aims to become Prime Minister. Our youngest's means "the LORD will provide abundantly;" one of his love-languages is gift-giving.

Nominative Determinism
New Scientist editor John Hoyland coined the term "nominative determinism" for cases of people who seem inexorably drawn to their profession by virtue of their name.[4]
Some wonderfully apt examples are attorney Sue Yoo, British neurologist Baron Brain, former Lord Chief Justice Igor Judge, and weather reporter Storm Field.

I think it's really important to be discerning with nicknames as well. "Princess," "Champ," or "Handsome" will have a more positive long-term impact than "Rascal," "Sniffy," or "Grublet." Words have power; names are significant.

I had an interesting experience when creating computer usernames for my boys. I thought that "bookworm" for the oldest and "mathsman" for the youngest were positive and appropriate. But the youngest was a bit peeved and told me he was a bookworm as well. And I noticed a clear drop in effort with the oldest's math lessons and realized the username had sent a subtle message that he wasn't as good at mathematics. I do think we should be able to compliment one child without the other feeling slighted. That seems more like a character issue to me. But it was fascinating that this had a noticeable effect on them both. When I asked my youngest to suggest a username later, he picked "TheEpicPianist." Choose your children's names, nicknames, and usernames carefully!

The Role of Naming in the Formation of Our Identity

—Paul Tournier[5]

Swiss physician Paul Tournier (1898–1986) writes in his book, *The Naming of Persons*, that to understand the pivotal function of names, we must recognize that naming a person conveys identity. He says that in a very real way, we become our names; we react to, and live in terms of, our names for our entire lives. Because of this, the name that a parent gives to a child takes on great significance.

Tournier seeks to provide parents with a better understanding of this God-given right and responsibility to name their child—a name which confers dignity as a person.

Throughout his life, the positivist culture of school, followed by the daily routine of work, will stifle this overflowing natural fantasy. At school, if he loses himself in his dream, he is scolded; he is letting his attention wander, and not listening to the teacher, who is talking about things that matter. Later on he will be a good doctor or a good workman only if he thinks about nothing but his work. Being concerned as I am now with old people, I see the result. Those who are dying of boredom, those who do not know what to do with the leisure time that retirement brings, are the ones who have had their creative imagination ground out of them by the mill of school and work. What a contrast with the child who peopled his mind with a teeming world of legendary beings!

Professor Viktor Frankl insisted on these frontiers of science where the study of man is concerned. Science, he said, is true in all it observes and describes in regard to man and his behavior, but it lies when it insinuates that man is just that and nothing more. It is right, for instance, when it says that man is a robot, comparable with a computer, but wrong if it claims that man is nothing but a robot. He is 'something more.' . . . Is there a single word that will adequately express it? . . . there is—the name, which is not only the symbol of the person: it is the person itself.

NOTES

1. John J. Ratey and Eric Hagerman, *Spark : The Revolutionary New Science of Exercise and the Brain* (New York: Little, Brown, 2008).
2. Mark Hancock, *Let Boys Be Boys* (Mache Convention 2023: Minnesota Association of Christian Home Educators, 19 May 2023).
3. Young, "When DAD Is the Teacher".
4. Tom Colls, "When the Name Fits the Job," *Today BBC News* (20 December 2011), http://news.bbc.co.uk/today/hi/today/newsid_9664000/9664697.stm.
5. Paul Tournier, *The Naming of Persons: The Fascinating Role of Names and Naming in the Formation of Our Personal Identity*, trans. Edwin Hudson (New York: Harper & Row, 1975), pp. 14, 80-83.

TRAINING A CHILD

A Long Obedience

I have some good news and some bad news about discipline.

The good news is that your child is going to turn out fine.

The bad news is that there is no silver bullet.

I am not an expert on raising children and encourage you to make use of experienced friends, support networks, and resources from trusted organizations for inspiration and practical advice. We have appreciated the wisdom and perspective of Gary and Anne Marie Ezzo from Growing Families.[1] Should I seem assured or prescriptive in anything I say, think of this only as applicable to my children and treat it as an idea to consider in your own family. And I must qualify my claim about children turning out fine. As parents, we have a responsibility to raise our children well, and we mustn't become complacent. As children grow older, they become responsible for their own decisions, and sometimes they don't turn out the way we hope they will. But I can say for sure that if you are educating your children at home, you are removing a huge variable introduced by external schooling, giving you much greater opportunity to influence them through your example, mentorship, and discipleship. And by doing this well, you can be confident your children will turn out fine.

Orepuki Trees

As the troubled philosopher Friedrich Nietzsche observed, *"things worth living for"* require *"a long obedience in the same direction."*[2] Eugene Peterson applied this principle to faithfulness and discipleship. I knew this concept as a child through the phrase "Orepuki Trees." My uncle taught at a country school in the tiny settlement of Orepuki, situated at the southern tip of New Zealand where a strong prevailing wind blew off the Southern Ocean. Exposed trees were permanently windswept, formed by the constant breeze.

Figure 9. Orepuki Trees. Photography by Four Seasons Garden UK (2012)[3]

In my experience, the task of disciplining children is that of undertaking a long obedience in the same direction. Pray for your children, consistently correct them, provide them with a loving home, encourage good behavior, and even if they seem like little monsters at times, they will eventually turn out alright.

I remember feeling rather shocked after a friend told my mother how wonderfully well-behaved my siblings and I were. I wasn't surprised that someone would consider us angels; we thought we were fairly well-behaved. But I was shocked by the astonishment in Mum's voice when she passed on the compliment. She could barely conceal her incredulity! I realized that the way others perceived us, as well as how we saw ourselves, was very different to what Mum had to deal with at home. She wasn't simply a passive observer and didn't only see us at our best; she also had to contend with our misbehavior.

The encouragement here is that as a parent, we are noticing all the faults of our children. We tend to focus on the bad and overlook the good, since we are dealing with our children every day and it is the poor behavior we must address. We don't need to correct them when they're doing the right thing. I've never sent my boys to their room because they were playing nicely together! When they are behaving well, it's easy to ignore them and get on with other things.

What we focus on, what we tend to remember most, is when they misbehave. But other people that only see them occasionally tend to overlook the bad and observe the good. Be encouraged!

Discipline

This isn't a book about discipline, so just a few comments on what I've learned.

The first is patience. I talked to someone who had lots of experience teaching pre-teen boys, and asked, *"How do you cope with poor behavior?"* She said, *"I take a deep breath and count to 10. Sometimes I count to 20."* Patience isn't a virtue that comes naturally to me, but I took that comment on board, and it helped. When I felt frustration and anger rising, I would close my eyes, take a deep breath, and count to 10. Sometimes I had to walk out of the room and remove myself from the situation until I had calmed down.

I did not find any silver bullet or fool-proof technique with regards to discipline. I tested lots of different methods: punishments, loss of privilege, incentives, and rewards. Nothing worked, as far as I could tell. By that I mean I didn't notice any immediate change in my boys' fundamental behavior.

My wife and I thought carefully about discipline. Most of the activities our children were doing were educational or worthwhile, and we didn't want to withhold these as a punishment. My oldest loved reading, and there was no way we were going to take away his books because of misbehavior. Screen time was already limited and mostly for educational purposes. And we avoided using jobs around the house or chores as discipline. We didn't want them to view contributing to the household or cleaning up their room as a punishment. In recent times, we have had some success in diffusing conflict by prescribing exercise or rest.

Corporal punishment was an approach we used early on. But even this did not seem to have much impact. I greatly respect Focus on the Family, and in their *Complete Book of Baby & Child Care*, they say about spanking that *"You should not need to take this course of action more than a few times during your child's life."*[4] I almost fell off my chair when I read that. It was certainly not my experience.

But here is my experience. As mentioned in Chapter Eleven, I have concluded that poor behavior in my children has as much to do with me as it does with them. Don't get me wrong—children are born with a sinful nature and are ultimately responsible for their own decisions. But what I mean is this: I began to see that my own insecurities had a negative effect on how my children behaved. In the early years of home education, I struggled with feelings of inadequacy at not having a job and failing to provide financially for my family. Were my children being disobedient and fighting with each other because of my emotional state? Words have power, but what impact was my attitude having?

So being an engineer, I conducted an experiment. I had learned as a teenager that I could choose my own emotions. As Victor Frankl said, *"In all situations . . . you always have the ultimate freedom to choose your attitude."*[5] So I chose to be happy for a week. And my boys' behavior improved. I went back to grumpy, and the fighting resumed.

Clearly, it's not that simple. And children's poor behavior is ultimately their choice. I don't think our environment should be an excuse—we are all responsible for our actions. But my own role became clear. I noticed that patient parents have relaxed children; uptight parents have high-strung offspring. My sister-in-law is the perfect example. She is absolutely in control; she knows what she wants and doesn't let her children get away with anything. But she is also an excellent teacher and is very relaxed and calm. The result is relaxed, well-behaved children.

Discipline requires patience, consistency, and love. There is no silver bullet, no panacea. Rather, it's a long obedience in the same direction. And we need to model the virtues we desire to see in our offspring. They are influenced by our own attitudes, emotions, and actions, whether positive or negative.

Our children are turning out to be wonderful young men.

Speaking Words of Life

People sometimes tell me they could never homeschool their children. They say they're not a teacher; they don't have the qualifications; they never learned enough themselves to instruct anyone else. That is not true. It is complete and utter nonsense.

There is one huge reason why you as a parent are your child's best teacher. It's because you love your child. You care about him, and you want the best for him. Education is not exclusively about teaching. It is not only instruction in academic knowledge. It is not primarily about delivering information.

If you remember nothing else from this book, remember this:[6]

> ## A child will remember how you make them feel much longer than they will remember what you taught them.

This has probably been the most challenging realization I have had on my adventure in home education. As an engineer, I'm all about knowledge and achievement and success. But when I'm berating my son for not getting a problem right and see the tears welling up, I am reminded that there is something more important than teaching my child through sheer force of will to remember a particular fact or technique. He may learn to do what I tell him, but end up hating the learning. And if he hates learning, even if he can do it competently, then I've won the battle but lost the war.

Loved and Valued

Mark Van Doren said that *"The art of teaching is the art of assisting discovery."* Teaching isn't about passing on facts. It's about guiding a child into a lifetime of discovery. They don't need you to know the answers. They need you to love them. And if your children know you love them, then you can teach them.

You've taught them from birth. You're teaching them every day. How to talk. How to play. How to act. How to treat others. You **are** their teacher. You always have been and always will be their primary teacher until they leave home, and sometimes well beyond. Taking responsibility for their academic education is no different. And if you don't know the answer to a particular problem, you can find out together, or you can teach your child how to find the answer himself.

So you **are** a teacher, you **do** have the qualifications, and you **do** know enough to be able to educate your children.

What you may not have are the skills to deal with educational bureaucracy and a classroom full of kids. I have enormous respect for schoolteachers, because there is no way I could handle twenty or thirty pupils at once, with their wide range of abilities and standards of behavior, and with limitations on how I could instruct and discipline them. While there are some benefits to group instruction, there are also disadvantages. A class needs to be taught at the level of the average child. It's like bowling—aim for the middle and hope to hit most of the pins on either side. But by definition, almost all children are either above or below average. Throughout most of my primary and secondary schooling, I was essentially ignored by my teachers because I was ahead academically. Eventually, I was moved up a year so I could come first in the class ahead of me. I understood my teachers needed to focus on those students who required extra help. But you don't need to compromise in that way when educating your own children. You can spend more time with them if they need it, without hampering twenty-nine other pupils. Or you can move your child ahead when they require more of a challenge.

But do so because you love them.

These days, there is no need to fear advanced subjects simply because you don't understand them yourself. Education is not about passing on your knowledge but about assisting discovery. There are so many excellent resources, including video lessons and online courses, that can fill in any gaps in your knowledge.

You are your child's best teacher. Be patient and encouraging without being patronizing or a pushover. And if you make them feel loved and valued, you will be successful in educating them.

And let me emphasize again what is perhaps my greatest failure as a teacher but what can be your greatest triumph. Make your children feel great about themselves during their lessons. Celebrate their successes, encourage them in their challenges. Speak words of life to them constantly. Ensure they feel loved and valued. They still need to work hard on their lessons, but they will do so from a foundation of security and confidence. We all want to do things we enjoy. Working hard does not come naturally to any of us. And schoolwork can be difficult and less than enjoyable at times. But how you make your child feel while doing their lessons will be what they remember the most.

Socialization

I was not planning to say anything about "socialization." And no doubt you'll soon understand why I used quotation marks. To me, it's not even a thing, because it's so obvious. If anyone cares to ask me, *"What about socialization?"* my response is, *"Yes, I agree that's one of the great advantages of home education."* My children are not the ones spending half their waking hours in a room full of their peers. Their social interaction is not only with children in their grade but with all ages, young and old. The invite list for their parties is not restricted to their classmates, but also includes elderly friends and adults from my Toastmasters club.

But I do understand this is an issue for some, and those exploring home education may have questions. Rather than say any more myself, I'll simply refer to a blog post which I think sums it up pretty well.

Debunking Myths About Homeschooling

—Stacey Wells[7]

Myth #1: Your child won't have a chance of socialization
Debunked: Homeschooled students will have plenty of opportunities for socialization. . . .
Think about it from a common-sense standpoint for a moment, if you will. In public school, children are tossed into a classroom with 20 to 40 same-age peers. They have one teacher and, if funding allows for it, sometimes a classroom aid as well. At any given point in the day, these children are all under the authority of usually no more than one or two adults. Unless there's a field trip, they aren't taken into the community. . . . In fact, everything about public school goes against the very grain of "socialization" as it is defined.
According to the first listed definition by the Merriam-Webster website, socialization means, "the process beginning during childhood by which individuals acquire the values, habits, and attitudes of a society." . . .
No, it's closer to the truth that the socialization our children receive in public school is more closely related to the second definition of socialization: "the action or process of making something socialistic: conversion to collective or governmental ownership and control."

NOTES

1. Growing Families International, https://growingfamilies.life.
2. Jonathan Wilson, "A Long Obedience in the Same Direction," *Leadership by Soul*, March 2011, https://leadbysoul.com/leadership/a-long-obedience-in-the-same-direction.
3. Four Seasons Garden UK. 2012. *Windswept macrocarpa trees of Orepuki (Southland New Zealand)*. Photograph. Flickr. https://www.flickr.com/photos/fourseasonsgarden /albums/72157629614536717/with/6935548786.
4. Paul C. Reisser, *Focus on the Family Complete Book of Baby & Child Care*, ed. Melissa R. Cox and Vinita Hampton Wright (Wheaton, IL: Tyndale House, 1997), p. 307.
5. Pattakos, *Prisoners of Our Thoughts*, p. iv.
6. Maya Angelou has been credited with the quote, "*I've learned that people will forget what you said, people will forget what you did, but people will never forget how you made them feel.*"
   According to Quote Investigator, https://quoteinvestigator.com/2014/04/06/they -feel, accessed 29 December 2022, this attribution is unsupported and the quote likely originated with Carl W. Buehner. In May 2000, a Cedar Rapids, Iowa newspaper printed a profile of a local teacher under the title "Educator of the Week." The teacher spoke a variant of the expression: "*Children may not remember what you've taught them but they'll remember how you made them feel.*"
7. Stacey Wells, "Debunking Myths About Homeschooling," *Homeschooling Mom*, 15 April 2020, https://homeschooling.mom/blog/debunking-myths-about-home schooling.

TIME MANAGEMENT

Don't squander the advantages that home education offers! Don't turn the learning experience into a mini-school!

There are advantages and disadvantages to almost anything, and I have found it's easy in the frenetic activity of daily life to squander the benefits of homeshooling, many of which relate to time management.

When I first began this adventure in home education and started thinking through our learning schedule, it became immediately clear that we could cover the material more effectively in far less time than could be achieved at school. After accounting for transport to and from school, downtime when switching between activities (it's quicker to move two children on to the next subject than twenty), working at the pace of the slowest class member, break-time, and extra-curricular activities, the seven-hour school day leaving at 8:30 a.m. and returning at 3:30 p.m. probably equates to only 15–20 hours of quality learning each week.

I found myself faced with a choice. I could take advantage of the light workload by completing lessons before lunch each day or by Thursday each week. Or else I could add additional activities to make the most of the time available. My struggle has always been that I want to add extra activities. And it's difficult, because there are so many worthwhile topics to include. We covered music, foreign language, logic, electronics, nutrition, discipleship, memorization, programming, seven-minute workouts, dance, cooking, and field trips. But it all adds up. Even an extra 10 minutes a day effectively adds an hour a week, and a few of these supplementary subjects can quickly turn an effortless 20-hour week into an intensive 30 hours.

Curriculum Creep Is the Enemy

So the first insight I learned about time management was to know my enemy. The enemy is curriculum creep, and I am constantly battling it. To win this battle, it is critical to be clear about your educational goals and know your Priority List as discussed in Chapter Thirteen—which subjects are foundational and which are ancillary.

To illustrate my struggle, at the end of each year I have my boys provide feedback on what they liked and didn't like about lessons that year, and what they would want included next year. Figure 10 shows a mind map one of my boys put together a couple of years ago, illustrating the range of subjects we managed to fit in and his suggestions of what to add the following year.

Structure Is Your Friend

The second essential I learned was that structure is my friend. Everyone is different, and some people may thrive on a more relaxed schedule. But in my case, I found I did better, and I believe my boys did better, when I set a fixed time to begin lessons and we followed more of a daily schedule. Of course, we always have flexibility if we need to change it. But if I simply started when I was ready, by time I'd checked my email and tidied up the kitchen and gotten myself organized, it might be 9:30 or 10 a.m. After a couple of hours, we would stop for lunch and take a break, and it would be 3 p.m. before getting underway again. We still needed to complete the work, so that meant lessons simply ran later, or would not be finished until Friday evening, or would need to be done on Saturday. But deciding to start at 8:30 a.m. each morning definitely helped us get through lessons and resulted in a more relaxed week. It also meant my boys knew what to expect and would regularly begin without me.

I guess I have always been leery of copying school—of using tactics like timetables necessary for a larger group but not needed in a home situation. But sometimes these things can help us, and probably in the first few years I missed the benefits of a daily schedule in my desire to avoid being too rigid.

This is the perfect example of my pendulum analogy. I have a saying that I only find the ideal balance in the brief moment when I hit the midpoint while swinging from one extreme to the other. My advice is to find the balance that works for you, to avoid being bound by a rigid timetable at one extreme or being too relaxed with zero structure at the other.

I tested the benefits of a schedule last summer. Even a three-month summer break can disappear with surprising swiftness. We had already spent May and June on three separate road trips, and I feared my boys would fritter away the final two months as I focused on writing this book. So I implemented a summer schedule.

I joined them at 8 o'clock for a devotional time, what we call the "Bible Block," then from 8:30–9:30 a.m. they chose two separate half-hour activities, whether piano, lessons, or another educational interest. At 9:30 they would go outside for football practice, and finish up at 10 a.m. by doing laundry or emptying the dishwasher. I figured that if there were no structure, they would hang around reading comics or playing computer games and not do much until mid-morning anyway. So in effect, this agenda didn't mean they had **less** free time. But it did guarantee that each day they read the Bible, did some learning, got some exercise, and completed their chores. And they could spend the rest of the day free from the burden of feeling like there were other tasks they really should be doing. I'm not sure they would quite agree, but I'm certain having this timetable actually gave them **more** time to enjoy their summer.

The Hidden Danger of Organization

The third aspect of time management that I have learned through hard experience is the subtle danger of being organized. Again, this is very much a consequence of my personality, and you might have a completely different experience. But being an engineer, I created a detailed spreadsheet-based weekly schedule with all learning activities listed on one page so we could easily monitor them and check them off. An example is shown in Appendix D. This was great for providing focus: *"Finish these activities and we're done for the week."* However, it also meant the emphasis was on ticking things off rather than savoring the learning experience. I would generally leave arts and crafts until Friday, both to provide a fun end-of-week project and to delay the activities I didn't consider to be core learning in case we ran out of time (a big "sorry" to you artists!). But when Friday arrived, we just wanted to get the schedule finished and be done for the week and too often, art became ten minutes of coloring (inside the lines) so we could check that box.

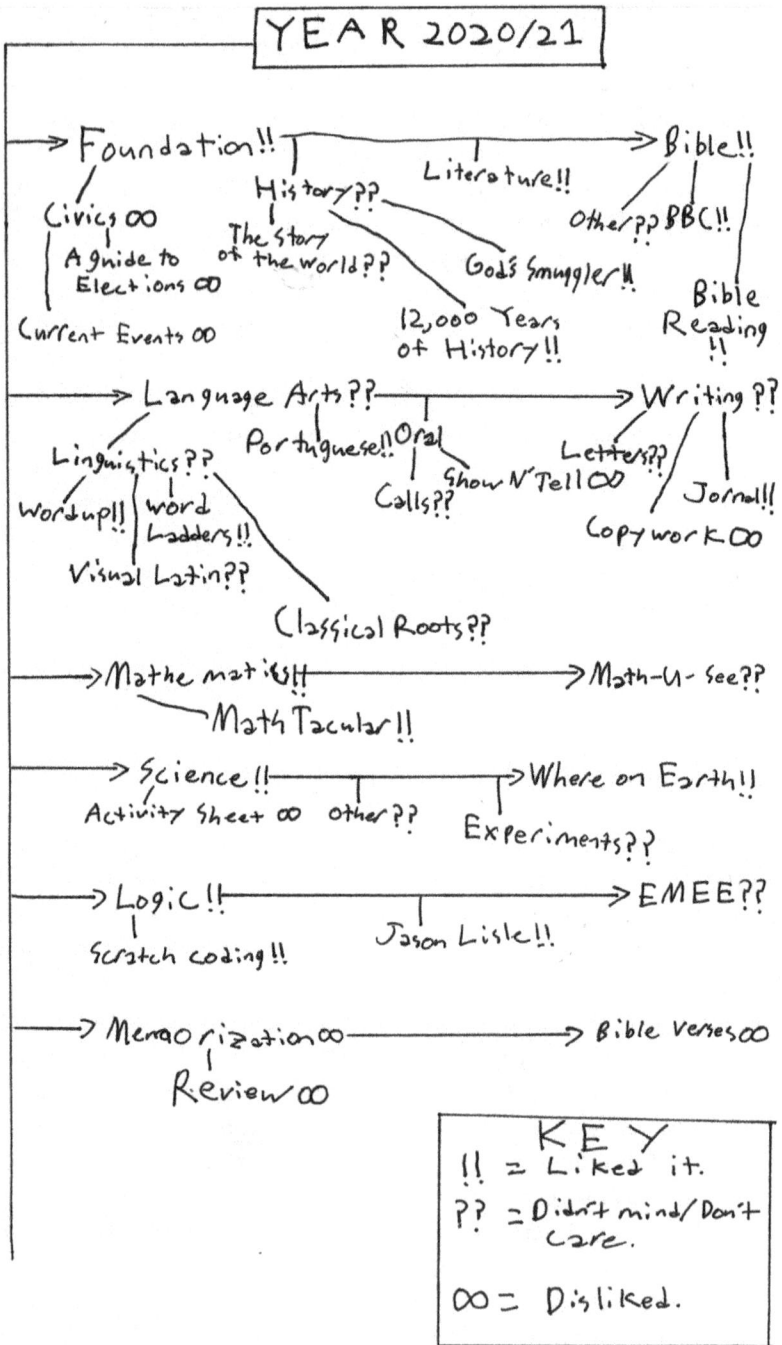

YEAR 2020/21

Foundation!! ──── Literature!! ──→ Bible!!
History??
Civics ∞   Other?? BBC!!
A guide to   The Story
Elections ∞   of the world??   God's Smuggler!!   Bible
Current Events ∞   Reading
              12,000 Years   !!
              of History!!

Language Arts?? ──────────────→ Writing??
Linguistics??   Portuguese!! Oral   Letters??
Wordup!! Word   Calls?? Show N' Tell ∞   Jornal!!
Ladders!!   Copywork ∞
Visual Latin??
            Classical Roots??

→Mathematics!! ──────────────→ Math-U-See??
      Math Tacular!!

→ Science!! ──────────→ Where on Earth!!
Activity Sheet ∞ other?? Experiments??

→ Logic!! ──────────────→ EMEE??
Scratch coding!!   Jason Lisle!!

→ Memorization ∞ ──────→ Bible Verses ∞
      Review ∞

KEY
!! = Liked it.
?? = Didn't mind/Don't care.
∞ = Disliked.

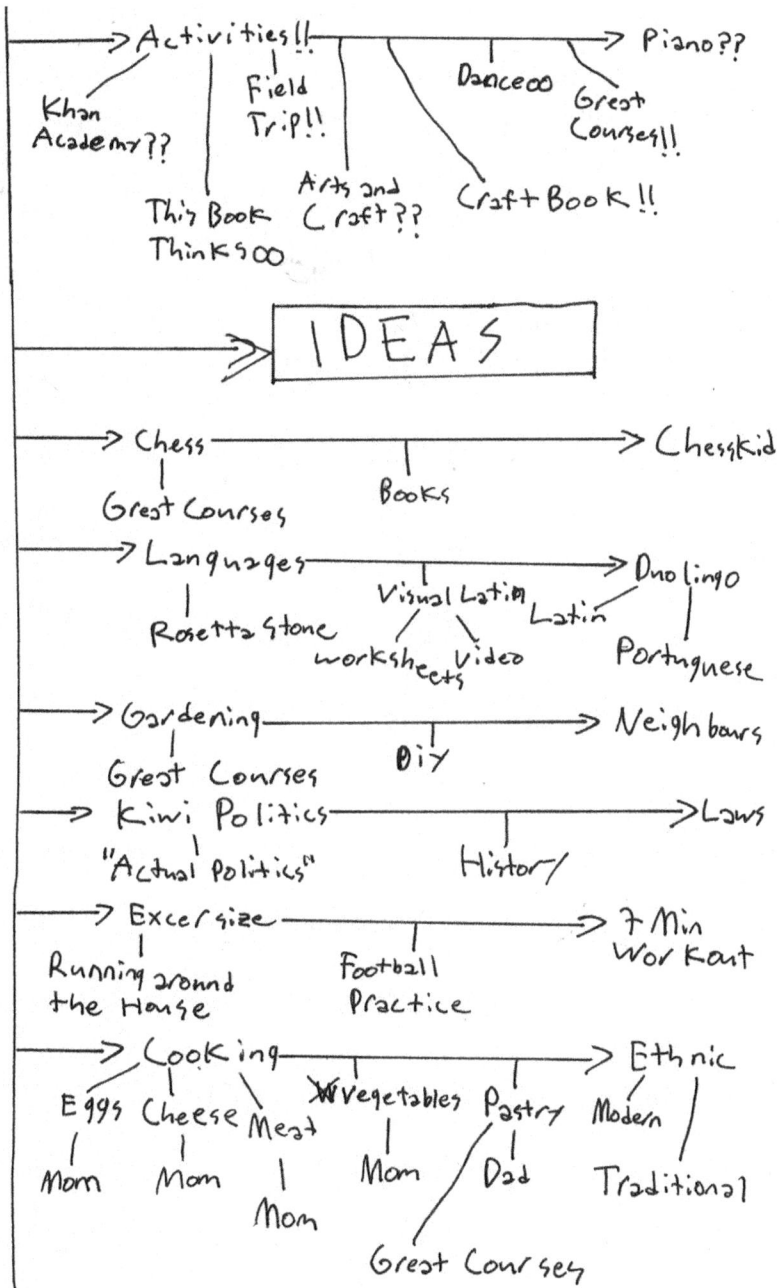

Figure 10. Year-End Review

CHAPTER NINETEEN

It might be too late for me. But I wonder—would the learning have been more enjoyable and more effective for my children if I had not had the schedule? We certainly wouldn't have gotten through as many activities. But completing tasks is not synonymous with learning. There will be a balance, and in my case, I did not seek the best solution while swinging between the extremes. My pendulum remained frozen at its zenith on the side of structure.

It's something I encourage you to think about.

And while we're on the subject of time and flexibility, I can tell you something else. Living in Minnesota, nobody is excited by the idea of getting up in the dark during winter and braving sub-zero temperatures to wait for a school bus. We appreciate being able to roll out of bed and launch into lessons without leaving the house (or even getting out of our pajamas).

PART 5

ABOUT SUBJECTS

*Tips and tricks, lessons learned,
and advice for the various subjects
we have studied over the years.*

LANGUAGE ARTS

Fencepost Model:	Winter (reading, handwriting)
	Summer (composition, comprehension,
	grammar, spelling)
Competency Model:	Incremental

In Chapter Fourteen, I introduced the Fencepost Model. We need to chip away at some subjects, little and often over the long haul. Others, however, can be left until your child is ready, and then taught in a more intensive fashion.

Language arts is where I truly put this philosophy to the test. Yes, I am biased toward math and science. And I do accept that perhaps it would have been a smart move to talk first with someone who was experienced in teaching language arts. But being a man, I didn't ask for directions. Being an engineer, I just knew I was smarter than the experts.

What Exactly Is Language Arts?

Those who know more about language arts than I do will point out that I am emphasizing many aspects of language arts by prioritizing reading and writing. According to the Charlotte Mason website, *"Language arts include the four main components of listening, reading, speaking and writing. Everything that relates to listening, speaking, reading, and writing in your selected language can be considered part of your language arts program."*[1]

The goal of language arts is "communicating ideas through language." So yes, in that sense I am certainly not neglecting language arts! Let me clarify what I'm talking about in this chapter.

Most traditional language arts programs cover the following skills as fifteen or more separate disciplines:

- Alphabet
- Listening Skills
- Phonics / Beginning Reading
- Parts of Speech
- Rhyming Words
- Sentence Structure
- Handwriting (printing and cursive)
- Punctuation
- Reading Comprehension
- Capitalization
- Writing Composition
- Public Speaking
- Vocabulary
- Proofreading
- Spelling
- Grammar
- Reference skills (alphabetizing; using a dictionary; etc.)
- Word study (homonyms, synonyms, prefixes, suffixes)

The Montessori Academy says that *"specific tools are used in language arts to analyze and describe the many written and spoken language forms. These include supportive strategies such as: workbooks, dictionaries, grammar guides, structural analysis activities . . . [and] online resources. These tools are often used in conjunction to help unravel the complex language arts process."*[2]

Yawn. Wake me up when we're done.

We included reading, handwriting, and public speaking as specific lessons, and that was about it. All other skills such as punctuation, reading comprehension, writing composition, and spelling may have been discussed along the way, but were not studied as formal lessons or discrete topics. The current chapter is specific to these aspects of languages arts. Perhaps we could refer to what I omitted as the "grammar" of language arts, as opposed to the "practice," although I also excluded creative writing which is certainly practice.

A Focus on Reading

As early as the first-grade curriculum, I felt the little and often approach didn't make sense for grammar or creative writing. Although at this stage my convictions were more intuitive than reasoned, I decided language arts would be a subject I could leave until my children were older.

The skills we emphasized at first were reading, mathematics, and science. My boys learned to write competently, which was taught primarily through copywork but also by means of journaling and writing letters. That covered my Level 1 Priorities. History and geography formed part of reading, and we also introduced foreign language (Portuguese) from an early age.

But apart from that, I basically ignored language arts for the first six years of their education. To the extent that I thought about it, my opinion was that the way to develop a love for great writing is by reading great writing, not by starting off doing simple writing exercises and trying to improve. If my children have read great literature and want to produce their own, then they will be motivated to learn how. And the older they are, the quicker they will pick it up. If they never have an interest in writing, then I don't think requiring them to compose a story every week is going to develop that interest. In fact, it is more likely to deter them.

My philosophy is that you learn grammar and language skills by reading. Anne Cunningham and Keith Stanovich report in "What Reading Does for the Mind" that vocabulary grows primarily through exposure to language, rather than direct teaching or study.[3] It's about learning by osmosis. And if you're reading well-written books (not merely comics and modern children's literature), then you'll know what great writing is like.

> **Develop a love for great writing by reading great writing.**

As previously mentioned, I used external exams as a sanity check. It is a requirement in my state for homeschooled children to take a nationally-normed test each year. Because my boys were working well above their grade level, I had them test at a grade or two higher than the expected level for their age. These tests included word analysis, vocabulary, language mechanics, and spelling, none of which we had covered in our lessons.

Norm-referenced tests report how test-takers compare to a standard sample group of students of the same age or grade level. These were the National Percentile Rank (NPR) results for the aggregate language score.[4]

Grade	Ethan	Jesse
2		95
3	99	86
4	95	95
6	99	97
7	86	94
8	96	
9	96	

Figure 11. National Percentile Rank Aggregate Language Scores

Again, my boys achieved these results without formal language arts lessons—no memorizing of grammar rules, no spelling lists, no comprehension questions. Simply lots of reading. It wasn't that I religiously avoided language arts. We did talk about some spelling rules like "'i' before 'e' except after 'c.'" I warned them against using grocer's apostrophe's, taught them to spell "honour" with a "u" and steered them away from the Oxford comma. We listened to the Schoolhouse Rock cartoons, and I would correct their writing. I defined words as we read together. But there were almost no formal lessons for the first six years, and their NPR results indicate they were doing just fine. I wasn't ruining them for life!

A Strong Start in Language

—Ruth Beechick[5]

Grammar scores do not correlate with quality of writing. Children who know the most grammar are not necessarily better writers. The parts do not add up to the desired whole.
But moving in the opposite direction does work. . . . Grammar is not a way to good writing; it is a tool that good writers use to analyze

writing. . . . He will learn from the good language models he studies, in the same natural way he learned to speak. . . .

A part-to-whole lesson on nouns, for instance, may teach a definition of nouns, list some nouns, and then give sentences for underlining the nouns. In this, the noun lesson is predominant and whatever meaning or significance the sentences may have is only incidental. But a whole-to-part lesson could begin with a paragraph from a history book which you chose because of its meaning and significance. Say that the child writes it from dictation and does well, so you decide to add on an incidental lesson about nouns. Discussing nouns in the passage gives an extra boost to vocabulary learning. You could notice proper nouns and titles, such as General Washington. In such a lesson, meaning is uppermost, and the noun learning incidental. But even in its incidental position it is stronger learning about nouns than in the other lesson.

In summary, a feature of the natural method is that it moves from whole to part. This kind of learning is stronger and more efficient. It is proven. It works.

The Three R's

—Ruth Beechick[6]

What is the natural method of learning to write? . . . How did he learn to speak? By listening and speaking. . . . Listening and speaking are to spoken language what reading and writing are to written language. If people ask you how children learn to write, here is the short, short definition to give them: Children learn to write by writing. . . .

It is better to wait until about seventh grade when children are fairly good writers, and then have some units on grammar. . . . Much research has shown that knowledge of grammar does not correlate at all with good writing. So reverse the order in your teaching. Teach your children first to write well and then teach them some grammar.

Language Intensive

By the seventh year, when my oldest was eleven and my youngest nine, we began to prepare for intensive work on linguistics by introducing

Latin and classical roots. The next year, we switched to a high school curriculum based on individual courses, one of which was Writing which included some spelling, grammar, and creative writing. But most of the language arts instruction was still done incidentally while working on essays and assignments for other subjects. I included written work in many of the high school courses. Classic Literature, for example, required a reaction paper for each of the eighteen assigned books, some of which were quite challenging such as *Pride and Prejudice* and *Robinson Crusoe*. Other courses, for example Church History, were assessed by four essays.

This is where the majority of language arts is being taught, by reading and writing. It is still an experiment in progress, but it seems to be working out okay and I'm comfortable with this approach.

In my view, breaking language arts apart into fifteen separate disciplines and teaching them individually is more likely to kill the art than illuminate it. This seems like another case of Newtonian mechanics run amok. I would rather my children learn language by reading great books.

It reminds me of a scene from the movie *Dead Poets Society* in which Robin Williams' character, English teacher John Keating, criticizes the textbook approach to analyzing poetry by its meter, rhyme, and figures of speech. He shocks his students by ordering them to rip the page out of their text. Poetry is to be felt and experienced, not analyzed and dissected!

The bottom line for me is to focus on the goal. What is the objective of language arts? It is the communication of ideas through language. Are my boys communicating effectively through language? Yes, they are. I don't really care about their result in the nationally-normed test. It gave me some comfort, but it's only a comparison with students who are learning language as a science, not an art. I want my children to feel the pleasure of great writing and experience the passion that Robin Williams brought to his classroom. When I have a four-year-old warn his aunt not to perch on the barstool because that's *"fraught with danger,"* when my eleven-year old critiques C.S. Lewis and explains how he could have written more effectively, and when my thirteen-year old brings me to tears with a reaction paper, then I know they're doing just fine in language arts.

Dead Poets Society ("Understanding Poetry" Scene)

[Keating]   *Mr. Perry, will you read the opening paragraph of the preface entitled "Understanding Poetry?"*

[Neil]   *. . . To fully understand poetry, we must first be fluent with its meter, rhyme and figures of speech, then ask two questions: 1) How artfully has the objective of the poem been rendered and 2) How important is that objective? Question 1 rates the poem's perfection; question 2 rates its importance. And once these questions have been answered, determining the poem's greatness becomes a relatively simple matter. If the poem's score for perfection is plotted on the horizontal of a graph and its importance is plotted on the vertical, then calculating the total area of the poem yields the measure of its greatness. A sonnet by Byron might score high on the vertical but only average on the horizontal. A Shakespearean sonnet, on the other hand, would score high both horizontally and vertically, yielding a massive total area, thereby revealing the poem to be truly great. As you proceed through the poetry in this book, practice this rating method. As your ability to evaluate poems in this matter grows, so will, so will your enjoyment and understanding of poetry.*

[Keating]   *Excrement! That's what I think of Mr. J. Evans Pritchard. We're not laying pipe. We're talking about poetry! How can you describe poetry like American Bandstand? . . . Now, I want you to rip out that page. Go on. Rip out the entire page. You heard me. Rip it out. Rip it out! Go on. Rip it out!*

Since I have opened the Pandora's Box of language arts, the next few chapters will cover reading, reading comprehension, and writing.

NOTES

1. Sonya Shafer, "What Exactly Is Language Arts?: Language Arts, Part 1," *Simply Charlotte Mason*, https://simplycharlottemason.com/blog/what-exactly-is-language-arts-language-arts-part-1.
2. "What Is Language Arts, and Why Is It Important," *Montessori Academy* (19 March 2022), https://montessori-academy.com/blog/what-is-language-arts, accessed 2 December 2022.
3. Anne Cunningham and Keith Stanovich, "What Reading Does for the Mind," *American Educator* 22, no. 1-2 (1998).
4. In case you're wondering, there is no Grade 5 because the test provider did not offer this level. Rather than missing a year or using an alternative test, the boys went from Grade 4 directly to Grade 6.
5. Ruth Beechick, A Strong Start in Language (Pollock Pines, CA: Arrow Press, 1986), pp. 5-6.
6. Ruth Beechick, *The Three R's* (Fenton, MI: Mott Media, 2006), pp. 42-43, 51.

READING

Fencepost Model:	Winter
Competency Model:	Incremental

My wife and I love books. We read widely, though not as frequently as we would like. Life gets in the way sometimes. Our dream is to take a year's sabbatical and tackle all the unread books in our library and on our wish list. We chose a literature-based curriculum because that's the way we wish we had been taught.

It's no surprise, therefore, that we consider reading to be **the** key skill to be mastered in academic education. It is the first discipline to be taught. When I was young, my mother said that I came up with some very interesting pronunciations because I was using words I read before hearing them spoken. Reading is the **foundation** for all other learning, since it **enables** all other learning. Being able to read well makes learning anything else so much easier.

Different Experiences

So we began reading to our children from birth. But we had two different experiences.

Our oldest child picked up reading very quickly. I don't even remember giving him formal lessons. We merely started off with simple books, and he took off. At the age of five, he became captivated by *The Princess and the Foal*, written by Stacy Gregg (a wonderful author and a childhood friend). This was a 270-page book with a reading age of ten to twelve. My oldest loved the story and read it over and over again. A year later, he picked up *The Lord of the Rings* and read through the entire trilogy as well as *The Silmarillion*. And a few years later, his favorite book was Jules Verne's *The Mysterious Island*.

So we never had to worry about him.

Reading Is the Key

—Zig Ziglar[1]

In 1994, I was invited to speak to a national convention in Nashville, Tenn., and I was picked up at the airport by a friendly limousine driver who had his 10-year-old granddaughter with him. It was "father/daughter" day, but the grandfather was playing father.

The little girl was pleasant and friendly, and I asked her what was the most important thing she could do to have a happy, healthy future. She responded with a question, "I don't know, but what do you think it is?"

I told her that if she would learn to love to read, it would make a dramatic difference in her life. I pointed out that if you love to read, you can learn anything you really want to know. Since I have read an average of three hours a day for the last 25 years, it's obvious I have a passion for the subject. The little girl was quite interested in what I had to say.

In January 1997, I was back in Nashville. The same limo driver picked me up at the airport and asked me if I remembered my conversation with him and his granddaughter. Fortunately, I did. He told me that his granddaughter had taken the message seriously and had become an avid reader, and her grades had substantially improved.

My first-grade teacher, Mrs. Dement Warren, taught me to read. My sixth-grade teacher, Mrs. J. K. Worley, taught me to love to read. I'm convinced parents should let their children see them reading good books, magazines and articles.

Children are great imitators. If they see their parents wrapped up in a good book instead of glued to the television set, they are likely to follow suit. Please consider it, parents. Show your love for reading, and your kids will do the same. That way I'll be able to see you—and the kids—at the top!

But our youngest was different. When he began formal education, I worked through *The Ordinary Parent's Guide to Teaching Reading* by Jessie Wise and Sara Buffington. This is an excellent resource which I highly recommend. Before we had completed the program, he was reading competently. But he hadn't been bitten by the bug. Although he could read and would do so when necessary, he wouldn't pick up books for fun or, as our oldest would do, take a book and disappear into the bathroom for an hour.

While this was not what we had hoped for, my wife and I knew we needed to be very careful with how we responded to having a reluctant reader in our family. Thankfully, we knew better than to assign lots of reading to him since this could easily turn books into a chore rather than a delight. We heard some wise advice along the way and surrounded ourselves with great books. We put book baskets in each bathroom beside the toilet. We made sure he would see us reading. We read bedtime stories as well. All kinds—*Uncle Arthur's Bedtime Stories*, poetry, children's books, *The Lord of the Rings*, *Pilgrim's Progress*.

And one day, when he was about seven years old, he picked up Christopher Healy's *The Hero's Guide to Saving Your Kingdom*. He loved it. It took only one story he really enjoyed for him to get hooked, and he has been reading ever since. We promptly bought the other two books in the series, and by time I got around to protecting them with adhesive contact paper, I had to patch the covers together. We have too many books to cover them all, so I only do this in rare cases for particularly well-used volumes. The *Hero's Guide* series was almost beyond repair by time I got to them!

Our youngest still doesn't read as much as our oldest. He tends to be more active and enjoys getting outside. He likes jokes and cartoons and trivia. But he does take a book and disappear into the bathroom. We used to call our oldest a bookworm, but the youngest now says he is the bookworm while our oldest is a bookworm-bear-goat-sheep.

Reading for Information

Now that we are doing high school course work, I am teaching my boys to operate at a university level which requires two skills with regard to reading: marking or noting important text, and absorbing large amounts of information quickly.

Books were always special to me. Folding a page as a bookmark was anathema. I never highlighted during my university career. I don't mark my Bible. But I do know it's a valuable practice when trying to understand and absorb information, so I bought a big box of highlighters and have been setting an example by marking and underlining and even writing comments in the books I now read. It has been harder to get my boys to do so, but we'll work on this habit over the next few years. I also gave them composition notebooks so they can make notes as they're reading. This too is a work in progress, but will establish habits that will prove useful later in life.

Getting through a large amount of reading is a skill that can be learned. Books are plentiful enough, but today we have the fire hydrant of the internet to drink from when researching for a paper. Simply knowing how to read is not sufficient. The question is how to get through a three hundred page book and find the one piece of information needed for an assignment. Thankfully, this is something I did learn while at university.

To read a non-fiction book in thirty minutes, follow this process:

1. Read the dust flap and back cover. This often touches on the key points.
2. Read through the table of contents, to understand how the book is structured.
3. Browse each chapter, reading the opening and closing paragraphs, the headings, and the opening lines of any section that catches your eye. Note anything particularly important to your assignment.
4. Go back and read in detail the most relevant sections until your half hour is up.

And that's how to read a book! How are you doing with this one?

Being able to read and get through material quickly is a great skill, one which my boys are learning and developing and putting into practice. I may investigate dynamic reading or speed-reading techniques; although I never learned to do this myself, I understand the concept and can see the benefits.

This leads us to the question of reading comprehension, which I will cover next.

Don't Force It

Before doing so, however, I want to highlight one caution. Despite my enthusiasm for reading and my conviction that it is the highest priority subject to learn, it should not be forced. It doesn't need to be the first thing a child learns. Ruth Beechick explains this well.[2]

> It is true that some children can learn to read remarkably early. But the fact that they can does not necessarily mean they should. Should is another question. One school district set up an experiment to help decide this question. Some kindergartners in the district received extensive instruction in reading. Others spent the same amount of time learning science. They melted ice. They observed thermometers in hot and cold places. They played with magnets, grew plants, learned about animal life, and so on. Books and pictures were available for these children if they wanted them, but no formal lessons in reading were held.
>
> And what did the school district learn? By third grade the "science" children were far ahead of the "reading" children in their reading scores. The reason? Their vocabularies and thinking skills were more advanced. They could read on more topics and understand higher level materials. The "reading" children, by starting earlier, used up a lot of learning time on the skills of reading, while the "science" children spent the time learning real stuff. And when they did begin reading, they were older and knew more and learned in a fraction of the time that the others took.

Dr. Raymond Moore cautions against allowing children to read too much before the age of eight, as young eyes are designed primarily for distance vision and have not developed enough for close work without strain.[3] Too much reading while young may actually damage their eyesight. Our experience does lend weight to this view as our early reader has required glasses since he was seven.

Let me try to swing the pendulum toward the middle ground by suggesting you should read a lot to your children, surround them with good books of all types, cover the basics of letters and phonics so that they have the necessary tools, and then let them pick up reading in their own time.

NOTES

1. Zig Ziglar, "Reading Is the Key," *Creators Syndicate* (23 November 2022), https://www.creators.com/read/classic-zig-ziglar/11/22/reading-is-the-key-a28a4, accessed 23 November 2022.
2. Ruth Beechick, *A Home Start in Reading* (Fenton, MI: Mott Media, 1985), p. 4.
3. Moore, Moore, and Moore, *Better Late than Early*, pp. 68-70.

COMPREHENSION

Fencepost Model:	Summer (literary criticism)
Competency Model:	Apprenticeship

Primary Level

Engrossed in a Story

Reading comprehension has always seemed like a strange subject to me. I can understand the pressure to administer this medicine in the classroom. If the class is asked to read a book, how else will you know that they did so? Do you simply ask them, and trust they're telling the truth? And how will you know whether they understood anything they read?

We all know what it's like to reach the bottom of a page and then realize we were thinking about something else and have no idea what we read. That is the fundamental reason for slow reading. Our mind gets bored and wanders, and we keep skipping back to check what we just "read." But the solution is not to intimidate a child into focusing on the book by the threat of a comprehension test to come. The real solution is to read books so interesting and enjoyable that the reader becomes engrossed in the narrative. When I was young, I would build a home-made flashlight from a battery and bulb and read under the covers after lights out. My best friend would bring a book to school which I would read during breaks and finish before the end of the day. My family won't believe it now, but I used to wake up at 5:30 a.m. to get ready for school so I could read for an hour before breakfast.

I would not have done any of that if I weren't understanding the stories. Yet I still dreaded reading comprehension. What if I couldn't answer the question? What if I didn't think the same way as the teacher about the book? I enjoyed reading, but not being tested on it.

I have observed the same dynamic in my children. The curriculum we used, typical I expect of most reading programs, reinforced understanding by including questions and vocabulary for every chapter of every book. The idea was to pose questions about what we were reading and have delightful discussions concerning the issues raised. This sounds wonderful in theory, and maybe it would have worked better if I were more of a conversationalist, or less focused on ticking off that box and being done for the day. But it totally didn't work for us.

As mentioned in Chapter Fourteen, I tried having my oldest, the prolific reader, write book reviews. He started off okay, but it became increasingly arduous. Neither of my boys enjoyed worksheets. If they'd completed a chapter in a science book, they simply wanted to move on.

I sensed that if I continued to push for reviews or reflection on their books, then it might turn reading into a chore. And so I dropped any type of reading comprehension. I did frequently give my opinion on what we were reading, and would explain difficult concepts or unusual words or sometimes review the vocabulary list provided with the curriculum. But not always.

Words in Context

A word divorced from its context will not be retained. I reckon my boys will learn vocabulary better by reading new words in a story and figuring out what they mean from context, than by being tested on a definition.

I can remember a class exercise when I was at primary school. We were given a word and asked to find out its meaning and include it in a sentence. My word was "affluence," and I wrote *"The boy relied on his friend's affluence for after-school treats."* I was mortified when the teacher told me this was wrong. Even today, that memory is etched in my mind, and I avoided using the term for decades before finally deciding I was right. I can guarantee I would have been better off if I had learned the word "affluence" through reading it in a book.

I once pointed out to my son the dust floating in a sunbeam and he told me, *"That's a dust mote."* He scampered over to the bookshelf and opened *The Princess and the Foal*, a book he hadn't read for years, to the exact page where the term "dust mote" appeared.

My wife and I are deliberate about employing words precisely and minimizing the use of generic terms such as "just," "thing" and that universal descriptive word, "good." Our boys also exhibit a rich vocabulary gained from their extensive reading. They occasionally check a definition in the dictionary, but usually learn new words from context as they are reading. Recently, one of them articulated a sentence which included both "authoritarian" and "totalitarian." When challenged, he correctly explained the difference between the terms. He wasn't simply throwing random words out there as synonyms to sound impressive; he had deliberately used both because they conveyed slightly different meanings that he wanted to include.

Reading for Enjoyment

During the first five years, I read aloud most of the books in our curriculum. My boys and I would sit together on the couch and I would read, and read, and read. As mentioned, I did explain some new words. I would occasionally comment on worldview or context or other such matters. Sometimes I would provide corrections to the text, particularly in science or history. I guess unconsciously, I modeled the behavior of being actively engaged when reading: questioning the worldview; not trusting that the author is always correct. And I demonstrated it's okay to become emotionally involved in the narrative. Although big boys apparently don't cry, my sons have seen me shed tears over a story. It was *Sadako and the Thousand Paper Cranes,* by Eleanor Coerr. I knew from the first page what was going to happen in the story. But still, at the dénouement, tears began to well up and spill down my cheeks!

So without tackling reading comprehension, how do you know whether your children are understanding the material? Basically, as a parent dedicated to your child's education, you just know. You aren't navigating a classroom full of students at various levels of reading ability. You can see how your children are going about reading. Are they eager, or reluctant? Are there particular types of books they like? Are they distracted while reading?

And I think your first task is to ensure that your children enjoy reading. If they don't want to read, it doesn't matter how much they comprehend.

> If your child laughs at something in a book, he is comprehending it. If he asks a question, he is thinking and comprehending. If he sometimes chooses his own books, on dinosaurs or whatever, he is comprehending. The point the "comprehension" people miss is that the child uses easy books during his early steps in reading. Of course he comprehends them.
>
> —Ruth Beechick[1]

But I did fret in the early years. I have experienced the frustration of asking my son about a book he is reading and getting a blank stare or an *"I don't know."* I stopped worrying though when, after reading *The Lord of the Rings* and *The Silmarillion*, my oldest explained his theory about who Tom Bombadil was. I stopped worrying when I misread a word from *The Lord of the Rings*, and he corrected me from memory. I stopped worrying when I heard my son laugh as he read *The Hero's Guide to Saving Your Kingdom*. When he spots a spelling mistake (he will be overjoyed if he finds one in this book) or when he is moved to tears while reading *King of the Wind* (Marguerite Henry), I know he is engaged and comprehending.

I continued to monitor their reading, the most important way being to see whether they are picking up books themselves. If they do, the war is won.

Secondary Level

These comments so far are relevant to the early years. Now as my boys are working at secondary level, literary criticism has become a relevant discipline. They are learning to critique and respond to novels. Their literature course requires a written reaction paper for each book they read. This gives me an excellent understanding of their comprehension and a chance to discuss and challenge their interaction with the book.

The Missing Key

The Matrix, a movie released in 1999, tells the story of mankind living in an apocalyptic world run by artificial intelligence. To prevent a human uprising, the AI computer has constructed a virtual reality known as the matrix. During the movie, characters move in and out of the matrix: sometimes they are shown in their ship, which is real; at other times, the action switches to the simulation in which the laws of physics can be altered.

I first watched *The Matrix* at a music festival. The last band ended well after midnight, and while waiting for the screening to begin, I dozed off. I woke up half an hour into the film and completely missed the opening which explained the dynamic between the real and virtual worlds. For the remainder of the movie, I was completely confused about why the characters kept switching between one setting and another, and why one reality didn't quite seem real. It made no sense to me until years later when I watched the first half-hour.

At this stage in my boys' education, they are reading more challenging literature by authors such as William Shakespeare, Charles Dickens, and Jane Austen. I don't want them to feel completely lost and slog through a classic having no idea what's going on, as happened to me when watching *The Matrix*. So, I provided study guides,[2] and we watched video summaries and movies (yes, the BBC version of *Pride and Prejudice*, as well as Bollywood's *Bride & Prejudice*) so they would be familiar with the background and plot before beginning to read. Some novels such as G.K. Chesterton's *Father Brown* mysteries might be spoiled by knowing what happens. But in general, anything that would help them better understand the story was permissible. It didn't seem like taking a shortcut or cheating, because the objective was for them to gain maximum enjoyment out of reading the book, not make it difficult for them. As they advance beyond secondary level, they will learn to analyze novels by themselves. But for now, the better they understand the literature, the more they will enjoy it.

And with them now being older and more capable of understanding, it made sense to me to introduce this sort of reading comprehension at an advanced level, rather than as something learned slowly by themselves over the years.

Quickly Is Key

Interestingly, my youngest somewhat disagrees with me! He thinks it would be better not to know the plot overview before reading a novel, and specifically cited *Jane Eyre*. But he agrees that plot summaries and background information are useful after finishing the book. I suspect the key is how quickly the book is read. He spent three months plodding through *Pride and Prejudice*, and I'm sure if he hadn't already watched the TV mini-series, he wouldn't have retained much of what he read.

After that, we worked on some techniques to read more quickly, such as using a bookmark under the line you're reading to prevent skipping forward, and consciously avoiding re-reading if your mind wanders. This made a significant difference, and he finished *Jane Eyre* in only two weeks and wrote an excellent reaction paper. This was his conclusion:

> *Great writing is for everyone: young and old; male and female; Eastern and Western; short and tall. Jane Eyre is acknowledged as one of the great books, and is worth the effort it takes to read.*

Some books do take a long time to read, and some require us to proceed slowly so that we can fully appreciate them. But in general, for a literature course, I think it is more helpful to read novels quickly.

Love Is THE Key

My conclusion on the matter is this: teach your young children to love books, and don't worry about comprehension. If they ask you to read a book, then they understand it. If they pick up a book themselves, the story makes sense to them. If they're not doing this, then read, read, read to them.

NOTES

1. Beechick, *The Three R's*, pp. 21-22.
2. CliffsNotes, SparkNotes and Max Notes are common brands which we use. There are many video options available, including ones from GradeSaver and Course Hero.

WRITING

Penmanship

Fencepost Model:	Winter
Competency Model:	Incremental

The Creative Process

I have always viewed the mechanics of penmanship as linked in some way to the creative writing process. The imagination is enhanced by the physical act of writing with pencil and paper, as it is with creating artwork or building a Lego tower. I have debated with myself for many years over the issue of when to allow my children to learn to touch-type and prepare assignments on the computer. But that day has still not come, even with them well into high school coursework and writing (and editing) substantial essays. I decided a number of times to "wait until next year" and always hesitated as I was not yet comfortable with their ability to express themselves through writing. There is a creative component that would be inhibited if it were not mastered before switching to a word processor. Similar arguments are made in support of cursive.

In addition, word processors are likely to correct spelling and grammar. I frequently disagree with the "corrections," and want my children to know how to spell and write properly before Microsoft molds them into its image.

Handwriting & Cognitive Development

—William Klemm Ph.D., Psychology Today[1]

Scientists are discovering that learning cursive is an important tool for cognitive development. . . . Other research highlights the hand's unique relationship with the brain when it comes to composing thoughts and ideas. . . .

There is a whole field of research known as "haptics," which includes the interactions of touch, hand movements, and brain function. Cursive writing helps train the brain to integrate visual and tactile information and fine motor dexterity. School systems, driven by ill-informed ideologues and federal mandate, are becoming obsessed with testing knowledge at the expense of training kids to develop better capacity for acquiring knowledge.

There is also a significant difference between paper and word processor when it comes to the process of creating written work, something I noticed many times during my university experience. On a computer, you tend to simply start writing. The order doesn't matter because it's easy to restructure and edit the document later. You also focus on the section you're currently typing, and there's a temptation to immediately edit and correct grammar and spelling as the word processor nags you and highlights your errors. My rule was always that if I were correcting spelling, then I was procrastinating. Fixing the spelling and layout should be a task for the final edit, once the text itself is completed and will no longer change. But you are pushed into the particulars when you start with a word processor. The process of writing on a computer therefore begins with the details.

In contrast, writing on paper forces you to think about the overall structure first. It lends itself to brainstorming and mind-mapping and free-form outlining and jotting down notes and ideas that get organized before the writing begins. Fundamentally, writing on paper starts with the big picture and moves in toward the details, whereas writing on the computer begins with the details and moves outwards toward the big picture. This book was conceived in my mind and birthed in pencil in a notebook, where I drafted an outline and wrote down notes for months before switching to software.

I have recognized this difference ever since I bought my first computer. When writing essays at university, it was always my intention to begin by drafting the assignment on paper before switching to a computer. But in most cases, I would default to typing from the start, usually to save time, and I often didn't even attempt an outline. I know from experience this is inherently what is going to happen when you have access to a computer, and I didn't want my boys to have this option and miss learning the creative process of writing papers by hand. It is inevitable that they will eventually use a word processor and default to beginning assignments there just as I did. And it wouldn't be realistic to demand a written outline from them first. But I don't want that to happen until they have mastered the skill of writing by hand.

This means their spelling and grammar need to be to a high standard, as they can't rely on the computer to fix it for them.

Quality and Style

The first step then is to learn how to write by hand. This was introduced at an early stage of their education. I did not teach cursive. I know that many classical teachers highlight the link between cursive writing and creativity, but my decision was pragmatic. Although I encourage writing by hand, I know most adults do very little of it nowadays. I remember sitting eight three-hour end-of-year exams during my first few years of university, and most of them required a lot of writing. Almost everything was done by hand back in those days before anyone owned a personal computer, and I earned a permanent ridge on my index finger where the pen rested, along with a callus on my pinkie where my hand would slide across the paper. But fifteen years later during an exam for my MBA, I wasn't the only one suffering from hand cramps as we were forced to write solidly for three hours.

I am not against learning cursive, but decided this was something my children could learn later if they wanted. In this case, I may be wrong.

Quality and style are also aspects I messed up. I ended formal writing lessons with my youngest once he could write competently, and left him to record journal entries and do copywork. However, the legibility of his handwriting was inadequate and did not improve naturally, and although we're working on it now, it's taking plenty of effort to change.

If I were to start over, I would definitely focus on quality of penmanship from an early age before poor habits became entrenched. And I would probably revisit the decision to stop at printing rather than continue on to cursive. I never learned to write well in cursive myself. The three of us are now attempting to remedy these defects by working together through the New American Cursive Penmanship Program, *Teach Yourself Cursive* by Iris Hatfield. Improvements are noticeable already, and I hope to prove it's never too late to learn a new skill.

Focus on quality of penmanship at a young age.

assiduously:	with careful and consistent effort; diligently or tirelessly
dénouement:	the final scene in a play or novel in which the plot is resolved
psychosomatic:	of the mind and body together

Creative Writing

Fencepost Model:	Summer
Competency Model:	Apprenticeship

The Natural Learning Method

While the psychosomatic link between pencil and imagination remains strong, creative writing itself is very different to the mechanics of penmanship. I have talked about how, in my first few years of home education while I was finding my way, I followed the curriculum more closely. Grammar and creative writing were incorporated from first grade. But I quickly questioned the value of this. It made no sense to me to teach a six-year-old the rules of grammar, hoping that over twelve years they would stick. It seemed pointless to include grammar in isolation. Obviously, examples were always provided with the exercises, but the approach was, *"Here's a grammar rule, and here's an example."* What I really wanted was a program that started with well-written literature, and then explained the grammar inherent in the completed work. More like, *"This is a great book, and here's how it works."* The curriculum also contained regular written assignments, with the intention that over the years, children would learn how to write in different styles such as a book report, an original story, or a newspaper article. My oldest was not enthusiastic about book reports and creative writing assignments, and I could see that forcing him to do this written work would be counter-productive in two ways. One, writing would become a chore for him. He would be doing it because he had to, which would put him off even more. And two, it would teach him to count words: *"How much do I need to write?"* Now that essays have been introduced into their lessons, I assiduously avoid specifying a length for any written assignment. It needs to be comprehensive to gain a high mark, but I don't want my boys to grow up counting the words. I'm hoping they progress to the point of needing to edit for succinctness to keep within a reasonable length, rather than edit to add verbiage in order to meet a minimum word count. During my theology degree, my greatest struggle was keeping essays within the allowable limit.

The Apprenticeship Approach

But how about the ability to write creatively? How did I prepare my boys for this discipline? I used the approach that I talked about when discussing the Competency Model on page 150 and assessment on page 166. Let me provide a recap.

I'm a big believer in Benjamin Franklin's approach. He became a great writer by copying great writing and then challenging himself to improve upon it. I think the foundation for great writing is reading great writing. As well as reading, I made sure the copywork my boys did when working on penmanship was based on stirring speeches and interesting poetry and notable quotes and Bible verses.

I figured this was a discipline for which the Apprenticeship Approach applied, and that the mechanics of creating written work could be taught more easily at a later stage of their education when it was really needed. We are now at that point, and it is taking some effort but is working out well. My boys are producing high-quality written work, with sometimes considerable assistance from me. But my assistance will diminish over the next couple of years until they are working at this level entirely by themselves. It isn't a smooth process. For some of the reaction papers in their literature course, it seemed as if I wrote the entire assignment. And then they would produce a well-written paper completely by themselves, but for the next book, they'd appear entirely lost and require a lot of assistance again. However, overall they are clearly improving and working more independently. In one year of applying the Summer Fencepost Model and the Apprenticeship Approach, I am confident they are writing as well as many students their age, and I expect their writing ability to develop rapidly over the next couple of years.

The Writing Process

I created a framework that my boys could use for any written assignment, which guides them as they outline, draft, write, and edit their papers. Some of the key points are the following:

- Read the topic sentence or essay question every single time you work on the assignment, to make sure you focus on and are answering the actual question. Refer constantly to the marking guide, which will put you on the right track with regards to the content of your work.

- Like a three-point sermon, your outline should (usually) contain three main arguments. Organize your research and ideas as bullet points around these headings.

- The first draft is created by turning each of the bullet points from your outline into a sentence. Write on one side of the paper, using every second or third line. This makes it easy to edit, rearrange and review the draft.

- The last sections to be written are the conclusion followed by the introduction. The conclusion summarizes what you've said. The introduction points the way toward the conclusion (which is why you need to know what you've concluded before writing the introduction).

- Edit carefully before writing out a final copy. It is revision and editing that makes for excellent writing. The A's are in the editing!

One final observation is that an aversion to writing does not mean your child will not write at all. I know there is value in students learning the various forms of writing, such as research reports, letters, creative stories, and essays. My boys didn't want to do these assignments.

> There is no great writing, only great rewriting.
>
> —Justice Louis Brandeis

But my youngest son is happy to write a letter to his pen pal, and our eldest likes blogging and has enjoyed creating a twenty-page script for a Christmas play.

As with reading, I've found it's a case of teaching them the mechanics so they have the ability, exposing them to lots of great writing, and letting them find the field in which they want to play.

NOTES

1. William R. Klemm, "Why Writing by Hand Could Make You Smarter," *Psychology Today*, 14 March 2013, https://www.psychologytoday.com/us/blog/memory-medic /201303/why-writing-hand-could-make-you-smarter.

CHAPTER TWENTY-FOUR

LANGUAGES

Fencepost Model:	Winter
Competency Model:	Incremental

It is frequently said that children find it easier to learn a foreign language than do adults. We believe that exposure to languages from an early age is important. Besides English, my wife is fluent in Portuguese and Spanish while I studied French and German at school. Languages are something that should be learned through consistent, regular practice. We introduced some Portuguese from birth, and short but official lessons from Grade 1.

Normally when I apply the Fencepost Model, it is to go against the status quo. This is again the case, as many schools delay foreign languages until high school. However, the value of learning foreign languages while young is widely recognized, and language immersion schools are well-accepted.

The Problem with Perfection

Language learning requires an attitude of starting small; of trying and failing while slowly building competence.

I tend to be a perfectionist. Engineers are probably inclined this way. The next time you drive across a bridge, be thankful that the engineer who designed it didn't settle for "80 percent is good enough." But when it came to languages, this tendency meant I was reluctant to say anything unless I was sure it was correct. It didn't help that I got caught out once.

I was on a mission trip to Fiji and was invited to speak at a church service. Before the trip, I had asked a friend to prepare a greeting for me in Māori, the native language of New Zealand. Even though I didn't speak Māori, I thought it would be a nice touch to acknowledge my Pacific homeland, so I practiced the greeting until I thought I had it memorized. But when I stood up to speak, I knew I hadn't practiced enough! *"No worries,"* I thought. *"No one here speaks Māori—I'll just do my best."* So I did, and a few times needed to use random words to fill in the blanks in my memory. After the service, a woman approached me. She was visiting from New Zealand, and she was Māori. I felt that sinking feeling as I asked her if she spoke the language. Of course she did, and I mumbled a mortified *"I'm sorry . . ."*

But to become fluent in a language, we need to shrug off these experiences. That is why children learn so much faster. They are less self-conscious and aren't afraid to practice and learn from their mistakes. Every language learner has a story like mine. One that taught me the difference that attitude makes occurred in Japan.

My close friends, Glenn and Heather, spent a year in Japan. Heather was a language teacher and spoke Japanese. Glenn didn't. But he was not an engineer, and was happy to simply try his best. I stayed with them on my way home from North Africa, where I had spent three months struggling to communicate in French because I couldn't remember enough to speak confidently. On one occasion, Heather was out and Glenn needed to make a call. He simply picked up the phone and used all of the limited Japanese he knew. I couldn't believe he didn't just wait for Heather to return home. That's what I would have done. But Glenn learned the language rapidly, far more quickly than I would have.

Being an extrovert definitely helps. But it's more than that. It's starting with what you know and building from there.

Progression

Our plan was for our children to first learn Portuguese, which many of my wife's family speak. Next, they would learn Spanish, which is widely spoken in the Americas and is an easy transition from Portuguese. Then they would learn French.

Things are not proceeding so well. The primary roadblock, I believe, is that they are not regularly exposed to situations in which they need to speak Portuguese, so although they are making progress, they are not yet comfortable with speaking it. Part of this is my fault. They take after me in wanting to be correct before saying anything. And because I don't speak Portuguese (and haven't been learning with them), I've been unable to push them on. It's hard to learn a language in isolation, and real-world application is key to mastery.

We started off using Rosetta Stone, which I do like. But the boys prefer DuoLingo, a free online service which gamifies the learning experience. For a while, they each chose a different language on which to focus: German and Latin. We bought a life-time, all-languages license to Rosetta Stone for each of them as a birthday gift. The Rosetta Stone license will be a resource they can use for a lifetime, even if they prefer to use DuoLingo for now.

Latin

A few years ago, I read *A Well-Trained Mind* by Susan Wise Bauer and started to appreciate the value of the classical *trivium*. I had previously dismissed any thought of learning Latin. However, I can now see the value of it and introduced lessons two years ago when we began our language arts intensive. A basic grasp of Latin provides a solid foundation for learning Portuguese, Spanish, and French as well as English grammar. I don't know that I'd begin in Grade 1, as I would with any living language. But I do think it is worthwhile to include as part of the language program. The goal now is to complete two credits in Portuguese and two credits in Latin through high school.

CHAPTER TWENTY-FIVE

ARTS & CRAFTS

Fencepost Model:	Winter
Competency Model:	Incremental

You have probably worked out by now that I am big on reading, science, and mathematics, but not so much on artistic endeavors. I claim that science and mathematics are creative pursuits—as my applied mathematics professor said, *"mathematics is the purest form of art."* Anyone who has explored the Mandelbrot set will know what I mean.[1]

It isn't that I ignored arts and crafts entirely. We did painting and coloring and building models and making collages and such. But it was more an activity to fit in at the end of the week rather than a subject that was intentionally taught.

One year, we visited my sister-in-law who has a degree in fine arts. I offered to coach her girls on science if she would teach my boys art. So for a couple of weeks, my children tackled the creative pursuits while her children enjoyed a range of science experiments.

Encouraging creativity and art is great for children. Despite my biases, I did check whether my boys had a natural inclination toward art. It's normal to do lots of hands-on activities with young children. And if a child is showing a particular interest or ability, then this should definitely be encouraged and purposefully developed. My boys did not show any notable aptitude in drawing. For a time, they got right into coloring (within the lines, like good engineers!), and I made sure there were plenty of art materials around. But this phase didn't last, and I was happy to keep the level of arts and crafts in our learning program to an acceptable minimum.

I did schedule some planned lessons. We worked through a manual called *This Book Thinks You're an Artist*, which I thought was brilliant. It is a workbook full of specific activities designed to promote creativity and show how art is accessible to everyone, and is far more than simply drawing. But I had to coerce my children into doing these projects. (To be fair, they didn't willingly do the activities in *This Book Thinks You're a Math Genius* or *This Book Thinks You're a Scientist* either.)

The one area where we saw genuine interest and promise was in music, particularly with our youngest. And so we have made a concerted effort to encourage and develop this talent. Our oldest has also shown real interest in cooking. To create an opportunity for him to develop these skills, we purchased a couple of Great Courses[2] programs on cooking as well as the movie *Ratatouille,* and we enjoy sharing his results whenever he practices! He has time in his schedule to pursue culinary arts if he chooses, and we will encourage it. But as with other artistic endeavors, it will be optional rather than required.

I have wondered whether there should have been more art in our program, or more specifically, whether my boys are deprived because I didn't include much of it. I'm honest about my biases toward STEM subjects. I do believe a solid grounding in technology and mathematics will be of greater benefit to my boys. And I know not everyone will agree with me. That's fine, by all means add more art into your learning schedule.

The issue is that there are limited hours in a day, and at some point we need to decide which subjects are more important and which are less so. I might argue that experimental science in the early curious years is more important than creative activities, but you might hold the opposite view. I might think there is logic and science behind my decision, but it is probably more about personal choice than I would like to admit! And I'm sure any decision reflects the teacher's interests as much as the children's.

So do what you think is best for your children, encourage any natural ability you see, and give them the opportunity to pursue the subjects they really enjoy.

NOTES

1. See "Fractals: The Secret Code of Creation," by Jason Lisle (2021) or https://youtu.be /taKaFUNJ6Ec.
2. The Great Courses, https://www.thegreatcourses.com.

CHAPTER TWENTY-SIX

MUSIC

Fencepost Model:	Winter
Competency Model:	Incremental

You'll Appreciate It Later

My grandmother was an experienced piano teacher and had played since she was a young girl. She gave all her grandchildren free lessons, and I was taught for a few years to the point where I began making significant progress. I still vividly remember the day this came to an end. Our piano was in the dining room, within sight of the TV in the lounge. I was about ten years old, and my favorite show had started when it was my turn with Grandma. I can still picture myself sitting at the piano, trying to get through the lesson while also keeping one eye on the TV. Grandma finally had enough and told me we were done, then stormed out of the room. Gratefully, I retreated to the lounge to watch the rest of the program, until my mother heard what had happened and made me immediately go and apologize. I didn't get to watch the end of the show.

We were done. Not merely with that lesson, but forever. And although I picked up guitar a few years later, I never went any further with piano. It still haunts me that my grandmother said I was her biggest disappointment because she could see the natural talent in me. I thought deeply about this as time went on, because I know if I had persevered for another two years, I would have reached the stage of being able to sight-read music and play anything, anywhere. I would have crested the summit and begun free-wheeling down the other side to the point where playing was a pleasure. I have always regretted that I didn't keep going; that I wasn't **forced** to continue piano lessons.

I have asked many people over the years whether children should be required to take music lessons for their own benefit. The piano is a foundational instrument, and I have always thought that a few years' tuition would provide a sound base for any later interest in music, irrespective of the instrument. But should they be compelled to practice if they would rather watch TV or play computer games?

The best answer I received was from a friend's mother who specialized in teaching piano to young children. Her view was that if a child showed natural ability, then it made sense to coerce them into continuing as they would appreciate it later, just as I would have. But if someone is simply not musical, then it would be pointless to require them to practice if they wanted to stop.

I figure that nurturing an interest in music is like lighting a fire. When the spark first ignites the tinder, blowing gently on the flame will provide oxygen that helps the fire grow. But if you blow too hard, you risk extinguishing the flame entirely.

Building a Foundation

With my limited and ancient experience, I started teaching my boys the piano. At first, it was with a beginner's book that color-coded the notes. By matching colored stickers placed on the keyboard with the colors in the music book, children could begin playing tunes immediately. We worked through this book for a year, and then moved on to some music primers, typically practicing ten minutes a few times a week. I was conscious at each stage that it needed to be fun; that I must avoid making piano seem like a burden.

After a couple of years though, I realized I was becoming the bottleneck and in danger of leaving them frustrated. So we found a piano teacher at our church who has been absolutely wonderful. She has a sound grasp of music theory, which I appreciate, but never overwhelms my boys. Sometimes I listen as she teaches and have heard her describe their playing as "perfect" when it certainly wasn't! But it's perfect for what she is trying to teach, and the boys have blossomed under her tutelage. Through her church connections, they have played at dance recitals and provided background music at Vacation Bible School. The youngest is aiming to become a concert pianist.

I don't know that either of my children began with a natural interest in music. We inherited a children's drum kit and it sat mostly unused, apart from the drumsticks being repurposed as swords. However, music is something that I think needs to be nurtured tenderly. It's certainly a case of applying the Incremental Approach and chipping away at the frozen ground rather than waiting for summer. I am pleased that both boys are well on their way to becoming accomplished pianists.

As touched upon in Chapter Thirteen when discussing our Priority List, music and sport are similar in the sense that neither are core academic subjects, but both provide tremendous benefits. Music aids the memory, improves coordination, enhances creativity, provides an emotional outlet, and develops a useful skill. Sport improves fitness, enhances mental health, teaches teamwork, develops leadership, and provides social connections. However, while we certainly encourage participation in sport, we place a higher priority on music as playing an instrument is a skill they will be able to use and enjoy for the rest of their lives.

MATHEMATICS

Fencepost Model:	Winter
Competency Model:	Incremental

Systematic Thought

Mathematics is a great example of a subject that should be taught little by little, consistently over the years. In terms of the Fencepost Model, it is a winter job. In terms of the Competency Model, mastery is gained incrementally over time.

Math is one of the core subjects I believe is necessary throughout a child's education. This isn't simply because it's important to know how to solve problems but also because mathematics trains the mind to think logically and systematically. I am forever telling my boys to do things systematically. If they are picking up sticks around the yard, they should cover the lawn in a defined pattern rather than wander around randomly looking for twigs.

I grew up at a camp and conference center, and groups that used the facilities would occasionally (or maybe, often) do a poor job picking up their rubbish. After they left, my siblings and I had the privilege of earning ten cents an hour collecting trash. We soon learned that the job was completed more quickly and thoroughly by walking methodically up and down the field than by looking around for the rubbish and picking it up haphazardly.

I want my children to develop organized minds that think systematically and logically, and mathematics is one subject that trains young thinkers in this manner. Logical thought is sorely lacking in society today.

Of course, I don't want to quash any creative tendencies they have. But one should not exclude the other. I don't see why a creative soul cannot also be logical and competent in mathematics. And a strong foundation in mathematics, like computers, is something which will benefit everyone, whether an artist, a musician, or a builder.

Some Advice

Mathematics is my passion. This makes me the wrong person to give advice to parents who may feel intimidated by the thought of teaching it. But I can offer two suggestions.

First, there are great resources and video instruction that will help children self-learn, with support and encouragement from a parent. We used Horizons Math[1] for the first six years, which did require me to teach the material. But then we switched to Math-U-See[2] which provides video lessons. My boys have enjoyed it and are doing well. I highly recommend Math-U-See.

Second, make a point of monitoring your children to ensure that the lessons aren't too difficult or too easy, but are just right. Check that your children are neither struggling nor becoming bored. It's hard to tell the difference, because both of these cases seem to produce the same outcome—a child who doesn't want to do mathematics.

If they have grasped a concept, then it becomes tedious to complete worksheets full of the same problem, and it's better to let them move on before they lose interest. I have seen many math curricula that include pages of practice problems. For my boys at least, they were not excited at doing page after page of something they knew how to do. In my view, if they have grasped the concept, then a couple of problems to practice it should be fine.

My nature is to want everything completed, every problem solved, every extra worksheet finished. But as time has passed, I have become more relaxed about my children completing every question. I now require my boys to demonstrate that they have attained a comprehensive grasp of the concepts in the lesson, with the test being a final check.

For example, let's say your child's lesson includes a worksheet of 30 problems. You could tell them that they may move on once they solve 10. If they get the first 10 correct, that's great. If they attempt all 30 and don't get 10 right, then you know they haven't understood and need some help. If they are struggling with a concept, then it's okay to proceed slowly so that they don't feel overwhelmed.

If they are not getting it, then doing more problems won't fix the issue and will leave them frustrated. They need to go back to the lesson and review the material being taught. With mathematics, it is better for your child to fully master the concepts even if it means only covering half of the course work in a year, rather than complete the program but not really understand the material. But don't get stuck either. If you reach an impasse, you can make the call to simply move on and return to it later. Most primary math curricula work in a spiral pattern, so you'll come back to the topic later on. Sometimes it takes a bit of time and space for a concept to take hold, and it may make more sense the next time you encounter it in your math program.

As Ruth Beechick says, *"The goal is to help children think and learn. If that is happening, whether you race through many selections or ponder on a few, matters not at all."*[3]

Tips & Tricks

I can't cover in this section all of the tips and tricks I used with my boys when teaching mathematics, but here are a few favorites that may be of interest.

Manipulatives

Addition and other basic concepts can be taught with beads or counters. I'm sure all mathematics programs start with manipulatives, which are essential in the early years. I made great use of Number Lines and Hundred Charts for addition, subtraction, and skip-counting. I would slip printed templates into a dry erase pocket[4] so they could be written on with a dry erase pen and reused. Some of these templates are in Appendix E.

Core Facts

Although in general I think it's better for children to learn by understanding rather than by repetition, there are some situations in which rote memorization is appropriate. Foundational building blocks like addition (how many in total) and multiplication (repeated addition) need to be known thoroughly, and there are some core facts I had my children memorize until they could recite them in their sleep. I kept drilling these because they are key for being able to do mental mathematics. This is what I considered essential:

- Addition Doubles (1+1=2, 2+2=4, 3+3=6 etc.)
- 10-Sums (2+8=10, 6+4=10, 9+1=10 etc.)
- Squares to 25^2

I also drilled single digit addition and multiplication tables up to twelve, but squares, ten-sums and doubles are what I consider to be the most important. Apart from these basics, I tried to avoid mindless rote-learning and endless repetition.

Patterns

Mathematics is all about patterns. You will see them everywhere if you are observant. The Hundred Chart is a great way to illustrate the patterns formed by skip-counting / multiplication.

1	2	3	4	5	6	7	8	9	10
11	12	13	14	15	16	17	18	19	20
21	22	23	24	25	26	27	28	29	30
31	32	33	34	35	36	37	38	39	40
41	42	43	44	45	46	47	48	49	50
51	52	53	54	55	56	57	58	59	60
61	62	63	64	65	66	67	68	69	70
71	72	73	74	75	76	77	78	79	80
81	82	83	84	85	86	87	88	89	90
91	92	93	94	95	96	97	98	99	100

Figure 12. Skip-Counting by Three and Nine

Here is another beautiful pattern, and there are more in Appendix F.

$$1 \times 1 = 1$$
$$11 \times 11 = 121$$
$$111 \times 111 = 12321$$
$$1111 \times 1111 = 1234321$$
$$11111 \times 11111 = 123454321$$
$$111111 \times 111111 = 12345654321$$
$$1111111 \times 1111111 = 1234567654321$$
$$11111111 \times 11111111 = 123456787654321$$
$$111111111 \times 111111111 = 12345678987654321$$

Figure 13. Patterns in Mathematics

Process

As the complexity of mathematics increases and the problems become harder to solve, following the process becomes ever more critical. A difficult problem will be introduced using a simple example in order to teach the method for finding the solution. If my children were able to solve these simple problems, they would often skip steps in the process or do it in their head. I am continually telling them to follow the complete process on the easy problems so that they learn the method and don't get stumped when encountering more difficult problems, ones they can't do mentally.

An example of this is word problems. They have been taught a process: underline the question, cross out irrelevant information, and circle the data. But if it's an easy word problem, they often don't bother because it seems too obvious. When faced with a difficult question, however, they often fail to follow the process of marking up the problem, and this makes it harder to solve.

So . . . learn the process on the easy questions and follow it rigorously so that you know how to tackle the tough ones.

NOTES

1. Horizons, https://www.aop.com/curriculum/horizons.
2. Math-U-See, https://mathusee.com.
3. Beechick, *The Three R's*, p. 63. Ruth Beechick was talking about language arts, but the comment is just as applicable to mathematics. In fact, I would suggest it's relevant to any subject.
4. I used Dry Erase Pockets from C-Line (https://www.c-lineproducts.com). Their website provides some downloadable educational templates. Job Ticket Holders, available at office retail stores, are essentially the same and work perfectly. Standard Sheet Protectors may also be used.

SCIENCE

Fencepost Model:	Winter (primary level only)
Competency Model:	Incremental

Competency Not Required

Although science was my chosen field, I don't think a child needs to study science to any particular level in order to become a competent and capable adult. Does that surprise you, especially since I included science in my Level 1 Priority List? Let me explain.

There are some disciplines in which I think everyone should become competent, let's say up to secondary level. Reading, writing, and mathematics are the main subjects in this category. I would add logic and computer skills, while economics and government should probably be included in the mix. In order to graduate from high school, proficiency should be achieved in these fields of study.

Other subjects contribute to a well-rounded education, such as music, history, literature, and art. However, I don't think every student needs to achieve a secondary school standard in these areas. If someone has a special interest or wants to pursue that discipline further, then by all means they should do so. But if they have no interest, then I don't think that requiring them to reach a high level of competence will add much value to their education.

A year of piano is enough basic exposure to music if a student is never going to touch an instrument again. He won't be a better person if he is required to pass three years of music theory against his will. And, perhaps surprisingly, I include science in this category.

But why did I make it a Level 1 Priority? Because the value of science is to open our eyes to the wonder of God's creation, to make us curious about the world and how it works, to allow us to begin to grasp our place in the universe, to provide the framework for imagination and creativity and language. Children need science when they are young, when they are curious, when they are little sponges soaking up all they see and hear and smell and touch and taste. That is why I think there should be a lot of science in the early years.

As children grow, however, and particularly at secondary level, literature and writing seem far more valuable and necessary than science. I don't understand the logic behind requiring three science courses in high school (except, you know, science is great).

I'm not saying students **shouldn't** take science. It will clearly expand their breadth of knowledge. I simply don't think there's any justification in requiring a student to meet an arbitrary standard or complete a specified amount of work in science if they will not continue beyond school. They will probably learn and remember as much from watching a fifteen-minute overview of all of physics[1] as they would from spending 120 hours on a high school credit course.

Include plenty of hands-on science while children are young.

The Harrison Academy Science Program

And with that out of the way, let me tell you what we did.

We did cover a lot of science, particularly in the early years, and went on plenty of field trips.

With field trips, I put greater emphasis on the experience than on the reflection. What I mean is that while I tried to make it an informative learning experience, I didn't require my children to complete a field trip worksheet or report afterwards. I do think this kind of deliberate reflection enhances the learning experience. I appreciate the value of a worksheet or field trip report. But as I found out with book reports, science worksheets really turned my boys off. And so we simply went on field trips and I let them enjoy it. We walked around in the woods and discovered diatoms by looking at creek water under the microscope.

We had an annual membership to the Minnesota Science Museum and would visit there frequently. We also went to the Children's Museum, aquariums, the Arboretum, and historical sites.

Inside the home, we investigated biology, chemistry, and physics. We undertook microscope work, built robots, tried chemistry experiments, tested magnets, and made motors. We worked on electronic projects from EEME, which I highly recommend. We took apart a broken laptop computer, built marble runs with Gravitrax, and made Lego towers. (Does that count as science?) We studied dinosaurs, creation science, and evolution. We discussed how faith complements science and how the Biblical account of a six-day creation and a global flood are strongly supported by the available evidence. I challenged my boys to understand evolution better than those who support it because you need to understand an opposing position before you can argue effectively against it.

We used a lot of Apologia material for our science courses.[2] I also really enjoyed the TOPS Learning Systems books, which present hands-on learning activities and experiments using everyday materials.[3]

So yes, we did do a lot of science. But let me reiterate that primary-level science is about curiosity and exploration and intrigue, not about comprehension or mastery, or reaching a particular standard of knowledge, or covering a certain set of topics.

Like history, science is a subject you could study your entire life and never learn it all. For that matter, you could explore any subset of any branch of science and still never reach a limit. My expectation is that if the basics are in place, any knowledge gaps can be filled in later. Doing well in mathematics and technology will provide a foundation for

> *All science is either physics or stamp collecting.*
>
> —Sir Ernest Rutherford,
> New Zealander and
> Nobel Prize-Winning Physicist

your children that will set them up for success in science, even if they have not done much at secondary level but decide at university to major in a particular scientific field.

So I'm not concerned about the level of competency my boys reach in science through to the end of high school. However, we will cover the state high school standard of three science courses, one with lab. And if they are interested, we will do more.

Engineering Resources
The quality and breadth of resources available to parents continues to grow, and children with an interest in science and engineering will find plenty of options to match their skill level and budget. Here are some favorite resources.

EEME
www.eeme.co
Hands-on kits and online lessons to teach kids electronics and coding.

KiwiCo
www.kiwico.com
Hands-on project kits to inspire the next generation of innovators and problem-solvers.

CrunchLabs
www.crunchlabs.com
Think like an engineer and build a new toy each month alongside former NASA engineer Mark Rober!

The Great Courses
www.thegreatcourses.com
A huge range of video courses, including "Do-It-Yourself Engineering."

NOTES

1. Arvin Ash, "All Physics Explained in 15 Minutes," (YouTube, 7 August 2020). https://youtu.be/TTHazQeM8v8.
2. Creation-based homeschool science curriculum: Apologia, https://www.apologia.com.
3. Hands-on science with simple things: TOPS Learning Systems, https://topscience.org. The founder made his start while teaching science and math in West Africa, where he didn't have access to a well-equipped science lab and learned to make do with limited resources.

CHAPTER TWENTY-NINE

COMPUTERS

Fencepost Model:	Summer (applications)
	Winter (programming)
Competency Model:	Incremental

It is easy to assume that children will be comfortable with technology simply by virtue of growing up in the digital age. That may well be true. However, technology is a topic which I think deserves separate and specific consideration. There are a number of aspects to this: using a computer for written assignments and course work; using other forms of technology such as a phone or programmable calculator; learning applications like spreadsheets and video editing; and programming.

Using a computer is quite different than programming, but I will cover both in this section.

Applications

I had expected to teach typing as part of our lessons. Being able to touch-type is a skill as basic in today's world as writing in cursive was to previous generations. But I kept putting it off. As discussed in Chapter Twenty-Three, my fear was that if I taught my boys to type, they would expect to do all their assignments on a computer. And I hesitated to open that door.

We control the amount of computer time our boys have. Although computer-based curricula seem to have a lot going for them, we didn't want our boys spending all day in front of a screen. Over the last few years, they have been doing an increasing amount of computer work, from video editing to Compass Classroom[1] courses to Vocabulary Quest[2] to managing their cookie-making business. It doesn't take them long to figure out a new application. But the core of their work is still completed with books and paper and pencil.

Apart from eventually learning to touch-type, I don't think they need any specific computer training. If they come across something they need to do, such as learn to use Excel formulas, it is simple to search for tutorials that provide training. Computer skills are easily self-taught.

Programming

The key question then is about more advanced topics such as computer programming.

As with mathematics, computer programming introduces a logical mode of thinking. While this is probably a subject that could be left until high school (summer in the Fencepost Model), I introduced it early so that my boys would become familiar with the type of thinking needed to create a program that solves a problem.

Back in the day, I learned to write code using BASIC and Pascal, before graphical user interfaces became available. I did miss the punch-card era, but not by much! Programming today is much easier. There are plenty of fun options for object-oriented languages that make programming enjoyable for children. We used Scratch, a block-based, drag-and-drop language specifically developed for children by MIT.[3] With a few simple activity books, my boys were creating programs and developing their own games in no time.

They have been using Scratch now for a few years. While they haven't advanced much beyond the basics, they have enjoyed it to the point of sometimes coding in their own time outside of lessons. That is all I want at this stage. If they show a particular interest, then they can progress to more advanced languages later.

However, at high school level I do want them to gain more exposure to programming languages and techniques. My expectation is that each child would do at least one programming course in high school. Website design, HTML, and maybe SQL for database work would be worthwhile next steps. In terms of programming languages, Python (for data science, AI, and machine learning) and JavaScript (for game development) are popular choices after Scratch. There are plenty of paid and free resources on the internet that make programming and computers fun and enjoyable, and it is a subject in which you can very quickly see results.

NOTES

1. Compass Classroom, https://compassclassroom.com.
2. Vocabulary Quest, https://vocabularyquest.com.
3. Coding for kids: Scratch, https://scratch.mit.edu.

CHAPTER THIRTY

LOGIC

| Fencepost Model: | Winter |
| Competency Model: | Incremental |

Critical Thinking in Schools

In C.S. Lewis's *The Lion, the Witch and the Wardrobe*, the Professor grumbles *"I wonder what they* do *teach them at these schools."*[1] He is talking with Peter and Susan about Lucy's account of visiting the fantastical world of Narnia, and says:

> *Logic! . . . Why don't they teach logic at these schools? There are only three possibilities. Either your sister is telling lies, or she is mad, or she is telling the truth. You know she doesn't tell lies and it is obvious that she is not mad. For the moment then and unless any further evidence turns up, we must assume that she is telling the truth.*[2]

Back in the 1940s, C.S. Lewis was concerned about the impact of modernist public education as articulated in his book, *The Abolition of Man*. The quote above clearly highlights his observation that schools were not teaching logic and critical thinking skills. If he were uneasy eight decades ago, what would he think now?

When education is provided by government, it will serve to further the goals of government. While a well-educated population is beneficial to a state, and ethical and civil citizens are desirable, it is also to a government's advantage to produce citizens who accept the role of the state, who do not question their leaders, and who obey those in authority.

During the last couple of years, we have seen with stunning clarity how Western populations, counter to all logic and scientific reasoning, have unquestioningly embraced an expanding state control and how debate and disagreement have been stifled. It isn't hard to see that it is in the best interests of governments to refrain from teaching logic in public schools.

I want my children to think logically and rationally, to question what they are taught, and to form their own conclusions. Homeschooling is often accused of being an avenue for indoctrinating young people. Ironically, as anyone who cares to look at the outcomes will see, it's clearly the public schools indoctrinating our children while home education provides an escape from sectarian, closed-minded thinking.[3]

As mentioned previously, my wife attended Georgetown University in Washington, DC. They are proud of their diverse student body and, after a recent election, boasted of the large number of their graduates who had attained public office. What Georgetown failed to acknowledge was that the vast majority of their elected graduates belonged to the same political party. They had recruited a disparate intake of students and molded them into a homogeneous voting bloc. The cohort may have exhibited a large variation of skin tone and gender, but they graduated with little diversity of thought.

Earlier I mentioned that everyone has a worldview, that every teacher has a paradigm and that it is a fallacy to believe any instruction is unbiased and value-free. I want to reiterate this point. It isn't a surprise that Georgetown has a perspective, or public schools subscribe to an ideology, or classical schools follow a particular approach. Of course they do. Homeschoolers do as well. The point is not to lambaste institutions for having a viewpoint. But what seems to be missing from the conversation is this: first, any acknowledgement that academic institutions are **not** neutral; and second, the need for students to learn critical thinking skills so that they can identify the biases in their teachers and question the prevailing narrative.

> *The amount of indoctrination that, that's happening in schools and universities is I think far beyond what parents realize. . . . Parents are just generally not aware of what their kids are being told, or what they're not being taught.*
>
> —Elon Musk[4]

The Harrison Academy Logic Program

Like mathematics and programming, logic is a subject that develops a systematic manner of thinking. Logical reasoning develops slowly over time, and even if it isn't being formally taught, children should be encouraged to think critically about every subject, with formal courses in logic being taken at secondary level.

I wanted to introduce logic early so that my boys would be exposed to the idea of thinking about thinking while they were young. We began with *The Thinking Toolkit* and *The Fallacy Detective* by Hans Bluedorn and Nathaniel Bluedorn, which provided a great introduction. These books were fun and taught them how to discuss, disagree and argue a position, how to use evidence and science correctly, how to spot pseudoscience, and how to reach their own conclusion. They learned about propaganda, statistical fallacies, making assumptions, and avoiding the question. They reviewed logical fallacies such as equivocation, the straw man fallacy, the *ad hominem* attack, and faulty appeal to authority.

Our expectation is that they will take one formal logic course during high school, and we have already started on Jason Lisle's *Introduction to Logic*. What I like about Lisle's course is that he begins the study of logic by looking at God's character and Word. Logic and rational thought are grounded in the nature of God. Therefore, believing in God and trusting in His Word, the Bible, is entirely logical. The "enlightened" world may suggest otherwise, but just as faith complements science, so faith is not separate from nor contrary to rational thought.

In our school, we teach logic.

Saving the World

Home education has an opportunity to produce the type of citizens this world desperately needs but is sorely lacking. We need young people who know what they believe and why they believe it, who are not deceived by illogical arguments, who recognize the role of science along with its limitations and know that questioning "the science" is how science is done, who can construct an argument and defend a position without resorting to *ad hominem* attacks, and who can express themselves clearly.

George Bernard Shaw said, *"The reasonable man adapts himself to the world: the unreasonable one persists in trying to adapt the world to himself. Therefore all progress depends on the unreasonable man."* It is considered unreasonable

> *When reason has no point of reference in society the next generation will embody the logic of unreason.*
>
> —Ravi Zacharias[5]

these days to question government, to question science, to question the accepted narrative. Therefore, all progress in the future will depend on unreasonable people who will do just that; on well-educated young people who have been taught how to think for themselves and who have the courage of their convictions to do so.

NOTES

1. Lewis, *The Lion, the Witch and the Wardrobe*, p. 50.
2. Lewis, *The Lion, the Witch and the Wardrobe*, p. 48.
3. *IndoctriNation: Public Schools and the Decline of Christianity*, ed. Charles LaVerdiere (Green Forest, AR: Master Books, 2012).
4. Bill Maher, "Elon Musk (Full Interview)," (YouTube, 29 April 2023). https://youtu .be/oO8w6XcXJUs.
5. Ravi Zacharias, *Deliver Us from Evil: Restoring the Soul in a Disintegrating Culture* (Dallas, TX: Word Publishing, 1996), p. 143.

BIBLE

Fencepost Model:	Winter
Competency Model:	Incremental

It is somewhat ironic that the subject which I consider the most important is the one about which I will say the least! Perhaps this is because I didn't approach the study of our faith as an engineer. It is simply a foundational part of everything we do. Perhaps as well, the way you include Bible in your day, or whether you do at all, depends on your own beliefs and perspective. Family devotions and discipleship are much more than an academic topic, and each family will approach it differently.

For us, the Bible Block is the first activity we do each day. We have used a wide variety of resources and methods over the years. For the first six years, we shared in devotions together, and memorization of Bible verses was on our schedule. Now, we each have a personal devotional time.

There are relatives on both sides of the family who have been missionaries, and they always have exciting stories to tell. We would call my uncle and aunt for "Missionary Stories with the Humes." They entertained my boys for a couple of years with their adventures in the remote mountains of Irian Jaya where my uncle was a pilot, and later in Banda Aceh following the 2004 Indian Ocean tsunami. My boys also enjoyed visiting another uncle and hearing tales of his time in the Arctic Circle, living in an igloo. If you know any missionaries, ask them to tell stories to your children.

Something I introduced early was a simple summary of the key theological doctrines. I had seen many resources which were much more comprehensive (it took us two years to work through the Westminster Shorter Catechism), but I wanted a simple overview.[1] And so I created a modest catechism of my own. Since we already have a Harrison Shorter Catechism, let's call this The Harrison Slightly Longer Catechism.

The Harrison Slightly Longer Catechism

What is it called?	**Creation.**
What is it?	Jesus created the world and the universe.
What does it mean?	God is in control of everything.

What is it called?	**Original Sin.**
What is it?	Adam sinned, and all people are descended from him.
What does it mean?	I was born with a sinful nature.

What is it called?	**Substitutionary Atonement.**
What is it?	Jesus died for my sins.
What does it mean?	Jesus took my punishment so that I can be forgiven.

What is it called?	**Repentance.**
What is it?	I accept that I have sinned, and I ask forgiveness.
What does it mean?	To turn around and go the other way.

What is it called?	**Eternal Life.**
What is it?	Jesus conquered death.
What does it mean?	If I follow Jesus, I can enjoy eternal life with Him.

NOTES

1. The "Big Thoughts for Little Thinkers" series by Joey Allen is also an excellent resource.

PART 6

ABOUT PERSPECTIVE

My wife and children provide their perspective,
and I finish up with encouragement
and key thoughts to take away.

THE FAMILY'S PERSPECTIVE

Wife & Mom's Perspective

They say choosing your spouse is one of life's most important decisions. Years ago, I was thinking about how I should make that choice. I knew the Bible commands wives to respect their husband, so I anchored my decisions on that point: *respect*. I decided a husband I could respect would be one that 1) was more spiritually mature than me (had a deep relationship with Jesus and knew the Bible very well); 2) was more intelligent than me (I had thought of pursuing a PhD so someone I wouldn't "leave behind" if I pursued further studies would be important); and 3) someone taller than me (I liked wearing heels and never wanted to tower over my man). Funnily enough, my mother-in-law later told me she was really pleased I married Craig because I fully appreciated and affirmed his love of learning. I've always thought it's awesome that he has five degrees! ☺ In hindsight I

> Life is full of choices, make good ones.
>
> —W. Yeargin, CEO of Correct Craft

believe these three criteria were divinely inspired for our situation as the LORD connected Craig and I across continents in an amazing way (a story for another time). After recently celebrating twenty years of marriage, I can say that despite the ups and downs of our time together, those three criteria have never faltered and neither has my respect for my spouse.

About the time our eldest was of school age I felt I was supposed to be doubling down on an entrepreneurial venture I had begun with a couple of my family members. I remember having a conversation with the LORD saying, "*If you want Craig to look after the boys, You need to tell him; I really don't want to be that messenger.*" We often have spent time at the end of a year or beginning of the next one to reflect on lessons learned and how the LORD might be directing us for the future. In early 2013, Craig told me the LORD had told him to look after the boys, so I knew the message had been delivered.

It's never bothered me that my salary has always been higher than Craig's. The LORD is the only source of our provision, and He can choose whatever channel He pleases for His purposes; it just so happens that so far in our married life that provision has been channeled through my employers. Craig and his family have always been great stewards of resources. I remember commenting to Craig at one point when I went back to full-time work outside the home that I would be bringing in the funds, but he would be using his skills to make sure those resources were well managed and grew over time. That definitely has been the case, and I've learned a lot from him.

I realize I'm writing about our marriage and finances and haven't quite got to the point about our homeschooling journey as such, but I think this is relevant context. We're speaking of home education centered around the family, and a strong marriage is a linchpin in any family. And marriages are often honed on the anvil of finances. Our marriage has endured because Jesus is our foundation, and when the storms of life buffeted us and we had to weather disappointments and hope deferred, we each chose to keep our eyes on the Author and Perfecter of our faith.

> Love does not consist of gazing at each other, but in looking outward together in the same direction.
>
> —Antoine de Saint-Exupéry, Airman's Odyssey

The LORD has given us shared dreams about the future. In the first few years of our marriage, we spent time praying and setting long-term goals. As it became clear that our original ideas of serving overseas were not panning out in the way we thought they would, we asked the LORD what we should be working toward instead. We set BHAGs we knew would take years to fulfill. In hindsight, it's clear we included several assumptions about how those goals would be achieved. One of them being that when we moved to the US, I would stay home with the boys while Craig would pursue his goals of working for a large consultancy.

As Craig shares in an earlier chapter, that didn't play out the way he'd hoped either, and he's had to process his disappointment. I've never been accused of being overly sympathetic. While I knew Craig felt sorry for himself and struggled with the depression resulting from receiving a God-given "assignment" different from what he'd dreamt of doing, I fully expected him to work through it with the LORD. And in time he has, especially in the last few years. They say love is an action, not a feeling, so I would say I chose to love him by staying in the race with him. Although I did not walk in his shoes, I know Craig's journey has not been an easy one. As he's been finding his way, it's been exciting to see the interesting, funny guy I knew he was slowly show up for our boys. They're now getting to see more and more of Craig's strengths, and it's awesome to see their admiration for him as a man and dad grow.

At the end of 2009, as our time in NZ was clearly coming to an end, I remember Craig received a word from the LORD that He was preparing a job for him that would use *all* of the training Craig had completed up to that point: in science, business, theology, and even his time as a football coach. It's clear to me today that job is the one he's fulfilling as a home educator and parent. He even used the piano lessons his grandma taught him! Today I'd say we're leaning into his role in a very positive way, and our family is reaping the rewards from growing young men of character and wisdom.

Our conversations early on about the purpose of education have shaped our attitudes toward lessons. One of the many books Craig read when wrapping his head around the idea of homeschooling was Dr. Sylvia Rimm's *How to Parent so Children will Learn: Strategies for Raising Happy, Achieving Children*. One of the ideas we gleaned from that resource was to speak to children with the expectation that they will be able to learn. We intentionally did not dumb down our language when speaking to our boys; we didn't distinguish between "kid-speak" and "adult-speak" in our home. We used our regular vocabulary and explained what we meant if they weren't familiar with a word. From a very early age, we've described our children as "good learners" which refers to a journey they're on and the skills they're developing rather than "being smart" which implies natural giftedness. We don't stress too much if they haven't mastered a skill at any given point—they will—they're good learners. Instead, we look for ways to better support their journey.

When our youngest was not yet showing as much interest in reading as our eldest had at the same age, Craig came across a suggestion that children will grow in their reading skills if there are lots of books around at their height. Soon each of our bathrooms had been updated with book baskets and the average time spent doing their business grew significantly. It's been great fun to have our youngest come out of the bathroom and share a bunch of facts or jokes he's learned from his latest reading. 😊 (Note: If you're looking for interesting books that you don't mind keeping in the bathroom, *Uncle John's Bathroom Readers* are great!)

From a practical perspective, the physical layout of our house has been conducive to juggling both work-from-home and home education needs. While we live in the suburbs and don't have much in the way of land, our house is a split level, so our office is upstairs on one side of the house and the learning center, where Craig and the boys do most of their work, is downstairs on the opposite side. As an extra precaution, I put a sign outside the office door to indicate whether I'm on a video or phone call. So although I've been working from our home office for the entire time the boys have been homeschooled, we've been able to manage the different spatial aspects well.

Because both of us are usually at home all day, we've made it clear that Craig is fully in charge of their schedules, and we've tried to be careful not to be caught giving different directions about the boys' priorities and responsibilities. When they ask me about extra computer time or doing early morning chess tournaments, I try to ensure Craig has approved that before responding. We've tried to take advantage of our unique situation by giving each other extra flexibility as well—I'm an early riser while Craig works late into the evening, so the boys and I usually have breakfast together before I start work, and then Craig takes over from there until dinner time when I am back on the scene. My presence at lunchtime varies depending on my meeting schedule. We have a bedtime routine we usually all do together.

I remember Craig was really frustrated at one point early on because he was trying to get the boys to do all the exercises in the math books. The boys hated the redundant tasks and took forever to complete them despite lots of nagging. Then Craig realized they might be bored. So he tested that hypothesis: he changed his tactics—if they finished a page of the exercises and got it 100 percent correct, they could move on to the next lesson rather than do multiple pages of reinforcement. It worked! They got through the work quickly, and the painful nagging was eliminated. Fast forward a few years and they're doing high school math years ahead of their age group.

While not a systematic occurrence, we have at times leveraged my liberal arts and multi-cultural background to add to the discussions the boys are having regarding different books they're reading. As it so happens I have read some of their fiction assignments, such as *Pride and Prejudice* and *Romeo and Juliet*, so we introduced my perspective by sharing insights about differences in social and economic strata as well as cultural nuances regarding an Italian's interpretation of Shakespeare's piece versus an American or British understanding, etc. My primary role as a parent occasionally morphs into that of a teacher as well. ☺

Craig and I do talk a reasonable amount about the thinking and planning he's doing for the boys, and while I do share my opinions or suggestions for his consideration, he is the one that has to work things out with the boys, so we try to discuss ideas in private beforehand and iron out any differences. That way when Craig introduces a new direction, I'm already on the same page and can be fully supportive.

Prior to 2020, when I told people Craig was homeschooling our boys, I'd make comments like *"If I were staying home, they'd be in a local school. I'm just not as organized and disciplined as Craig is."* I no longer believe that is true. We've both undergone a transformation in our understanding of the incredible gift our sons are receiving by being educated at home. Yes, we've been able to travel as originally envisioned and have enjoyed many special memories together. But we've now also journeyed through the crises of last few years together, we've talked through the many challenging situations and when we didn't have all the answers, we helped them think critically, lean into wisdom from above, and engage in spiritual warfare. I have no doubt that by keeping our children home, we protected them from the trauma inflicted on so many others in the school systems as adults processed their fears and governments experimented with lockdowns and social distancing among other myriad restrictions. Arguably, we have provided them with a much more resilient perspective to face challenges in the future.

> For God has not given us a spirit of fear, but of power and of love and of a sound mind.
>
> —2 Timothy 1:7 NKJV

We are living through an extraordinary chapter in history, and it is our privilege to contribute to a new reformation of society, to a return

> *Dream no small dreams*
> *for they have no power to*
> *move the hearts of men.*
>
> —Johann Wolfgang
> von Goethe

to God-honoring values, to build families that are resilient and honorable. In contrast, the open assault on traditional values should not surprise us: throughout history, usurpers have always attacked those who kneel only to the Most High God. Yet those who rely on Biblical supernatural power and courage to withstand the onslaught of evil will not bend to tyrants and so-called elites. Ultimately, our children and our children's children will rise or fall on the strength of their foundation in Jesus Christ and that is what is at stake with their education in the most holistic sense.

So we are building a lighthouse within the new monastery movement. Our Harrison Family Team is being intentionally cultivated. From the memories we make on our field trips (e.g., visiting all major waterfalls in the Twin Cities areas and enjoying a stirring rendition of Handel's Messiah in St. Mary's Basilica) and road trips (e.g., travelling 4,000+ miles through eight different states), to instilling a sense of shared ownership and accountability for resources (both boys contributed to buying our house), to setting the table formally and learning etiquette fit for the (late) Queen, to praying together and discussing our spiritual journeys, little by little our boys are progressing on their journey toward maturity.

Reflecting back to the early wisdom we received from our more experienced homeschooling friends, today I'd say we educate our children at home because we are *for* our children and our grandchildren, *for* our family and *for* our future. We are delighted to grow with our sons as we strengthen our family team, and I very much look forward to continuing to enjoy the wonderful men Ethan and Jesse are becoming.

A Thirteen-Year Old's Reflections

Hello. I'm Ethan, the oldest son of Craig and Edelweiss Harrison. My first memory of schooling is taping a cut-out of the Sphinx to a yearbook. I don't remember education as being anything other than home, and I still can't imagine any other options that I would have picked for myself. Even as I complete high school and college level courses while just becoming a teenager, I am truly grateful to my Dad and Mom for choosing this way. Being homeschooled means I am learning not just the normal stuff, math, science, essays, and history, but am also learning about God and the history of the Christian church and catechisms. And politics! Yes, politics and government structure are frequent topics in our discussions around the dinner table. Homeschooling is such a blessing.

These are the key benefits of our homeschooling journey that have presented themselves to us in due time: Flexibility, Choosing the Curriculum, and Family time.

Flexibility

Flexibility has got to be one of the most important aspects of our nine-year homeschooling journey. It was the key reason why Mom and Dad started homeschooling; and it's been almost crucial to our education. Car trips are our most common trips, but we have also traveled to New Zealand and flown to the Florida Keys. If we were going to a public school, we wouldn't have had that option. The number of trips we have taken to the historical places and places of natural beauty and wonder all over the Continental United States means trips are basically part of our education. We can just pack some lessons for the road or catch up at home. And we have freedom of flexibility at home as well. Whenever our cousins come over for Christmas or Thanksgiving or when we go over to their place, we can take that week off. Me and my brother are chess enthusiasts; often we are allowed to compete in lengthy online chess tournaments. And when I joined a football (soccer) club, lessons can fit around it. Now we aren't allowed to do every chess tournament that pops up, or skip lessons on an excuse, but we have freedom to create our own schedule that fits our specific wants and needs.

Choosing the Curriculum

Another major element is the fact that I (and my brother) can influence the curriculum. Last year, Dad let us each pick one course. My elective course, the one I got to pick, was on New Zealand politics. I got a couple of books about Kiwi history and culture and am writing three essays and making an oral presentation. I was born in New Zealand, and it's always been close to my heart. I have set a long-term goal to become the Prime

Minister one day. I wouldn't have been able to pick a course like this in a public school in the US.

At the beginning of the year, we talk over all the courses and curricula and discuss new methods and evaluate old ones. We have tried multiple ways of allocating time to different subjects, and we test them almost like a scientific experiment, testing them for weeks or months, then trying a new way. The first was a simple spreadsheet that had all the tasks we had to complete for the week, and when we finished them, we just ticked it off. That was very simple, but it had a few vital flaws. There was no motivation to finish quickly. When we got behind schedule, we didn't catch up. We were using this method for about seven years, and when we started high school courses, we knew this had to change. So we switched to a method with half-hour blocks. We would sit down, study one subject for a block or two, then go on to a different one. Pretty soon, we hit a snag. There was nothing to keep us from just staring into space and waiting for the time to pass. And then it would take us a few minutes to get into the next subject, so the half an hour block was really a twenty-minute block. Seems almost like schools. So, after a year went by and we weren't even halfway done with the courses, Dad decided to try hour-long blocks. The reason behind longer blocks was more time focusing as opposed to waiting for the bell to ring or getting into it. There was definite improvement in the amount of time focusing, but it still lacked perfection. After much planning, thinking, and discussion, we hit the jackpot.

Our new system is based on goals. Weekly goals that we would set at the beginning of the week, and we had to finish by the end. We would still record the time that we spent, but the emphasis was on completing the goals, not sitting through until the clock ran out. This was powered by the proven best motivation we have discovered: computer time. Since I like to play chess on the computer, the goals would be run on the basis that I wouldn't get much screentime until I finished my weekly goals, and then I could play chess. This has worked very well despite a bit of dissension from me and Jesse.

Family Time

One of the most important things for almost all homeschoolers is the fact that you get way more family time together than a public school schedule would allow. Family is one of the most important elements in society and is a crucial part of education and development—both personal and social. You just can't have family "beliefs" together with the public school's way of teaching. Remember, the purpose of education is to convey knowledge and "to raise your child in the way of the LORD." "Train up a child in the way he should go; even when he is old he will not depart from it" (Proverbs 22:6). With you teaching, with you choosing the curriculum, and with you having weekly, daily, and hourly one-on-one access to your child(ren), that is "raising your children in the LORD." "You shall teach [the ways of the LORD] to your children, talking of them when you are sitting in your house, and when you are walking by the way, and when you lie down, and when you rise" (Deuteronomy 11:19). "The fear of the LORD is the beginning of wisdom, and the knowledge of the Holy One is insight" (Proverbs 9:10). "Apply your heart to instruction and your ear to words of knowledge" (Proverbs 23:12).

A final thought. As the oldest son, I have slightly different experiences from my younger brother. The most obvious is I started first and so am ahead of him in some subjects, for example, mathematics. We all have different personalities, and that is one reason why regular schools aren't the best option: they can't cater to hundreds of different styles. I like working alone and at my own pace; Jesse likes being with people and doing things quickly. These differences flavor the way we work and learn. If you are starting homeschooling, don't forget to incorporate these elements into your mindset. It will greatly impact your decisions.

So overall my experience of home education has been very positive. I am still learning at home, but I don't expect my attitude to change.

Input from an Eleven-Year-Old: My Side of the School

Hi! I'm Jesse, the youngest son of Craig and Edelweiss Harrison. I want to take some time to tell you about my side of our homeschooling journey.

When Dad decided to start homeschooling, he thought we didn't need to do preschool or kindergarten and went straight to elementary. Then we discovered some problems. The way we were doing it was having a big sheet with all the activities we were supposed to do that week and we ticked them off when they were done. That started off fine, but as we slowly got behind schedule, we never caught up until the end of the year. The reason was because we had no motivation, no reason to work hard. We continued this way for years, trying things to see if they motivated us, but nothing was working. Finally, by the time we reached high school, we knew this had to change. Dad developed a system where we did lessons in half an hour blocks and did forty-two blocks a week. However, there was another problem. There was nothing stopping us from just waiting for the timer to ring and then calling that a block.

Our latest system uses goal-setting. At the beginning of the week, we make a list of the lessons we are going to do that week. If we finish them by Tuesday, we are done for the week. And as for motivation, we don't get any time on the computer until we have finished our goals for the week. This works splendidly. And that's where we are at.

I have never been to a public school, so I do not know that side of the story, but I have been homeschooled for eight years, and if there is one thing I have learned from being educated at home it is that we have the flexibility to do next to anything we want. For example, I have been to New Zealand twice and both trips were during the typical school year. We go on frequent car trips and a good portion of them are during the school year. This also gives us the freedom to play sports if we want to, even during regular class time. We aren't tied to a fixed schedule, so we can work around things and do lessons on the go.

Family is mentioned in the Bible one hundred times. This is a big deal. In the classical education system, children are sent away for most of the day and only see their parents in the mornings and evenings. Because we are homeschooled and our Mom works from home, we see each other every day. This helps build our, as Dad put it, family team. Having family to back you up and support you in every decision and situation. I can't imagine what it would be like going to school and not having someone to rely on.

One of the main differences between public school and homeschool is you get to pick your own material. For example, on our first year of high school me and my brother talked with Dad about which courses we were going to do. In a public school, you are given a curriculum and expected to learn it, whether you're interested in it or not. Below are some further thoughts on a selection of courses I've taken.

Classic Literature—For this course we read eighteen books and wrote an essay about our reaction to each one. My final score was 87. I have noticed that sometimes when I read faster, I got a higher mark. For instance, I read *Pride and Prejudice* in a few months, and got an 83. I read *Jane Eyre* in a few weeks and I got an 87. I read *Oliver Twist* in a few days and got a 91! I think the reason behind this is if you are reading a book for a bit, then taking a break, then coming back to it, you see less of the change in the story, and when you write the paper, you are less likely to write about character development in the book. So it isn't always better to take tons of time. My Dad used to think it was best for me to watch or read an overview of the novel I was about to read before I read it in order to help me understand the book. But what I realized was it was more enjoyable for me if I only saw the overview after I read the book because the overview gave away the plot.

History of the Christian Church—In this course I read seven books plus the Westminster Shorter Catechism and wrote four essays on them. I got an 86. The main obstacle to completing the course was the Westminster Shorter Catechism: it took about half an hour for a chapter and there were sixty-four chapters! This meant it would take more than thirty hours! And I think it might have! Our method was to do one chapter when we got up and one after lunch. Using this method we were able to move through it quickly. My older brother Ethan has always read faster than me, and it was very noticeable when he was done with all the books in a month, except the catechism. However, this did not mean he got the course done first. In fact, I did. The reason was I like writing essays a <u>lot</u> more than him.

Writing I—This course consisted of working through various materials based on writing. This course was organized very loosely but was mostly a couple of Jonathan Rodgers courses, a note-taking workbook, Spelling-U-See and a grammar workbook provided by Sonlight. I don't have many thoughts on this course because we didn't do much other than work through the books. Because it was so loosely organized, I don't know what my mark was because Dad hasn't figured out how to grade this subject yet.

Piano—This course included piano lessons by our teacher, music theory, practicing, sight-reading, and performance. We had three recitals, and I wrote an essay on a composer (my favorite—Rachmaninoff). Piano is my absolute favorite course. I love piano and was playing for fun and being taught by my music teacher for a few years before we created a formal course. If you want to become great at something you love, it is worth hours and hours of practice. I got a 90. ☺

Biology—This course was Apologia Biology including the lab and lectures. This course has taken by far the most time because it included experiments and a three-hour lecture for each of the sixteen modules. This didn't take time because it was difficult but because there was just so much information to take in. This was my least favorite course for one reason: dissections. We had to do four dissections, which I absolutely abhor. I got an 81.

Algebra I—For this course we used Demme Learning's Math-U-See Algebra 1. Math is probably the subject I am best at. Math-U-See has come up with a very good system for learning math that we have used since sixth grade. Using this method has helped me understand the course as well as get consistent good marks. We basically just followed through the workbook the whole way. I got a 93.

We have used numerous resources over the years, but these are some of the best: Rosetta Stone, a site where you can learn almost any language you want; the Great Courses, a shop where you can get a series of instructional videos on all kinds of subjects; Sonlight, the place where we got almost all the resources for the first five or so years of homeschooling; Duolingo, pretty much like Rosetta Stone but more kid friendly; Scratch, an online coding platform that is both fun and helps you learn to code (until they banned us for disagreeing with the LGBTQ+ ideology they were pushing); and Demme Learning, which has lots of good courses to choose from.

If this has not been made clear, no matter how good of an alternative homeschooling is to public school, there is still a lot of effort needed. Public schools are too far gone to save; we need a reformation in the school system. Instead, homeschools are our best bet.

CHAPTER THIRTY-THREE

THE FINAL ENCOURAGEMENT

Not What I Wish I'd Known

"Ka mua, ka muri"—walking backward into the future—is a Māori proverb describing the time-honored concept of looking to the past to inform the future.

As I share my pilgrimage in home education with you, I pray that it encourages you in your journey. I don't know where you are at right now. Perhaps you are a veteran homeschooler, in which case many of these concepts and experiences will already be familiar to you, and I trust you have agreed with some ideas, disagreed with others, and found ones which cause you to think in a different way. It could be that you are beginning your journey in home education, and I hope you have found information and inspiration that encouraged you and strengthened your resolve to undertake this adventure. Maybe you are not sure whether this is for you; I urge you to prioritize what is best for your children. Perhaps you are a homeschooling dad—I pray you will cherish this time with your children and know your true worth as a man. Your children and family are blessed to have you taking on this role.

Throughout this book, I have sought to explain the thought process behind my decisions. I didn't want it to be a how-to manual or a volume of advice. I want you to think for yourself, understand the way I went about things, and leverage my experience to assist you with deciding on the best course of action for yourself and your children in your own unique circumstances. I don't want you to apply my solutions thoughtlessly to your situation, but rather to think through the issues and arrive at your own conclusions.

And I want to be clear that this is not what I wish I had known before starting. If it were, the implication is I would have been able to "get it right" if I had realized when I began homeschooling what I understand now. Yes, there are things I wish I would have done differently. But that's called life, and we may find that what we want to change is what most makes us who we are.

I remember reading about Neroli Fairhall, who won a gold medal in archery for New Zealand at the 1982 Commonwealth Games. In 1984, she became the first disabled athlete to take part in the Olympics, having been paralyzed from the waist down in a motorcycle accident in 1969. At a post-event press conference, one cynical journalist asked Fairhall if it were a help or a hindrance to shoot from a wheelchair. Fairhall's answer has become one of the great quotes in New Zealand sports. *"I don't know,"* she said. *"I've never shot standing up."*[1]

I don't know how the experience would have turned out for my boys if I knew then what I know now, and I want you to guard against the danger of thinking you might "get it wrong." Yes, I think we all need to learn from others, and I hope this book is informative for you. But you have your own journey to take. You will make your own mistakes and have your own successes. And you are going to do just fine.

No condemnation. You are your child's best teacher.

No Condemnation

There is a fine line between being motivated by a book and feeling intimidated. I have read many volumes intended to inspire, which in fact leave me thinking, *"There's no way I could do that!"* And so, as I close this book, I want to urge you to maintain a sense of perspective. As I read through what I've written, I hardly recognize the reality of my own situation. It doesn't feel so triumphant in the daily grind of lessons and grading and discipline.

Remember some key concepts:

- Everything you read by homeschoolers will have been written to **encourage** you. We believe in the value of home education, and we believe in your ability to provide that education for your children. To express this in the negative, nothing homeschool authors write is intended to overawe you or condemn you or suggest you are not capable enough. It isn't about doing something right or wrong, although it may be about doing something better. Remember, there is no condemnation for those who are in Christ Jesus (Romans 8:1). Commit your education journey to the LORD, and he will direct your paths and bring success to your plans (Proverbs 3:5-6, 16:3).

- However you choose to go about home education, it needs to work for you as the teacher as much as for your children. Parents are key to the success of this venture, and they need to be committed to making it work in order for their children to thrive. So if a suggestion doesn't resonate with you, then maybe it's not for you. If you try something and it doesn't work, then learn and adapt and move on. Think about what inspires you, because enthusiasm and a love of learning is contagious. You can't expect your children to be excited by learning if you are grumpy about teaching them. As they get older, these maxims will apply less and less because your children will be studying more independently and will be able to follow their own interests. But as you start off and while your children are young, make sure your method of home education works as well for you as it does for them.

- Do not become bound by other people's expectations. There is far more to raising children than filling them with academic knowledge. You have one duty—to raise your children well in the fear of the LORD (Proverbs 22:6). You know what is best for your family, and you have been given the responsibility by God to nurture and educate and train your children. You are ultimately accountable to God, not to others and certainly not to the state. Measure your success by the standard of the Bible, not by the standards of a homeschooling book. Be guided by what you believe is right for your family, not by other's expectations.

Never let what someone else wrote make you feel inadequate. Allow it to inspire you, without intimidating you. I'm going to tell you a secret, and although I can't speak for other homeschool authors, I suspect most would agree with me.

Our home education program isn't as perfect as it may sound. The examples and advice I have included in this book focus more on what was successful than what failed, because it's more helpful to you if I share what has worked for me. But be assured that not everything went so well. I didn't sort out our basic educational philosophy until I started writing this book. The results may not have been quite as stellar as I have suggested. My children are not perfect, and neither am I. Actually writing ideas down and figuring out how to explain them has been helpful to clarify and straighten out my own thinking. I reflected a lot over the years, wrote down notes here and there, and changed my mind at times. I may have learned some things too late to be of benefit to my children.

I imagine most of us suspect as much about the authors we read, but it's easy to forget. Like my mother's friend complimenting my Mum on the behavior of her children, we often see the best of others without knowing the truth about what it's like at home. Our house is not always as tidy as it is when we receive visitors. So be encouraged and inspired by others without feeling despondent about your own reality.

In this book, my aim has been to provide a perspective lacking from other literature. I have never read anything written about home education by an engineer or by a father who is the primary homeschool teacher. Whether you are an artist or an engineer, a mother or a father, the primary teacher or a supportive spouse, I trust the insights I have gained will offer a different perspective on the process of home education and will enrich your own journey.

Child's Best Teacher

My sister-in-law provided an important lesson when she shared with me about her home education experience. Her first daughter is very much the artist who would be quite happy having zero structure during the learning day. While this suits the creative nature of my sister-in-law, she does recognize that some structure is required to ensure lessons are completed. Her second daughter, however, is more inclined toward mathematics and a clear plan with goals and specific tasks are needed for this one to thrive. As the third begins her schooling, my sister-in-law is still trying to figure out the best approach for this child.

Our conversation was a helpful reminder of a number of the advantages we have teaching our offspring. We know our children best and have the opportunity to figure out how they learn most effectively. We are in charge of the program and can adapt it to suit the learning style of our children. We can offer them individual attention, and give them freedom or structure as they need, and challenge them and hold them accountable. My sister-in-law also reminded me to keep the main thing the main thing—to remember that education is not merely academic. She is much better than me at being sensitive to her children's needs, while I tend to focus on the program and the lessons. This entire book is about my perspective. But the point is not whether I'm right. The point is for your children to be educated well, for them to be raised and instructed in religious, moral, social, and intellectual matters.

As I've explained earlier in this book, I don't have the temperament to be a teacher. You might not either. But like me, you can do it anyway.

People have said they could never homeschool because they don't have the educational training that I have. That's simply not true. An academic background may even prove to be a barrier. Simply knowing something doesn't mean you can teach it. Teaching isn't about delivering information; it's about instilling a love of learning. It's about assisting discovery, and sometimes the experience for your child might just be better if you don't know the answer yourself and you need to learn together.

You are your child's best teacher.

If you love your children, are committed to raising them well, and want what's best for your kids, then you absolutely are your child's best teacher. Education is not only about academics. If we understand that education is training in character, faith, and knowledge, and if you are training your child in character and faith, then you certainly can train them in knowledge as well.

This doesn't mean you are necessarily your child's best math teacher, or science teacher, or music teacher. There are resources available and alternative solutions to cover areas in which you're not so confident. The language of Classical Conversations is very helpful, that you are the "Lead Learner." You don't need to know everything. We used to tease my Mum that "teachers know everything." They don't. Voddie Baucham observed that no parent is good enough, because we are all fallen and completely dependent on God.[2] In other words, being your child's best teacher has nothing to do with your ability.

The key question is not whether you are skilled at being a classroom teacher; it's whether your home is the best environment for educating your child. If you decide it is, then don't compare yourself to a school-teacher. A classroom full of pupils is very different to a house full of children.

There are plenty of wonderful professional teachers who do a great job instructing their class. Many young people have been positively impacted by their teachers; some have had their lives changed. These teachers deserve our respect and gratitude. And I dare say, some of them do love their students. There are children without loving family homes, for whom a good teacher can make a huge difference in their lives.

But no matter how skilled the teacher, no matter how much they invest in their students, you have home-court advantage. You have known your child far longer—most likely from birth. Your child will always be your child and will never graduate out of your family. You care for your child and want the best for him or her even more than the best teacher ever could. You are not doing it for money; you are sacrificing your time and effort without being paid. You are responsible for your child's growth in character.

Academic knowledge is only academic knowledge. There are many ways to obtain it, and it is important. Believe me, having spent almost two decades at university, I do appreciate the value of academics. But that is not the most important thing a child needs in order to grow. They need a parent's love. And if you love your child, then you are absolutely qualified and capable of educating them.

Love is more important. If you remember nothing else from this book, remember this:

A child will remember how you make them feel much longer than they will remember what you taught them.

NOTES

1. Neroli Fairhall, https://www.olympic.org.nz/athletes/neroli-fairhall, accessed 4 December 2022.
2. Voddie Baucham, *How the Gospel Can Transform Your Family*, *Homeschool Family Relationships Summit* (10 October 2022).

Appendices

Family Team Workbook

Sample pages from the Family Team Workbook are shown. The full workbook is available at https://books.qrx.group.

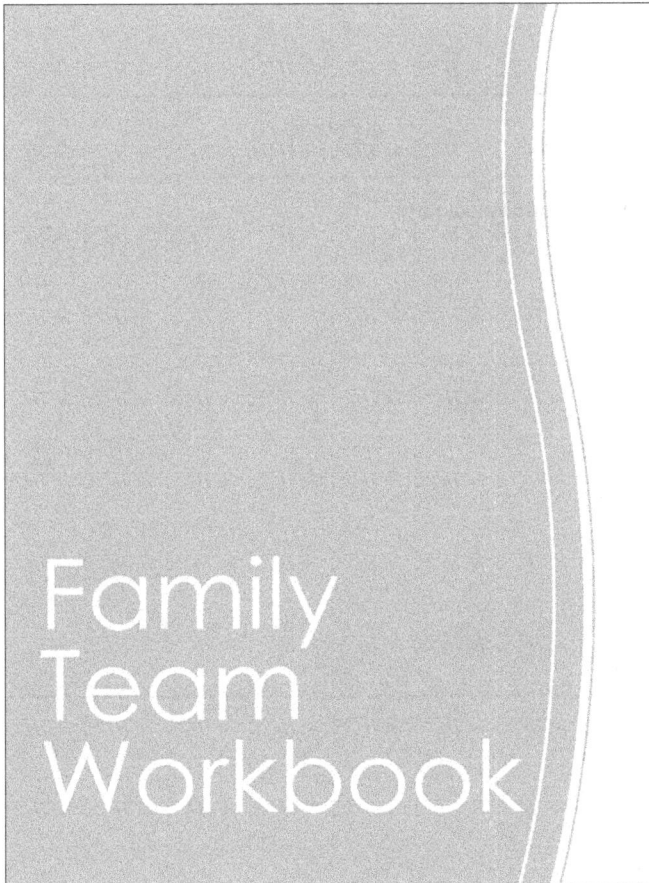

MISSION STATEMENT

What we should be doing as a family

MOTTO

A good motto for our family

FAMILY VALUES

What should our top values be?

Who are our role models?

ABOUT ME

What I'm good at

What I dream about doing

ABOUT MY SPOUSE

What I really appreciate about my spouse

What my spouse loves doing

APPENDIX B

Sample Course Syllabus

Sample pages from a syllabus are shown. Examples of course syllabi are available at https://books.qrx.group.

Syllabus
1 Credit Course

NEW ZEALAND POLITICS

Course Description

New Zealand politics will be studied in the context of the history of New Zealand, and a comparison between the cultural values of New Zealand and the United States of America.

Course Outline

The course requires a commitment of 120 hours over a 36-week educational year.

Method

The learning in this course will be undertaken by reading the two primary resources, conducting research as required by the assessment questions, and completing the course assessment.

Resources

The primary resources will be:
o *The Penguin History of New Zealand*, by Michael King
o *Fairness and Freedom: A History of Two Open Societies: New Zealand and the United States*, by David Hackett Fischer

Other resources will be consulted as required.

Learning Outcomes

Upon completion of the course, the student will have gained a sound understanding New Zealand's history and government system, as well as a comparison of the cultural values of New Zealand and the United States.

SAMPLE COURSE SYLLABUS

Assessment

Assessment will comprise three essays and an oral presentation, each contributing 25% to the final grade.

Essay 1

What events in New Zealand's early history shaped the nation's culture?

Marking Guide	
Spelling & Grammar	5
Layout & Presentation	5
Writing & Penmanship	5
Is the essay structured well?	15
	20

Percentage of Final Grade

...system of government.

Essay

De...

Marking Guide	
Spelling & Grammar	5
Layout & Presentation	5
Writing & Penmanship	5
Is the essay structured well?	15
Is the question answered thoroughly?	20
How well is the evolution of the system of government described?	25
Does the essay demonstrate an understanding of the source material?	25
Total	100
Percentage of Final Grade	25

287

Secondary Program

Sample files are available at https://books.qrx.group.

High School Programme

GRADUATION REQUIREMENTS

Objectives

While our educational goals go far bey_____ ___ _____ ____
requirements, the objectives that _____ and Bloomington School District b____
- To create a compelling C_____
- To Satisfy Minneso____ ___ expectations for a well-rounded educationa_ ___
- To meet our per_____

Requiremen____

	State / District	College Admission	Expectatio
Literature	Classic Literature		Literature I
	Literature II		Literature IV
Langua__ Arts	Writing I		
	Language Arts II		
Histo__	Church History		History II
			History III
Math	Algebra I	Pre-Calculus	Calculus
	Geometry		
Science	Algebra II		
	Biology (with lab)		
Languages	Ci___ ___cs / Chemistry		
	Art		
Other	Physical Educa__		
Electives			

Overview

Ethan
Credits: 9.0

Course	Assessments	Hours	Score	Grade	Credits
Algebra 1			87	A	1.0
Geo			93	A	1.0
	Complete			A	1.0
	Complete	80		A	1.0
of the Christian Church	Complete	257		A	1.0
sic Literature	Complete	233			1.0
riting I	0 / 6	148			1.0
New Zealand Politics	Complete	167	87		1.0
Biology	Complete	267	81		
Algebra 2	Complete	187	86		0
Physical Education I	Complete	133	100		
Piano I	1 / 5	78	13		
Pre-Calculus	23 / 35	154	53		
Classical Roots A&B	Complete	56	93		
American Literature	0 / 10	27	0		
History of the United States	0 / 4	11	0		
Portuguese I	0 / 4	51	0		

sse
ts: 7.0

Course	Assessments	Hours	Scor
story of the Christian Church	Complete	201	
ic Literature	Complete	244	
I	0 / 6	123	
	Complete	117	
	Complete		
	Complete		

Sample Weekly Schedule

A Microsoft Excel spreadsheet of this weekly schedule is available at https://books.qrx.group.

Learning Schedule		Week 36				
2019	Date Planned		14 May	Wed, 15 May 178	Thu, 16 May 179	Fri, 17 May 180
	Teaching Day				Week 36 Day 4	Week 36 Day 5
	Sonlight		15/5 | Rev 18	36 Day 3	□ _/_ Mat 27:32-	□ _/_ Mat 28
HL	, Eastern Hemisphere	8/5 | pp.396-402	■ pp.40...		y 21	□ _/_ Rev 22
	ury Slessor					
	Eastern Hemisphere Notebook					
	100 Gateway Cities	2/5 | p.68	■ p.70	▶		□ _/_ p.110
	Current Affairs					
Literature	+ The Mad Scientists Club	13/8 | pp.592-607	□ _/_ pp.608-619			
	The Horse and His Boy	6/5 | Ch.11	■ Ch.12	■ Ch.13	Ch.15	
	Water Sky	25/4 | Ch.7	□ _/_ Ch.8	□ _/_ C	hs.12-13	
	All the Small Poems	25/4 | p.191	■ p.193			nal
Language Arts / Writing	+ Journal	13/5 | Journal	■ Journal	■ Journal		
	+ Copywork & Dictation	10/5 | Mem. Verse				
	+ Writing & Research Project		■ Write	□ _/_ Res		
	+ Journal	13/5 | Journal	■ Journal	■ Journal		
	+ Copywork	10/5 | Mem. Verse	■ Literature	□ _/_ Prc		
Oral	+ Rosetta Stone: Portuguese	13/5 | 20 min	□ _/_ 20 min	■ 20 min		
	+ Speaking	21/6 | Call Opa	■ Call Uncle Shane			
	+ Zoology 1	14/5 | pp.228-229	⊠ p.230	□ _/_	T.16	
	Food & Nutrition					
	Improve Your Survival Skills					
	Exploring, History of Medicine	1/5 | Ch.18	□ _/_ Ch.19			
	...ons: Math 4	9/5 | L.157	■ L.158	_/_ Knowledge	□ _/_ Review	
	... Pre-Algebra	14/5 | L.30			□ _/_ Walker Kit Centre	
	...ain Ques...	9/5 | 15 min		■ Card for Dr Anna		
	+ Piano			■ 5 Activities		
	+ Piano Adventures Primer	13/5 | p.71	□ _/_ 20 mins	□ _/_ 20 mins		
	Date Completed	13 Aug 2019				

□ Planned   ■ Completed   ⊠ Revoked   + Extension   ↔ Moved

Preparation

⚲ Map   🕐 Timeline   ↑ Timeline Figure

| Ethan | Jesse | □ |

* For direction and teaching notes, see Sonlight Instructors Guide, Horizons   □
Math Teacher's Guide and Exploring Creation Notebook.   □
* Record notes and observations on the reverse.   □

Printed 4/07/2023

Math Templates

Mathematics templates are available at https://books.qrx.group and https://www.c-lineproducts.com/templates/template-dry-erase-pockets .html.

Number Chart: 1 - 100

1	2	3	4	5	6	7	8	9	10
11	12	13	14	15	16	17	18	19	20
21	22	23	24	25	26	27	28	29	30
31	32	33	34	35	36	37	38	39	40
41	42	43	44	45	46	47	48	49	50
51	52	53	54	55	56	57	58	59	60
61	62	63	64	65	66	67	68	69	70
71	72	73	74	75	76	77	78	79	80
81	82	83	84	85	86	87	88	89	90
91	92	93	94	95	96	97	98	99	100

Number Line: 0 - 19

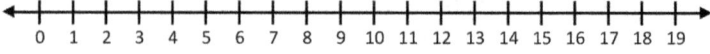

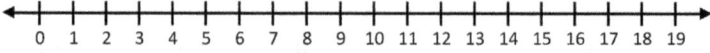

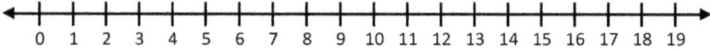

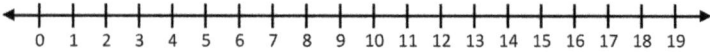

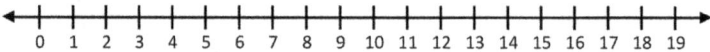

| | | | | | | | | | | | | | | | | | | | |
|0|1|2|3|4|5|6|7|8|9|10|11|12|13|14|15|16|17|18|19|

| | | | | | | | | | | | | | | | | | | | |
|0|1|2|3|4|5|6|7|8|9|10|11|12|13|14|15|16|17|18|19|

| | | | | | | | | | | | | | | | | | | | |
|0|1|2|3|4|5|6|7|8|9|10|11|12|13|14|15|16|17|18|19|

| | | | | | | | | | | | | | | | | | | | |
|0|1|2|3|4|5|6|7|8|9|10|11|12|13|14|15|16|17|18|19|

| | | | | | | | | | | | | | | | | | | | |
|0|1|2|3|4|5|6|7|8|9|10|11|12|13|14|15|16|17|18|19|

The Beauty of Mathematics Worksheets

$1 \times 8 + 1 = \square$

$12 \times 8 + 2 = \square\square$

$123 \times 8 + 3 = \square\square\square$

$1234 \times 8 + 4 = \square\square\square\square$

$12345 \times 8 + 5 = \square\square\square\square\square$

$123456 \times 8 + 6 = \square\square\square\square\square\square$

$1234567 \times 8 + 7 = \square\square\square\square\square\square\square$

$12345678 \times 8 + 8 = \square\square\square\square\square\square\square\square$

$123456789 \times 8 + 9 = \square\square\square\square\square\square\square\square\square$

$1 \times 9 + 2 = \square\square$

$12 \times 9 + 3 = \square\square\square$

$123 \times 9 + 4 = \square\square\square\square$

$1234 \times 9 + 5 = \square\square\square\square\square$

$12345 \times 9 + 6 = \square\square\square\square\square\square$

$123456 \times 9 + 7 = \square\square\square\square\square\square\square$

$1234567 \times 9 + 8 = \square\square\square\square\square\square\square\square$

$12345678 \times 9 + 9 = \square\square\square\square\square\square\square\square\square$

$123456789 \times 9 + 10 = \square\square\square\square\square\square\square\square\square\square$

APPENDIX F

$9 \times 9 + 7 = \square\square$

$98 \times 9 + 6 = \square\square\square$

$987 \times 9 + 5 = \square\square\square\square$

$9876 \times 9 + 4 = \square\square\square\square\square$

$98765 \times 9 + 3 = \square\square\square\square\square\square$

$987654 \times 9 + 2 = \square\square\square\square\square\square\square$

$9876543 \times 9 + 1 = \square\square\square\square\square\square\square\square$

$98765432 \times 9 + 0 = \square\square\square\square\square\square\square\square\square$

$1 \times 1 = \square$

$11 \times 11 = \square\square\square$

$111 \times 111 = \square\square\square\square\square$

$1111 \times 1111 = \square\square\square\square\square\square\square$

$11111 \times 11111 = \square\square\square\square\square\square\square\square\square$

$111111 \times 111111 = \square\square\square\square\square\square\square\square\square\square\square$

$1111111 \times 1111111 = \square\square\square\square\square\square\square\square\square\square\square\square\square$

$11111111 \times 11111111 = \square\square\square\square\square\square\square\square\square\square\square\square\square\square\square$

$111111111 \times 111111111 = \square\square\square\square\square\square\square\square\square\square\square\square\square\square\square\square\square$

SELECT REFERENCES

Books

The Abolition of Man, C.S. Lewis (1947)

The Abolition of Sanity: *C.S. Lewis on the Consequences of Modernism*, Stephen Turley (2019)

Already Gone: *Why Your Kids Will Quit Church and What You Can Do to Stop It*, Ken Ham, Britt Beemer and Todd Hillard (2009)

Areopagitica; and Of Education, John Milton, George Sabine (ed.) (1951)

Battle for the American Mind: *Uprooting a Century of Miseducation*, Pete Hegseth and David Goodwin (2022)

Better Late than Early: *A New Approach to Your Child's Education*, Raymond Moore, Dorothy Moore and Dennis Moore (1975)

The Brainy Bunch: *The Harding Family's Method to College Ready by Age Twelve*, Kip and Mona Lisa Harding (2020)

Building a Christian World View: *God, Man and Knowledge*, W. Andrew Hoffecker (ed.) (1986)

Classical vs. Modern Education: *A Vision from C.S. Lewis*, Stephen Turley (2016)

The Coming Rise of Christian Education: *How Political and Religious Trends are Fueling a Surge in Christian Schooling*, Stephen Turley (2019)

Education: Does God Have an Opinion? *A Biblical Apologetic for Christian Education & Homeschooling*, Israel Wayne (2017)

Homeschoolers' College Admissions Handbook, Cafi Cohen (2000)

The Household and the War for the Cosmos: *Recovering a Christian Vision for the Family*, Chris Wiley (2019)

How to Parent So Children Will Learn: *Strategies for Raising Happy, Achieving Children*, Sylvia Rimm (2008)

I Don't Have Enough Faith to Be an Atheist, Norman Geisler and Frank Turek (2004)

IndoctriNation: *Public Schools and the Decline of Christianity*, Charles LaVerdiere (ed.) (2012)

The Kingdom Agenda, Tony Evans (1999)

Live Not by Lies: *A Manual for Christian Dissidents*, Rod Dreher (2020)

Love & Respect: *The Love She Most Desires; The Respect He Desperately Needs*, Emerson Eggerichs (2004)

Men Without Work: *America's Invisible Crisis*, Nicholas Eberstadt (2016)

The Naming of Persons: *The Fascinating Role of Names and Naming in the Formation of Our Personal Identity*, Paul Tournier (1975)

Powerful Inspirational Motivation, Gerald Bradley (1993)

Prisoners of Our Thoughts: *Viktor Frankl's Principles for Discovering Meaning in Life and Work*, Alex Pattakos (2010)

The Return of Christendom: *Demography, Politics, and the Coming Christian Majority*, Stephen Turley (2019)

SELECT REFERENCES

The Right Side of History: *How Reason and Moral Purpose Made the West Great*, Ben Shapiro (2019)

The School Revolution: *A New Answer for Our Broken Education System*, Ron Paul (2013)

The Second Mayflower, Kevin Swanson (2008)

Setting the Records Straight: *How to Craft Homsechool Transcripts and Course Descriptions for College Admission and Scholarships*, Lee Binz (2010)

So You're Thinking About Homeschooling: *Fifteen Families Show How You Can Do It*, Lisa Whelchel (2005)

Socialism: *The Real History from Plato to the Present*, William Federer (2020)

The Three R's, Ruth Beechick (2006)

The Underground History of American Education: *An Intimate Investigation into the Prison of Modern Schooling*, John Taylor Gatto (2017)

The Well-Trained Mind: *A Guide to Classical Education at Home*, Susan Wise Bauer and Jessie Wise (2009)

What if Jesus Had Never Been Born? *The Positive Impact of Christianity in History*, D. James Kennedy and Jerry Newcombe (2001)

Websites

Apologia https://www.apologia.com
BB New Zealand https://www.bb.org.nz
Classical Conversations https://classicalconversations.com
Compass Classroom https://compassclassroom.com
CrunchLabs https://www.crunchlabs.com
Demme Learning https://demmelearning.com
EEME https://www.eeme.co
Family Renewal https://familyrenewal.org
Family Teams https://familyteams.com
Gather & Grow https://gatherandgrow.us
Generations https://www.generations.org
The Great Courses https://www.thegreatcourses.com
Growing Families International https://growingfamilies.life
Homeschool Legal Defense Association https://hslda.org
Horizons https://www.aop.com/curriculum/horizons
KiwiCo https://www.kiwico.com
Math-U-See https://mathusee.com
Memoria Press https://www.memoriapress.com
Moore Academy https://www.moorefoundation.com
Ron Paul Curriculum https://www.ronpaulcurriculum.com
Scratch https://scratch.mit.edu
Sonlight Curriculum https://www.sonlight.com
The Boys' Brigade https://boys-brigade.org.uk
TOPS Learning Systems https://topscience.org
Trail Life USA https://www.traillifeusa.com
Vocabulary Quest https://vocabularyquest.com

SELECT REFERENCES

Additional Resources

Homeschooling Market Survey Analysis. Hanover Research (March 2021).
What Is Homeschooling? HSLDA Action (Purcellville, VA: 2022).
U.S. Supreme Court. "Pierce v. Society of Sisters." In 268 U.S. 510, 1925. https://supreme.justia.com/cases/federal/us/268/510.
"What Reading Does for the Mind," Anne Cunningham and Keith Stanovich, *American Educator* 22(1-2), (1998): 8-15.
"The Lived Experience of Evangelical Christian Homeschooling Fathers in Fulfilling the Biblical Role of Disciple-Maker: A Transcendental Phenomenological Study," William Farrington, Doctor of Education dissertation (Liberty University, 2020)
Good Soil: A Comparative Study of ACCS Alumni Life Outcomes, David Goodwin, *The Classical Difference* (27 January 2020). https://www.classicaldifference.com/good-soil.
"Building Monasteries in the New Dark Ages," Rory Groves, 28 August 2021. Audio Recording. https://gatherandgrow.us/product/building-monasteries-in-the-new-dark-ages.
"Schoolhouse Rocked: The Homeschool Revolution," Garritt Hampton (Vision Video, 2021). DVD.
"Home Instruction: The Size and Growth of the Movement," Patricia Lines. Chap. 1 in *Home Schooling : Political, Historical, and Pedagogical Perspectives,* Jane Van Galen and Mary Anne Pitman (eds.) (Ablex Publishing, 1991).
"We Are Losing Our Children: Remarks to the Southern Baptist Convention Executive Committee," Thomas Pinckney, Southern Baptist Convention (Nashville, TN: 18 September 2001). https://dev.schoolandstate.org/Knowledge/Faith/Pinckney-WeAreLosingOurChildren.htm.
Gen2 Survey: A Spiritual and Educational Survey on Christian Millennials, Brian Ray (NHERI, 2015).
"The Myth of Neutral Education," R.C. Sproul, *Christian Education* series, Ligonier Ministries.
"Can Values Be Taught? The Myth of Value-Free Education," Margit Sutrop, *Trames. A Journal of the Humanities and Social Sciences* 19(2), (2015): 189-202. https://doi.org/10.3176/tr.2015.2.06.

INDEX

10,000-hour rule 16

A

activity, physical 130, 143, 177, 179, 236, 272
affirmation 113, 178, 188, 235
Age of Reason *See* the Enlightenment
Allen, Tim 46, 105
analytical approach 48, 49, 50, 51, 60, 67, 82, 206
Aquinas 36
Aristotle 33, 52, 69
arts & crafts *See* subject:art
Asimov, Isaac 65
Athens *See* worldview:Greek
Augustine 33, 36, 69, 131

B

Bauer, Susan Wise 230
Beechick, Ruth 204, 213, 218, 239
behavior 119, 177, 183, 186, 187, 188, 190, 217, 274
Benda, Václav 13, 133
Bennett, William 75
Bible xviii, 5, 17, 27, 32, 36, 40, 45, 49, 55, 90, 94, 95, 97, 110, 124, 135, 137, 138, 158, 195, 212, 225, 245, 252, 259, 264, 268, 273, *See also* subject:Bible
Bjorkman, Nancy 171
Bloch, Arthur 72
Bluedorn, Hans 252
Bluedorn, Nathaniel 252
book report 149, 168, 225, 244
Boyer, Chris 87
boys xiv, xvii, 109, 145, 176, 177, 178, 179, 187, 217
Bradley, Gerald 70, 121
Brandeis, Louis 227
Bunyan, John 120
Burns Family Studios 45

C

Calvin, John 47
Cameron, Kirk 45
Campolo, Peggy 94
Camus, Albert 115
career xvi, 3, 5, 6, 7, 30, 75, 83, 94, 95, 102, 106, 108, 109, 110, 111, 112, 116, 129, 142
Carlson, Allan 134
Carman, Davis 144
Carson, Clarence 72
Casap, Jaime 143
Chan, Yong Kang 96
character 26, 29, 73, 182, 252, 261, 275, 276, *See also* ethics
Chesterton, G.K. 26, 37, 219
Christendom *See* society:Christendom
Churchill, Winston 26
coaching xvii, 5, 261
coercion 149, 150, 181, 189, 213, 234
Coerr, Eleanor 217
Coleridge, Sir Paul 74
companionship 37, 120, 121, 125, 161, 191
Competency Model 146, 150, 167
    Apprenticeship Approach 150, 152, 166, 225
    Incremental Approach 150, 167, 236, 237
computer 6, 66, 76, 177, 181, 182, 183, 195, 221, 235, 247, 262, 266, 268, *See also* subject:computer
Comte, Auguste 54
cooking 162, 193, 232
courage 31, 108, 109, 253, 264
Covey, Stephen 118, 121
creative writing *See* subject:creative writing
Cunningham, Anne 203
curriculum *See* homeschool:curriculum
Czechoslovakia 13, 133

INDEX

D

Darwin, Charles 49
de Saint-Exupéry, Antoine 260
de Tocqueville, Alexis 47, 53
Dead Poets Society 206, 207
Demme, Stephen 161
Desmet, Mattias 51
devotions 19, 195, 254
Dewey, John 47, 52, 54, 57
dialogue 178
Diamandis, Peter 57
discipleship 10, 27, 28, 36, 37, 38, 40, 60,
    91, 158, 185, 193, 254
discipline xxi, 10, 19, 113, 185, 186, 187,
    188, 190, 272
dishwasher xx, 143, 195
Disney 45
Dreher, Rod 133
DuoLingo 230, 270

E

Eberstadt, Nicholas 84
education
    agenda *See* school:agenda
    Biblical 10, 28, 30, 34, 37, 38, 40, 43,
        47, 60, 61, 65, 73, 75
    Classical Education 27, 28, 30, 31,
        32, 38, 39, 43, 62, 147, 158, 251
    cost 6, 70, 71, 75, 81, 136, 157
    definition 23, 25
    early US 47, 52
    for all 17, 37, 47
    Greek academy 8, 27, 30, 39, 40, 62,
        See also worldview:Greek
    Hebraic Model 9, 15, 27, 28, 32, 36,
        37, 39, 71, 75
    Modern 15, 27, 28, 32, 37, 39, 43, 56,
        60, 250
    Prussian 52
    purpose 22-27, 38, 54, 129, 132, 168,
        176, 261, 267
    structure 43, 52, 71
    values xviii, 10, 11, 16, 30, 32, 43,
        55, 56, 57, 60, 67-69, 73, 76, 138,
        191, 251, 264
Eggerichs, Emerson 123
Einstein, Albert xviii, 48
Eldredge, John 109

emotion 22, 27, 28, 47, 96, 112, 115-122,
    123, 188, 217, 236
encouragement xv, 3, 82, 83, 86, 107, 119,
    120, 121, 165, 178, 180, 186, 190, 231,
    232, 236, 238, 271, 272
Engels, Friedrich 53
engineer xiv, xv, xvii, xviii, xx-xxi, 4, 5,
    82, 117, 119, 141, 188, 189, 195, 201,
    228, 229, 254, 274
engineering xx, 162
Enlightenment, the 13, 28, 29, 30, 49, 51,
    59, 60
ethics 29, 34, 44, 56, 67, 76, 250,
    See also morality, work ethic
Evans, Tony 68
Ezzo, Gary & Anne Marie 131, 185

F

Fairhall, Neroli 272
faith xviii, 9, 13, 15, 28, 29, 33, 49, 55, 58,
    72, 124, 131, 134, 138, 245, 252, 254,
    260, 275
family 131, 135, *See also* education:Hebraic
    Model, society:family
    Biblical model 27, 34, 98, 135
    structure 17, 92, 98, 104
    team 135, 264, 266, 268
Farrington, William 36, 111
father
    example 28, 36, 102, 103, 107, 115,
        185, 212
    identity 83, 93, 95, 101, 105, 106, 110
    laborer 84, 97, 102
    protector 10, 15, 43, 55, 76, 91, 96,
        100, 110, 112, 263
    provider 91, 92, 93, 95, 96, 98, 102,
        110, 111, 188
Federer, William 74
Fencepost Model 146, 148, 167, 201, 226,
    228, 237, 248
Fernandez, Joaquin 60
Fichte, Johann 52
field trip 83, 191, 193, 244, 264
finances 70, 82, 91, 92, 96, 98, 102, 103,
    111, 113, 260
fishing 141
Focus on the Family 187
force *See* coercion
Forrest Gump 172

INDEX

ABOUT THE AUTHOR

Craig Harrison was born in New Zealand and has one wife, two children, and five university degrees including a PhD in Physics, a Theology degree, and an MBA. Over the last few years, he has become a Distinguished Toastmaster and a Maxwell Leadership certified coach, has canoed in the Northern Minnesota Boundary Waters and is halfway through building a workbench in his garage. He is an avid reader, a huge fan of *The Lord of the Rings,* and a passionate although at times frustrated football enthusiast. Maybe next time, England will win the World Cup and Queens Park Rangers will return to the English Premier League.

Craig has worked as a research engineer, a football coach, a business consultant, and an Uber driver, and for the past 12 years has lived in Minneapolis, Minnesota where he homeschools his two boys.

You may connect with Craig through his LinkedIn profile:
https://www.linkedin.com/in/cbharrison
or by email:
books@qrx.group

Resources related to this book are available at:
https://books.qrx.group

www.ingramcontent.com/pod-product-compliance
Lightning Source LLC
Chambersburg PA
CBHW060246100426
42742CB00011B/1656